Praise for *Becoming a Mountain*
Winner of Kekoo Naoroji Book Award
for Himalayan Literature

"Climbing out of the ache and nightmare of a vicious, life-threatening attack at his home in the Indian hill town of Mussoorie, Stephen Alter writes beautifully of his forays into the Himalaya. By turns rigorous and enlivening, his ascents, circumnavigations, and retreats deliver him back to himself, refreshed, chastened, healed, and fully alive. A wondrous book."

—Gretel Ehrlich, author of *Facing the Wave*

"In the tradition of the best nature writers, Stephen Alter combines an intimate knowledge of the landscape and a scrupulous attention to detail with a profound awareness of its sublime and sacred nature that underlies and unites it all."

—Anita Desai, author of *The Artist of Disappearance*

"A gorgeous piece of writing: Richard Haliburton's thrilling adventure stories combined with Annie Dillard's close observation of nature combined with Anne Morrow Lindbergh's quiet philosophical and personal reflection. I don't think anyone could write about a personal journey through nature more beautifully or thoughtfully."

—Alan Lightman, author of *Mr g* and *Einstein's Dreams*

"A lovely and compelling book, a delight to read. No writer describes a Himalayan quest with greater insight and clarity than Stephen Alter. . . . His radiant vision of the mountains includes the joy of walking, natural history, violent storms, and local myths and religious ceremonies, all filling him with bliss and exhilaration, as they do the reader."

—George B. Schaller, vice president of Panthera and author of *Tibet Wild*

"In this book Steve Alter beautifully illuminates the power of the Himalayas to heal, and to inspire."

—Chris Anderson, TED curator

"A rich, satisfying memoir that plumbs the depths—and acknowledges the limits—of both man and mountain. . . . [Alter] convincingly brings to life the culture, terrain, flora and fauna of the Himalayas . . . [and] offers a multifaceted consideration of life's tough truths and stunning splendors."

—*Kirkus Reviews*, starred review

"Beautifully written . . . a source of joy to anyone interested in knowing about Nature and our connection with it, especially if mountains are involved."

—*Bookpleasures.com*

"Writing with the precision and passion of a poet, Alter narrates his experience in the mountains that he loves. His descriptions of treks and expeditions to Nanda Devi and Mount Kailash in Tibet, among others, are interwoven with insights on how we interpret ourselves in the ceaseless exploration called life."

—*Times of India*

"From the moment I opened it, this book was the start of a journey that would take me outside myself . . . as only the mountains can do. It's a deeply felt, personal story of traveling on many levels, and Alter weaves the threads of the spiritual, physical, and emotional into a cohesive narrative whole. . . . If only desecrators of mountains and those who aim to 'conquer' them would read this book!"

—*Outlook*

"*Becoming a Mountain* is an extraordinary travelogue . . . Instead of 'conquering and colonizing high places,' he tries to 'become like the mountains.' This constitutes the book's distinctive core and is a wonderful prescription for wayfarers and travelers."

—*Hindu Business Line*

"A rich narrative in which myth and memory mix with vivid descriptions of the natural world . . . Alter's evocative language and the range of his references make us understand what mountains can mean."

—*Telegraph*

Becoming
a Mountain

Also by Stephen Alter:

NONFICTION

All the Way to Heaven: An American Boyhood in the Himalayas
Amritsar to Lahore: A Journey Across the India-Pakistan Border
Sacred Waters: A Pilgrimage Up the Ganges River to the Source
of Hindu Culture
Elephas Maximus: A Portrait of the Indian Elephant
Fantasies of a Bollywood Love Thief: Inside the World of
Indian Moviemaking

FICTION

Neglected Lives
Silk and Steel
The Godchild
Renuka
Aripan and Other Stories
Aranyani
The Phantom Isles
Ghost Letters
The Rataban Betrayal
The Dalliance of Leopards

Becoming
a Mountain

Himalayan Journeys
in Search of the Sacred
and the Sublime

STEPHEN
ALTER

With a New Foreword by Alan Lightman

Arcade Publishing • New York

First North American Paperback Edition 2019

Photograph of Flag Hill courtesy of Aaron Alter

Arcade Publishing books may be purchased in bulk at special discounts for sales promotion, corporate gifts, fund-raising, or educational purposes. Special editions can also be created to specifications. For details, contact the Special Sales Department, Arcade Publishing, 307 West 36th Street, 11th Floor, New York, NY 10018 or arcade@skyhorsepublishing.com.

Arcade Publishing® is a registered trademark of Skyhorse Publishing, Inc.®, a Delaware corporation.

Visit our website at www.arcadepub.com.
Visit the author's site at stephenalter.net

10 9 8 7 6 5 4 3 2 1

Library of Congress Cataloging-in-Publication Data is available on file.

Cover design by Georgia Morrissey
Cover photo: Coni Hörler

ISBN: 978-1-62872-909-2
Ebook ISBN: 978-1-62872-542-1

Printed in the United States of America

For Ameeta

As we look at the Himalaya from such distance that we can see things whole and in their just proportion, the pain and disorder, squalor and strife, vanish into insignificance. We know that they are there, and we know that they are real. But we know also that more important, and just as real, is the Power which out of evil is ever making good to come. . . . This is the true secret of the Himalaya.

Francis Younghusband

Writing is, I suppose, a superstitious way of keeping the horror at bay, of keeping the evil outside.

Paul Bowles

*The face of the landscape is a mask
Of bone and iron lines where time
Has plowed its character.
I look and look to read a sign,
Through errors of light and eyes of water
Beneath the land's will, of a fear
And the memory of a struggle,
As man behind his mask still wears a child.*

Stephen Spender

Contents

Contents

Foreword
by Alan Lightman

For many years, my wife and I have spent our summers on an island in Maine. It's a small island, only about thirty acres in size, and there are no bridges or ferries connecting it to the mainland. Consequently, each of the six families who live on the island has their own boat. My story concerns a particular summer night, late, in the wee hours, when I was out in my boat coming to my home on the island. I had just rounded the south end of the island and was carefully motoring toward my dock. No one was out on the water but me. It was a moonless night, and quiet, and the sky vibrated with stars. Taking a chance, I turned off my running lights, and it got even darker. Then I turned off my engine. I lay down in the boat and looked up. A very dark night sky seen from the ocean is a mystical experience. After a few minutes, my world had dissolved into that star-littered sky. The boat disappeared. My body disappeared. And I found myself falling into infinity. I felt an overwhelming connection to the stars, as if I were part of them. And the vast expanse of time—extending from the far distant past long before I was born and then into the far distant future long after I would die—seemed compressed to a dot. I felt connected not only to the stars but to all of nature, and to the entire cosmos. I felt a merging with something far larger than myself, a grand and eternal unity. After a time, I sat up and started the engine again. I had no idea how long I'd been lying there looking up.

That experience, or something similar to it, will be familiar to many readers. In Hinduism, it's called *darshan*. Being in the presence of the sublime and accepting that blessing. Stephen Alter's book, while filled with personal adventures in the Himalayas and close observations of nature, is most deeply about his quest for *darshan*. "I see myself in this mountain and feel a part of its immensity," he writes, "as well as a greater wholeness that contains us all in the infinite, intimate bonds of eternity."

Like me, Alter is what one might call a "spiritual atheist." That is, he does not believe in an all-knowing and intentional Being who governs the universe, and yet he has experienced *darshan*.

We have arrived at our beliefs by different paths. Alter's grandparents and parents were Presbyterian missionaries, who ventured to the hill station of Mussoorie in northern India, in the foothills of the Himalayas. There, Alter was born and grew up. From an early age, he was a writer. For various reasons, he rejected traditional religious beliefs, but every morning he looked out at the snow-covered Himalayas. He trekked their winding paths and translucent slopes. His spirituality is easy to explain.

By contrast, I grew up in a suburban American city and was the little scientist—doing experiments in my home-made laboratory. From an early age, I adopted a purely scientific view of the world. By that, I mean that the universe is made of material and nothing more, that the universe is governed exclusively by a small number of fundamental forces and laws, and that all things in the material world, including humans and stars, will eventually disintegrate and pass away.

Early in his book, Alter writes: "Instead of defining a mountain in human terms, we must allow ourselves to be defined by mountains. . . . Essentially, we must erase a prevailing bias of separation from the world and move beyond the divisions of perception and reality." I would like to try to unravel the meaning of these sentences from my vantage as a scientist, but also as a spiritual person.

Over the centuries, science has succeeded by separating the observer from the observed—in other words, separating perception from reality.

The ruthlessly reliable laws that govern the swing of a pendulum were arrived at by isolating the pendulum within a box, and then analyzing its swing from outside the box. The "observer" is a disembodied being, immune to emotion, who objectively measures and analyzes the swing of the pendulum, arriving at a mathematical rule for its behavior. Once that law is found, it may be applied to all pendulums. The law does not depend on any particular pendulum, and the "observer" has ceased to have any significance at all. The nameless observer was only an artifice to discover the universal law, the underlying nature of reality. The pendulum exists in all its pendulumhood whether observed or not. In other words, there's a reality out there, independent of our perception of it. So that's the scientific view.

But Alter invites us to dissolve into the mountain, to "become" the mountain, to lose the distinction between observer and observed—just as I lost all sense of my self that night in Maine. I believe we should accept such experiences, whether we completely understand them or not. In fact, we should honor them. The mind may be nothing but the brain, and the brain nothing but a special arrangement of a hundred billion neurons or so, all humming along with their electrical and chemical energies. But what majesties that material thing is capable of. Art, music, philosophy, science, wonder, mystery—and the ability to lose its own material self and join with the sky. The ability to forget, for a moment, its fleeting existence and imagine eternity.

A few years ago, I visited Alter and his mountains. My wife, Jean, and I stayed with him and his wife, Ameeta, in his family home, "Oakville," in the little village of Mussoorie. Mussoorie is essentially a two-dimensional world, almost all vertical. A ribbon of a path winds around the mountain going up and going down. Houses are situated on the occasional spots where the land grudgingly spreads sideways for more than a few feet. At Oakville, the Alters were charming and gentle hosts. We had lovely meals together and talked of the days when the milk wallahs and wood wallahs would deliver their cargoes to each house, weathered men bent over with heavy metallic milk containers or piles of wood on their backs, trudging the steep paths up and down the mountain. It was October, and the air was cool and crisp. Some days, I would go out the back door, cross the few precious feet of level ground, walk through a little gate, and find myself perched on the side of the mountain. There, almost hanging in space, was a stone bench. Alter often sat there, and his father before him. And beyond, the Himalayas, its ranges in horizontal layers, the closest deep purple, the more distant gradually paling and dimming until they faded into the sky. I was again falling into infinity.

A Note on the Himalayas

The pronunciation and spelling of the word *Himalayas* has been a matter of dispute from the time it was first translated into English. In Sanskrit *Hem* or *Him* means "snow" and *alaya* denotes the "place of." When I was a boy, we were taught to stress the second syllable (*Himaalaya*), rather than swallowing the vowel (*Him'laya*) as many people do. We believed this was the correct pronunciation, though it differed from the original Sanskrit. As for spelling, many purists assert that Himalaya, without the *s*, is more accurate and gives the mountains a singular grandeur. Common usage has devolved into the plural form that I have chosen for this book. My purpose is simply to avoid confusion among readers who may not be aware of the arcane nuances of this debate. In the end, of course, no matter how we transliterate their name, the Himalayas will always rise above the perverse inadequacies of language.

Becoming
a Mountain

FLAG HILL

Distant Prayers

If the red slayer think he slays,
Or if the slain think he is slain,
They know not well the subtle ways
I keep, and pass, and turn again.

Ralph Waldo Emerson

Birthright

The true face of the mountain remains invisible, though its southern aspect presents a familiar profile. Two corniced summits, with a broad intervening ridge draped in snow, fall away more than ten thousand feet into the valley below. From certain angles and at certain times of day, just behind the eastern peak, a pale, indistinct shadow becomes visible, the hint of something else beyond. This is the third summit, hidden but higher than the other two by a couple hundred feet. During the dry seasons—late fall and early spring—dark gray shapes begin to appear on the mountain. Avalanches have carried away the snow, and ice has melted, revealing the underlying strata of rock tilted skyward by interminable forces of geology.

I have looked at this mountain all my life, sometimes at dawn, or midday, or dusk, even by moonlight, yet there is no way that I can accurately describe its presence, whether I use poetry or the contentious languages of religion and science. Both the mountain's myths and its natural history have an elusive, enigmatic quality. I have sketched it in pencil, pen, and watercolor, but each time I have failed to express a convincing vision of what this mountain represents. Over the years, I must have photographed those twin summits several hundred times, but none of my camera images seems to capture anything more than a faint suggestion of the mountain, mere ghosts of light. I know that it stands there, but what it means is beyond my comprehension. Yet, constantly, I see myself in this mountain and feel a part of its immensity, as well as a greater wholeness that contains us all in the infinite, intimate bonds of eternity.

～

At the beginning of October 2012, we buried my father's ashes in the cemetery on the north side of Landour ridge, facing the Himalayas. He and my mother had chosen our family plot years before. Two of my uncles were already buried there, on a terrace overshadowed with deodar trees. My father's grave looks out upon a snow-covered mountain called Bandarpunch, the monkey's tail, which takes its name from an episode in the *Ramayana*. This is the most prominent peak we see from our home in Mussoorie, a broad massif with twin summits rising 20,722 feet above sea level.

When my father died, on June 19, 2011, I was attempting to climb Bandarpunch. Our expedition, comprised mostly of staff from Woodstock School, was organized by the Nehru Institute of Mountaineering (NIM), in Uttarkashi. Before I reached base camp, a wireless message came in from my wife, Ameeta, patched through on the radio at NIM. My father's condition had suddenly grown worse. For a year and a half he had struggled with skin cancer, which had spread to his throat and other parts of his body. We knew that he was dying, but I didn't expect it would happen so soon.

During our last conversation, on the morning I left for Bandarpunch, my father could barely speak, though he told me to be careful on the mountain. He was worried about my safety, even as he faced his own mortality. We talked for half an hour over a poor connection following an early monsoon storm, the line rasping with static. My mother translated his hoarse words through their speakerphone. A month before, I had traveled back with them to their home in Wooster, Ohio, after my father made a final visit to Mussoorie. Dad joked that his cancer was a result of the Indian sun and the consequences of having white skin. He reminded me to take sunscreen with me on the expedition.

Setting out for Bandarpunch, I wasn't sure if I would speak to my father again. His last trip to Mussoorie had been an emotional visit. We gathered at Oakville, the family home my parents had bought thirty years ago, where Ameeta and I now live. It is a sprawling old bungalow built by a British officer around 1840, surrounded by twenty acres of forest. Until their retirement, when my parents moved to

Ohio, they had lived at Oakville. Every year they returned for several months. In Mussoorie, my father went for a walk each day, religiously circling the ridge in view of the snows, but this time Dad's legs were so weak he had trouble standing. I drove him around the top of the hill so he could see the Himalayas one last time.

A year later, putting his urn in the ground, I felt an overwhelming connection to these mountains, this place that we call home. Once again, my mother had traveled halfway around the world, carrying his ashes, just as she first ventured here from Pennsylvania to Mussoorie, sixty-five years ago, to marry my father. Dad was born in Kashmir, in 1926, a child of the Himalayas. His parents were Presbyterian missionaries, and my father followed in their footsteps. He spent most of his life in the mountains, as a teacher and principal at Woodstock School, then later working with village communities in the surrounding hills, promoting drinking water projects, public health, education, and environmental awareness. Laying his remains to rest in sight of the high Himalayas seemed to finally close the circle.

In one of our family albums is a photograph of my father as a young man, standing on the grass-covered slopes near the Darwa Pass, directly in front of Bandarpunch. The mountain rises up in the background like an enormous white tent. On our expedition, I carried a snapshot of my father, intending to bury it in the snow at the top, if I got there. But the wireless message pulled me back, ending my chances of climbing Bandarpunch. After I returned home, seventeen others in our group made it to the summit.

Retreating from the mountain, I trekked back down to the road head at Sukhi. Along the way, I collected wild irises and pressed them inside my notebook, where they still stain the page. Alone on the trail, I wept and grieved, imagining my father in the last hours of life, sustained by my mother's presence, my brother and sister-in-law, and the hospice nurses. After I finally reached the motor road, I hitched a ride to Uttarkashi and retrieved my jeep, which was parked at NIM. From there it is a four-hour drive to Mussoorie. I got to Oakville at eight in the evening. When I called Ohio, my brother Joe picked up the phone and told me that Dad had died a few minutes earlier, about the time that I reached home.

Death brings out the oldest truths and does away with any pretense of sentimentality. Of course, I wish that I'd been able to reach the summit of Bandarpunch, though I have no regrets about turning back. Losing my father has been a far greater challenge than any mountain I might try to climb. Besides, most of the pleasure would have come from telling him that I'd made it to the top. I'm not a serious mountaineer and am much happier looking across at Himalayan peaks rather than testing myself against rock and ice.

My father's illness and his death made me intensely aware of our separation and the physical distances that we have put between us as a family. India and the United States seem farther apart than ever before. Wooster and Mussoorie are almost opposite points on the globe. My grandparents originally came from Ohio and Western Pennsylvania—and before that our forefathers emigrated to North America from Switzerland and Scotland—but I have never felt any strong associations there, no ancestral tug of war.

I was born in Mussoorie. These mountains are my birthright. Our family has lived here for almost a century, since my grandparents first spent a summer in Mussoorie in 1916. Ameeta and I both studied at Woodstock School, though we had little to do with each other then. Later, we met again in Landour and were married. Our son, Jayant, was born here, and for the first few years of their lives both of our children were raised at Oakville. Shibani, our daughter, attended Woodstock as a boarding student. Even when we lived in other parts of the world—in Hawaii, Egypt, and Boston—we returned to Mussoorie for family visits every year. Finally, in 2004, Ameeta and I came back to India and made Oakville our permanent home. Yet, despite all this, I am conscious of my own dislocation, the foreignness of settling here in the foothills of the Himalayas. Sometimes it feels as if I have taken on an assumed identity. Earlier, growing up in India, I never felt that I belonged anywhere else, despite my American passport. Whenever I left the Himalayas, an instinctual urge pulled me back, a sense of surety that this was home. Only in recent years have I begun to experience doubts and discontentment, the uneasy, persistent ache of alienation.

My attempt to climb Bandarpunch was driven mostly by a need to overcome the physical and emotional trauma of a violent incident that happened at Oakville three years earlier, when Ameeta and I were stabbed and beaten by four intruders. Even as I mourn my father, I find myself returning to those brutal memories. This is something I would rather forget. The indelible experience of our attack still evokes a sense of violation and loss . . . as if I have become a stranger within the sheltering mountains of my birth.

Recovering Memory

The image that keeps coming back at me is a disjointed pantomime of threatening figures silhouetted against the early morning light. One of them is waving a pistol. In that brief instant, the gun looks fake, as if carved out of wood. Only later do I realize it must have been a crude pistol, known as a katta, which fires a single twelve-bore cartridge. Behind the first attacker is a second man with a knife that is unmistakably real. Two of the men have knocked Ameeta to the floor. Her screams wakened me a few seconds ago. Throwing off the bedcovers and running to the kitchen, I plunge from sleep into a waking nightmare. None of the intruders' faces are visible, only the flailing black shapes of their arms, like a demon with a dozen limbs.

Even now those men keep rushing at me, again and again. I run toward them, swearing, hurling whatever comes to hand, plastic pill bottles, a folding umbrella. We collide outside the bedroom door, next to the ironing board. This is where the image ends, a five second loop of memory that sends a spasm of fear through my body every time it is projected inside my skull. Unwillingly, I see the violence repeated over and over again, a flashback of gesticulating arms like shadow puppets. Ameeta's cries and my panicked curses are the only sounds. The attackers remain silent, mute in their savagery. Remembering these moments is an unconscious reflex, an involuntary twitch of the mind, retracing shadows indelibly tattooed upon my brain. What follows has a sequence, a narrative that I've recounted dozens of times ... for police, for journalists, for friends, for strangers. Yet this jagged fragment of memory is torn from the rest of the story, like a piece of shrapnel embedded forever in my mind.

～

July 3, 2008. 5:30 a.m. We were asleep. Wakened by a knock at the kitchen door, Ameeta assumed it was the baker who delivers bread three mornings a week. She didn't check the time, seeing it was beginning to get light outside. On monsoon mornings curtained with mist, it is impossible to tell the difference between 5:30 and 7:30 a.m. Instead of the bread man, three strangers were at the door. Opening the latch, Ameeta asked them what they wanted. They said they were painters sent by the carpenter who was remodeling one of the rooms in our home. We didn't need painters, Ameeta answered, puzzled. The contractor who was overseeing the renovations would be coming later in the day. If they were working for him, she told them, they should wait until he arrived.

"Where is Bauji?" asked the taller man. He had long hair and a gaunt face. Ameeta noticed he was fidgeting, restless. "Bauji?" She didn't understand. "Where is Uncle?" another man asked. Realizing who they meant, Ameeta told them I was asleep. At this point, they pulled the screen door open and forced their way inside. A fourth man who had been hiding behind a corner of the wall leapt up and joined them. He was wearing a knitted ski mask, with holes for his eyes and mouth. Defending herself against the attacker's knives, Ameeta was cut on both hands. When they shoved her to the floor, she twisted one of the men's fingers. He cursed under his breath saying she'd broken it, then kicked her in the face, leaving her dazed. Soon afterwards, they tied Ameeta's wrists and ankles. One of the intruders slashed her legs, cutting through her jeans. He also stabbed her just below her ribs on the left side. Blood began pooling on the kitchen tiles.

By this time I had been wrestled to the floor as well. With the butt of the pistol, one man kept hitting me on the head. Each blow felt like the crack of a spoon against an eggshell but much harder. Though it didn't knock me out, my eyes lost focus. Three of the attackers were on top of me. They worked quickly, efficiently lashing my hands and feet with cotton cords. As they started to gag me, I bit one of their fingers. Again, there were blows to my head. One of the men kept whispering in my ear, telling me to keep quiet. "Chup ho jao!" He said nothing else, and his Hindi carried no trace of an accent. A few seconds later, he tried to smother me, pushing down on my mouth and nose with one hand. In a panic, I began to kick and struggle again.

The warning was repeated in my ear: "Be quiet!" As they dragged me to my feet, I could see Ameeta lying on the other side of the kitchen. She was completely still, one of the attackers crouched beside her. Earlier, I had heard her groan, and I thought she might be dead. All of this was a blur of shadows as I was hauled into the dining room. The intruders paused for a moment beside the cast iron stove, holding me up, my legs dragging on the parquet floor.

"Where is the money?" they demanded in Hindi. "Where is the locker? Where do you keep your money?"

I could barely speak through the gag and my voice was muffled. "There is no money," I told them. "Take whatever you want . . . laptops, cameras."

With my hands tied, I gestured toward the glassed-in porch that Ameeta used as an office and my study nearby, an alcove between the living and dining rooms. Seeing the windows on the porch, I imagined that, if I could get close enough, I might be able to throw myself against the panes of glass and escape outside. But the intruders pulled me into the inner hall. I could hear someone opening a door, searching through the house.

"Take the TV if you want," I told them, trying to point. "Leave us alone." But they kept asking where the money was hidden, voices calm but insistent, as if they were still inquiring about painting the house.

Entering the TV room, the masked man switched on the light. Our television set was too heavy for them to take away, but I saw one of the men pull it aside to check if anything was hidden behind. As he turned to look at the others, I caught a glimpse of his smirking features. He was in his early twenties, clean shaven, with wavy hair and a dark complexion. I noticed scars of acne on his cheeks. Though I didn't recognize him, the impression that remains is the cynical amusement on his face, as if he took sadistic pleasure in seeing me bound and bleeding.

Immediately, the light was switched off. I was yanked back into the central hall and thrown to the ground. This room is darker than the rest of the house, with narrow windows that open onto an entryway. One of the attackers pinned me to the floor, my face scraping against the rough jute matting. Again, he began to smother me. Unable to breathe, I tried to fight back, but he dug his elbow into my neck. The choking sensation was worse than the blows to my head. At that moment, I felt sure I was going to die. Never before had I experienced such complete helplessness and terror, expecting my life to end in a final, deflating moment as my breathing ceased. Fully conscious, I almost wanted my mind to go blank, to escape the suffocating pressure in my throat and chest. After more than a minute, which felt like an hour, the man unclamped his hand and asked again, "Where is the money?"

Another member of the gang was standing over me, and I could just make out his lanky figure against the light from an open doorway. It was the man wearing the mask. "Tell us where the money is or we'll shoot your wife—madam ko goli mar dengey!" As I gasped for breath, I remember thinking it was strange that they called Ameeta "madam" after they had beaten and stabbed her. Once again, I told them we had no money in the house.

When the masked man raised his arm, I clearly saw the knife he was holding as if it were a cutaway shot in a black-and-white film. The mirror in the hall reflected light from the sharpened steel. A commando knife with an eight-inch blade and decorative serrations near the handle, it was the kind of weapon one sees in martial arts films, or violent video games.

Knowing that I was going to be stabbed, I rolled onto my left shoulder, still under the weight of the other attacker. Desperately, I kicked at the masked man. I was wearing only what I sleep in—a T-shirt and undershorts. My legs, tied at the ankles, were white in the shadows. Convinced that I was going to die, I didn't want to give up without some sort of resistance. The masked intruder stabbed me six times on the legs, though the only wound that I recall receiving is the last. I saw him avoid my thrashing feet, then brace himself before lunging forward. Bringing the blade of the knife down on my right thigh, he ripped open a deep gash, twelve inches long.

There was no pain. In shock, my body must have switched off those nerves. All I could feel was a numb sensation of skin and muscles separating like a damp newspaper being torn in half. Instinctively, I reached down and touched the wound, though my hands remained tied. The blood felt warm and my fingers probed inside the gash for a second or two, until I drew back in horror. Unlike the smothering, this felt as if it were happening to someone else, or another part of me. It didn't hurt at all.

After the stabbing stopped, the man who was holding me down must have taken the knife from the other attacker, for he began pressing it against my throat. Somehow, I squeezed my hands under his wrist, fingers clenched around his grip and the hilt of the knife. I could feel the serrations on the lower part of the blade cutting into my palm. Unable to see my attacker, it felt as if I were grappling with my own shadow. There was something intimate and obscene in the way he held me in his arms. For a few seconds, the man began to smother me again but then gave up. I tried to pretend to be dead or unconscious, which was impossible, for I was afraid to let go of the knife and my breathing was coming in shallow groans. Twenty minutes must have elapsed from the time I had been knocked down in the kitchen until now, though it seemed much longer. The man who held me had become an inseparable companion, my anonymous partner in this gruesome embrace. I could feel my blood, slick against his skin, making his knuckles slippery. All I knew of him was his voice, but he no longer spoke. His breathing was close against my ear. We lay still for several minutes, as if exhausted, drained of anger and aggression.

Then, without warning, he let go. The knife was suddenly withdrawn. My attacker pulled away and jumped to his feet. The last thing I saw was his figure rushing out of the hall toward the kitchen, from where he and the others had entered.

Here was my only chance.

I rolled over on the jute matting and pushed myself off the ground. With my wrists and ankles tied, I had trouble getting to my feet, but when I did I was able to hop across to the double doors that open into an outer hall. This is the main entrance to the house, though seldom used. As I struggled with the barrel bolt at the top of the door, I kept expecting my attackers to return. The bolt finally slid open, and I hopped clumsily out into the entryway. Ahead of me was another door, but before I could reach it I tripped and fell. My blood was smeared on the slate flagstones. Forcing myself upright again, I stumbled forward. The outer door was bolted too, and I stretched both arms over my head to open it before leaning down to twist the brass doorknob. Seeing daylight encouraged me, the chance to escape those threatening shadows. Each movement seemed impossible, though I continued to feel no pain. Only the fingers of my right hand were working. There was a heavy dullness in my legs.

Hobbling outside onto the front steps, I pulled the gag from my mouth and sucked in the monsoon air. Immediately I began to scream, shouting for help. Our cook, Ajeet, and the gardener, Ram Lal, live a hundred yards from the main house. Each time I yelled, I kept thinking the attackers would hear me and come back.

Eventually, I saw a figure running toward me. My vision was blurred by blood from cuts above my eyes. I couldn't tell who this person was, believing it might be one of the attackers returning to finish me off. Our jeep was parked a short distance away. If I could reach it and blow the horn, someone might come to our rescue. Hopping across the yard, I reached the door of the jeep but collapsed before I could open it. My head hit the ground and I lay there dazed. Seconds later, when I turned to face the approaching figure, I saw it was Ram Lal. He hadn't recognized me because of the blood. "I thought someone was dressed all in red," he told me later, but at that moment Ram Lal couldn't speak, breaking down in tears. I had to shout at him and tell him this was no time to cry. "Call someone to take us to the hospital!" With one hand still covering his face, Ram Lal turned and ran for help.

After that, I lay there for a while, drifting in and out of consciousness. Others came and went. I remember Ram Lal's son, Vinod, touching my shoulder, then stepping back. Ajeet and Ram Lal struggled to untie my hands and feet, then finally got a knife and cut the cords. At the sight of the blade, my fears returned. I asked them to bring towels to staunch my bleeding. Someone put a cushion under my head. Guddi, Ajeet's wife, ran over and broke down wailing. Chris Cooke, our neighbor, kneeled beside me. I asked him about Ameeta. He reassured me that she was all right. They had found her in the kitchen, unconscious but alive. A short while later a car arrived. When they lifted me inside, I fainted, eyes rolling back. Next thing I remember, Ajeet was slapping my face, telling me to wake up. All the way to the hospital, he and Chris kept talking to me, trying to keep me alert as the car raced down the steep driveway, around hairpin bends. I can't recall what I said to them, but I was babbling, unable to believe I was still alive.

⌘

August 3, 2008. Exactly a month has passed since the attack. For the first time, I am attempting to type with both hands. My left wrist was cut to the bone, tendons severed. This injury must have happened soon after I began struggling with the intruders, but I have no recollection of receiving this wound.

Swollen and stiff, my hand looks mummified, dry skin stretched taut, peeling and stained yellow from iodine. The raw scar forms an upside-down L on the back of my wrist. Across the top is the cut from an attacker's knife, at right angles is the surgeon's incision, the two coming together in a misshapen scab. My left arm is weak, flaccid, and trembling from having been immobilized for the last four weeks. Yet, these fingers, which were limp a month ago, are now working, pecking at the computer keyboard like an arthritic hen feeding on consonants and vowels.

My hand is grotesque. It feels as if it isn't part of me. The wound makes it look as if someone else's hand has been attached to my wrist—amputated and transplanted from a corpse. I can see the red marks of stitches on my skin. The re-joined tendons are tight as guitar strings. Traces of dried blood remain beneath my nails. There are cuts on my fingers. After typing each phrase, I pause to rest. Today is the first time I have tried to write down what happened. The physical act of typing these words gives me hope, because the whole experience was entirely physical—being hit and stabbed, having my hands and feet tied, being suffocated by a stranger's hand, his fingers pinching my nose, his palm clamped over my mouth, the knife at my throat. There was nothing intellectual or literary about what happened to us. It was as real and tactile as the clumsy pressure of my injured fingers tapping these computer keys.

⁓

In many ways I have received a second life, for I was treated at the same hospital in which I was born. It's almost as if everything were starting over again. The Landour Community Hospital is a landmark from my childhood, a place where I came for inoculations and blood tests, annual physicals and occasional X-rays. Twice I was carried to this hospital in a dandie, or sedan chair, with injuries that required stitches—a gash on my chin when I was eight years old and, again, a few years later when I slipped and fell down the side of the hill, cutting open my forehead. I've had my arm set in plaster at the hospital after it was fractured in another fall. There were illnesses too that confined me to the wards—chicken pox, measles, paratyphoid. I have plenty of reasons for hating the Landour Community Hospital, even if it is my birthplace. The three-story building, set against a steep hillside, has always been dark and gloomy, smelling of disinfectant and medicines.

Carried into the emergency room, I vaguely remember being placed on a gurney and lying there while a doctor was called. The hospital had recently been renovated and the medical facilities upgraded with a new surgery wing. One of the improvements was an elevator, but it wasn't working yet. After the doctor arrived, I was wheeled up

15

a ramp at the back of the building and into the operating theater on the uppermost floor. Dr. Samuel Jeevagan was on call. I had never met him before. In his surgical mask and green scrubs, he seemed anonymous, though I remember his calm, reassuring voice, so different from the whispered threats of our attackers. Before he started cleaning my wounds, the doctor bowed his head and prayed, along with all of the nurses. Lying there on the operating table, drifting in and out of consciousness, I can't recall the words of his prayer, but it felt as if I were outside myself for a while, a detached omniscience separating me from my injured body.

Though I had eight major stab wounds, as well as dozens of minor cuts and bruises, there was still no pain, which was a good thing because the anesthesiologist was on vacation. Dr. Jeevagan told me later that he didn't want to sedate me because both my ears were clogged with blood and he thought I might have suffered a concussion. As it turned out, the blood was from the lacerations on my forehead and had collected in my ears. One of the things I do remember is a nurse asking to be excused because the sight of my wounds was making her feel light-headed. After the prayer, Dr. Jeevagan began his work with methodical patience and precision, checking my injuries one by one and dictating a description of each for his assistant to write down. These observations would form part of the police report, and it made me feel as if I were listening to my own post-mortem.

Dr. Jeevagan warned me each time he injected local anesthetic before he began the process of cleaning. Because I had fallen in the dirt outside our house, there was mud and gravel in the wounds. These had to be flushed out and disinfected before being stitched. It was a slow process but I had no sense of time. Afterwards, I learned that I was in the operating theater for five hours, but while it was happening, I was only conscious of the doctor and nurses circling around me, working their way clockwise from wound to wound. They began with the injuries on my forehead and then sewed up a cut on my right arm, where the attacker's knife had sliced my bicep. From there, they moved on to my legs, beginning with a large gash on my left calf, which had bled the most. Another cut extended across my knee and upper thigh. There was also a stab wound near my groin. The only injury I could remember receiving was the knife entering my right thigh. Each time the anesthesia was injected, I felt the pinprick of a needle followed by numbness, as if someone were pressing down on my limbs.

From time to time, Dr. Jeevagan would step outside. Only after an hour did I realize that he was also treating Ameeta in the room next door. When he finished stitching her wounds, he let the nurses wheel her to the entrance of the operating theater so that we could speak to each other. Because of the way I was lying, with my head turned to one side, I couldn't see Ameeta, but we talked for several minutes—awkwardly asking if everything was okay. Just to hear her voice was a huge relief; to know she was alive. The last time I'd seen her, she was lying unconscious on the kitchen floor with an attacker hunched beside her. After our neighbors found Ameeta, she was brought to the hospital in a separate car. Her injuries were not as severe as mine, but she had lost a lot of blood from the wound in her side and her hands had been slashed as she fought off her assailants.

The final two wounds of mine were the most serious, and the doctor had saved them for last. The cut on the back of my thigh, which I was dreading, was about a foot long and very deep. Fortunately, my femoral artery hadn't been severed or else I would have quickly bled to death. During the surgery I was given several units of blood, as well as a steady drip of saline solution. From time to time, one of the nurses moistened my lips with a washcloth, but I wasn't allowed to drink. Lying on the operating table, I felt as helpless as I had been when the attackers pinned me to the floor. Rolling me onto my side, the doctor began working on my thigh, cleaning and repairing the muscles with internal stitches before closing the wound. From time to time, Dr. Jeevagan kept asking me questions to see if I was still alert. At one point, he asked me if I minded that the stitches on some of the wounds would leave a scar. I told him I didn't care. "Just get it over with," I said. It was only when he was cleaning the cut on my thigh that I felt a severe jolt of pain, when he probed an inner nerve. The shock was so sudden, I shouted and the doctor apologized, pausing for a moment before he continued.

Throughout the procedure, I tried to make conversation but felt as if I was talking to myself. Occasionally, my breathing became rapid, moments of discomfort and agitation, but by this time the fear had left me. I knew that we were safe in the hospital, no longer at the mercy of our attackers.

My left hand was the last injury the doctor stitched together. Afterwards, Dr. Jeevagan admitted that he knew it wasn't fully repaired. Until he began treating this wound, I thought it was nothing more than rope burn, imagining that the lack of feeling was because the cord, which the attackers had used to tie my hands, had cut off my circulation. In fact, it was much more serious. The knife had sliced across the back of my wrist, cutting through each of the tendons connected to my fingers.

Two days later, when the doctors removed the bandage and splint, my wrist went limp and my hand dropped without feeling. It was one of the most frightening moments of the whole experience. More than the sight of stitches and swelling, it was the lack of sensation and the inability to move my fingers that made me understand how badly I had been cut. Instinctively, I reached out with my other hand to try and support my lifeless palm and fingers, which felt like a rubber glove filled with porridge. By now, Dr. Matthew, an orthopedic surgeon, had returned to Mussoorie, and he performed a second surgery to reconnect the tendons. This time, instead of local anesthesia, he gave me an injection in my neck that blocked all sensation in the nerves up and down my arm. It was delicate repair work and took several hours. Both ends of each severed tendon had to be retrieved and stretched to the point where they could be fastened together.

However, on that first morning right after the attack, when I was finally wheeled out of the operating theater, the only thing I cared about was that we had survived. Even as I lay there in shock, feeling the sutures pinching my wounds, I was already stitching together a story in my mind, imagining what I would say to our children and my parents. I also knew that I would eventually write about the experience, and it was important to remember the details as precisely as possible so I could relate the horror of what happened and answer the questions I would be asked. Out of the raw terror of that morning, I was trying to compose a coherent version of events. I remember thinking how hard it would be for people to believe that I felt no pain. Already the narrative was taking shape in my mind, a reordering of chaotic, confused memories and disconnected images that I would piece together to make some sort of sense of what had happened, a garbled sequence of events that needed to be rendered along a thread of time.

The random cruelty of our assault was matched only by the overwhelming expressions of love and concern that we received in the aftermath. The doctors and staff at the Landour Community Hospital were exceptional in their skill and compassion. Family and friends gathered in our hospital room while we recovered. The townspeople of Mussoorie, many of whom I'd known since childhood, formed a crowd outside the hospital while we were in the operating theater. When I finally emerged from surgery, the hall was filled with familiar faces looking down at me as I was wheeled toward our room.

Amazingly, I continued to experience very little pain, even after the medicines wore off. It took several weeks, however, before I could walk more than a few steps without feeling as if I were going to fall apart at the seams. Five hours of surgery with local anesthesia gave me a new appreciation for what my body could endure. The resilience of human muscles and tissue is remarkable, especially their potential for physical regeneration.

At the same time, there is a need for inner healing too. Being an atheist, I never felt any compulsion to ask for help from god while I was being attacked. I do not say this as a boast or in an effort to discredit the beliefs of others. It is a simple fact. If there was any time in my life when I might have turned to a higher power to save me, this was it. Yet I did not feel any need to ask for divine intervention or solace. Afterwards, there were many who came and prayed over us, including a faith healer who insisted on holding the tips of my fingers to give me a dose of "astral energy." Immobilized by my wounds and stuck in bed, I had no choice but to let our well-wishers call upon god for healing. Despite all this, I knew that my recovery wasn't linked to any religious power. Even as my tendons, muscles, and nerves began to heal themselves, my psychological sinews were also undergoing a process of self-repair. Here too, it wasn't faith that offered comfort but a knowledge that the human mind can overcome the worst forms of trauma and think beyond anguish and mortality.

As soon as I was able to take the first few steps from my hospital bed to the window of our room, looking across at the steep ridgeline of Mussoorie, I began to convince myself that I would be able to walk again. Though the wounds in both my legs made it impossible for me to support my weight for more than a few seconds, I knew that I had been able to hobble outdoors, immediately after the attack to call for help. My injured body had been driven by adrenalin and shock, as well as a desperate instinct to remain alive. Now, I had to persuade myself that I could overcome these wounds. The damaged muscles would one day carry me up a hill, just as they had done before. These fingers, which were all but lifeless, would soon be able to write again.

But where would I walk and what would I write? It wasn't a heroic impulse that gave me hope, or some sort of spiritual urge to relate a testimonial of healing and conviction. Instead, there was an instinctual need to simply get up on my feet again and feel the weight of gravity, the uneven incline of a mountain path. Equally important was a desire to tell my story, picking out the words on a keyboard. There was no question that the attack had already changed me, even a few hours after it was over. For one thing, I knew that I would never feel invincible again. Yet, somehow, I wanted to set a physical goal for myself that took me beyond mere survival and challenged my body to become stronger because of my injuries. Someday, I wanted to out-distance my fears and leave behind the horror, to reach destinations that would prove I was whole and well again. . . .

⁓

Healing is a journey like any other, a slow, solitary quest leading toward a distant, unattainable summit. Afterwards, when you tell your story, the act of narration dictates coherence and chronology. But while traveling, while flesh and mind repair themselves, there is no clear itinerary. Weeks and months of

*wandering are punctuated by abrupt arrivals and prolonged departures. Your
body is a map with routes sketched out in veins and arteries, with mountains
and valleys of muscle and bone. Walking these trails you grow stronger. Your
pain diminishes, returns, then eases once again. Yet, even before you arrive at
an expected point of culmination, when you are finally well again, or when
you find yourself at the top of a mountain, the story is just beginning.*

❧

News of our attack spread quickly. Television channels picked up the
story, and, within a few hours, it was being reported all over India in running type at the bottom of the screen: AMERICAN WRITER AND
WIFE STABBED IN MUSSOORIE. Along with the crowds from
town, journalists besieged the hospital. Reporters and TV crews arrived
at our house, filming a pool of my blood in the yard and, inexplicably, a
bent spoon that lay near the flowerbeds, as if this were a weapon used in
the assault. One of the reports in the *Times of India* uncharitably referred
to us as "soft targets." After surgery, Ameeta and I had been moved from
the operating theater into a large room in a newly furnished wing of
the hospital. Seeing her bruised and bandaged brought back the frightening sequence of events. We touched each other and wept, reaching
across from one bed to the other. Both her hands had been badly cut,
the tendons of her left thumb severed. Ameeta's lip was swollen where
the attackers had kicked her in the mouth.

For the first time she told me how she'd heard the knock at
the kitchen door and quickly got dressed before going to answer it,
explaining what had happened while I was still asleep. We had shared
this nightmare, and, between us, we began to piece it together again.
Ameeta's immediate memories of the men who attacked us were
much clearer than mine, and for her their faces and voices were more
frighteningly real, still vivid from her conversation through the screen
door and the unexpected violence of their sudden assault as they burst
in upon her. Feeling the bandages on each other's hands, we spoke in
hoarse whispers, partly because of our injuries but also because it was
something that nobody else would be able to understand.

21

There was no time for us to be alone because well-wishers were already arriving, though the doctors had put up a sign on the door: NO VISITORS. Two guards were posted outside. Nurses came and went, checking blood pressure, changing bottles of saline drip, and injecting antibiotics through catheters in the backs of our hands. Coming out of surgery, I was thirsty and asked for tea. Though my tongue was sore and my teeth still hurt from the pressure of the gag, it was a relief to sip the tea as a nurse held the cup to my lips. The police came in to question us, the station house officer (SHO) from Mussoorie and two constables, all of them looking anxious and uncomfortable. We told them what little we could. Ameeta had seen the men, but for me they had been only shadows. She described the attackers carefully, especially the man with the thin face and long hair who had spoken to her through the screen door. The police kept asking about their accents. "Were they Nepali? Did they sound Muslim?" Already they had formed a profile in their minds based on prejudices and preconceptions.

Over the course of the day, more policemen came to see us, each officer more senior than the next: the DSP, deputy superintendent of police: the SSP, senior superintendent of police. The ACP, assistant commissioner of police, arrived with a video crew in tow. It was only when he had been questioning us for a while that we realized these videographers were journalists. They were hustled out of the room by the guards, which led to an argument in the hall. By now, every time the door opened a dozen cameras were thrust inside, as photographers tried to get a picture of us in our hospital beds. Finally, I lost my temper, shouting in Hindi and calling them "bloody fools!" an insult I never use, except as a joke.

The doctors cleared our room a couple of times, insisting that we needed to rest and warning that there was danger of infection with so many people coming and going. But the first two days in the hospital were like a circus, a constant stream of townspeople and politicians coming to express their sympathy and concern. Everyone kept saying, "We never imagined that something like this would happen in Mussoorie." Emotionally, it was exhausting, and I went from casual banter to sudden tears without being able to control myself. I suppose it was good to keep talking about what had happened, telling and retelling the events. As I listened to Ameeta's account of the attack, I tried to fit my own memories to hers, struggling to comprehend what had taken place. Each time we described the assault, it seemed as if we had peeled another layer off the story, though we never got any closer to the truth.

The Uttarakhand state government offered to evacuate us by helicopter, suggesting that we should move to a better equipped hospital in Dehradun or Delhi. But we declined, now that the surgery had been completed and we were out of danger. A close friend and neighbor, Sanjay Narang, sent food from home, and two of his staff, Harish and Rama, attended to us constantly. Though the mobile telephone signal was intermittent, we were finally able to speak with our children in America and to my brother, Joe, who relayed messages to other family members. My parents were traveling and only learned what happened three days after the event. Two of Ameeta's sisters flew in, from Australia and London, while our daughter, Shibani, boarded a plane in Boston to be with us.

The whole experience took on a surreal quality, our bodies battered and barely able to move, but around us a frenzy of activity. Always there were the questions, a repeated inquisition from visitors, police, and journalists: "Did you recognize them?" "Were they after money?" "How did it happen?" "Are you all right?" We had no answers to any of these questions. None of it made sense. For a while, I almost felt as if we were suspects in the crime, accused of hiding something, our replies inadequate. I also realized how impossible it is to reconstruct a complete chronology of facts.

Ameeta was released from the hospital a few days before me, and she went home with Shibani and her sisters, Dolly and Mona. Though attempts had been made to clean things up, there were still bloodstains on the walls and carpets. Furniture had been moved about, both by the intruders and the police who investigated the scene of the crime. A bottle of gin had been taken out of the drinks cabinet and half of it had been drunk. Cupboards were open, and the piano had been pulled apart. Returning to Oakville, Ameeta had to relive each moment of the attack, seeing the screen door through which the men had entered. The police claimed to have searched for fingerprints, but even though Ameeta asked them repeatedly about these, they said no useful evidence had been recovered, not even from the bottle of gin that had clearly been handled by the attackers. In a clumsy effort to collect blood samples, the police had chipped out a large piece from one of the tiles on the kitchen floor. Coming back to see me in the hospital, Ameeta laughed when she told me what they'd done, but later she berated one of the senior police officers, asking him what his investigators had hoped to discover underneath the tile when the whole floor was covered in blood. It almost felt as if our home had been broken into once again.

Two policemen were assigned to the case—Inspector Tamta, an officer from Dehradun, and Kukreti, the SHO in Mussoorie. These men interrogated us more than a dozen times over the next three months. They were pleasant enough, always polite and respectful, but it soon became clear that they were clueless. Tamta and Kukreti were caricatures of bumbling policemen, flourishing a lot of bravado, claiming to have uncovered leads that took them nowhere and questioning suspects who provided no information. Most of our conversations were in Hindi, and like our attackers the police referred to us as "madam" and "uncle." Kukreti, in particular, had a way of asserting his points with random words of English. "Hum ko un ka poora modus operandi maloom hai!" or "Suspect ko hum ney tackle kiya!" They were ruthless in their investigation, rounding up dozens of day laborers, carpenters, and other workmen who lived in one of Mussoorie's slums. This area is known as "Butcher Khaana," because it lies near an old slaughterhouse. Since we were having work done at our house and the attackers had pretended to be painters, our contractor's men were all suspects, and they were hauled off for questioning. At one point, Tamta and Kukreti were so aggressive in their sweep of suspects that the local Congress Party politicians, who had visited us in the hospital and promised swift justice, took out a protest march against police excesses.

During the investigation, we experienced episodes of absurdity interspersed with moments that brought back the full terror of that morning. On our second day in the hospital, Tamta and Kukreti ushered in a team of so-called sketch artists who were supposed to use a computer program to create an image of the suspects. For almost three hours Ameeta spoke to them, describing as precisely as possible the men she'd seen, correcting the images on the laptop screen. The process began with a slideshow of faces, from which she picked a person who vaguely resembled the attacker. Then the chin was narrowed, eyebrows raised, hair lengthened. The nose or mouth were taken off one face and transplanted onto the other. It was a slow, frustrating process, and in the end the composite image looked like an androgynous cartoon character. They repeated the exercise over three days before the picture was finally printed in the newspapers. On the third day, as the sketch artists were leaving, they said goodbye with hesitant smiles and handed us their business cards.

"Actually, we're not sketch artists," they confessed. "We're karate instructors." One of them had a cousin who was a computer technician with the Delhi Police, and they had learned how to use the Identikit program from him.

Several weeks after the incident, when we had been discharged from the hospital, Tamta and Kukreti arrived at Oakville, announcing they had a suspect in custody who fit the description Ameeta had given. We were put in a police van with tinted windows and driven a half mile from our house. At the side of the road, with two constables keeping guard, stood a young man they had apprehended. Ameeta stared at him through the darkened glass. At first, she was convinced that he was one of the attackers, then doubt began to skew her memory. Finally, in frustration, she rolled down the window and spoke to the man, asking if he recognized us. He shook his head, but the frightened insolence in his eyes brought back the sickening immediacy of the attack and left us anxious for several days.

Perhaps the most unnerving aspect of any form of violence is the sense of estrangement that follows, as if your identity has been violated. Mussoorie has always been my home, the town where I was born and raised, yet the attack made me acutely aware of being a foreigner. As the police officers conducted their investigation, the lineup of suspects included innocent people we had known for years, as well as anonymous faces. Rumors, theories, and speculation about possible conspiracies behind the attack ranged from absurdly farcical suggestions to hints of disturbing intimacy. At times, I felt as if I was not just a victim but also a witness and even a suspect in my own murder mystery.

Various theories circulated in Mussoorie about the motives for this crime. One of the riddles was that nothing had been stolen from our house. We had no cash, but there were other valuables they could have taken. Only at the last minute, as the intruders were leaving the kitchen, one of them reached down and snatched Ameeta's wedding ring off her finger. Because so little had been stolen, it was suggested that the attack had been set up to frighten us out of our home. There were whispers about the land mafia trying to force us to sell Oakville, which didn't make sense because nobody had approached us to buy the house and, being a family property, it wasn't ours to sell. There was also a rumor that I had uncovered corruption by building contractors and the attack was a warning that I shouldn't reveal what I knew. Here too, the theory was farfetched. Though I had discovered, mostly by accident, some illegalities related to construction projects, it was unlikely that anybody else knew I had this information.

For a while, everyone in Mussoorie was assumed guilty until proven innocent, and a number of young men who lived near us were kept under surveillance by the police. Nothing seemed to come of it, only false leads and speculation that failed to congeal into logical theories. After a time, I no longer cared if the attackers were arrested. They had come and gone anonymously, disappearing into India's population of more than a billion, out of which it would be impossible to identify anyone. Though I have no proof, I believe they were petty criminals from the plains who came up to the mountains in search of easy victims. The man who wore the ski mask was probably from Mussoorie, a local accomplice who showed them where we lived. More than likely they were after money to buy drugs, which is why they didn't take our cameras or computers. They wanted cash, which we didn't have in the house. Of course, this explanation is as much conjecture as any other and I can't prove it, unless one of the men is eventually apprehended, which isn't likely to occur.

But more than deductive reasoning and puzzling over guilt and innocence, there were larger questions that began to form in my mind. As a child, I was taught that I must forgive those "who have trespassed against us." Was I really willing to forgive those men? I can honestly say that I feel no desire for revenge and have given up on the idea that our attackers will ever receive justice, despite Tamta and Kukreti's best or worst efforts. At the same time, I know that if I were ever attacked again, my first instinct would be to kill those men. Never before had I come face to face with evil. Even now, I have difficulty using that word, though there is no doubt in my mind that the men who attacked us were undeniably evil. Unlike obtuse moral debates in religious or philosophical discourse, this form of evil was not an abstract concept or some form of spirit possession. It was real and present. The man who held me down and tried to smother me was evil. Those who kicked and stabbed Ameeta were equally evil. And yet, at the end of it, like us, they were also human.

⁐

Having been touched by evil leaves you with a sense of anger and violation, as well as a constant fear that the evil might return. While we were still in the hospital, Ameeta was disturbed and unsettled by some of the people who came to visit us, not knowing whom to trust. In the confusion of rumors and unsubstantiated theories about the attack, we began to doubt even some of our friends, who we thought were hiding the identities of the intruders, protecting them from the police. Gradually, after returning home to Oakville, the worst of our fears and suspicions diminished, though they never completely went away. Perhaps if our attackers had been arrested and Ameeta was able to identify them, it might have given us a more complete sense of closure, though some of the anxieties would probably have remained.

Even today, almost five years after those events, when Ameeta and I talk about our attack, we recall how it changed our lives. There are things that we can say to each other that we would never be able to explain to anyone else. At times, those terrifying memories draw us closer together, and at other points, they seem to pull us apart. Some days we withdraw into ourselves, struggling to forget. Silence heals, but it also preserves the pain. We ask ourselves what would have happened if one of us had died, or both of us, bleeding to death on the floor of our house, with our hands and feet tied. Having survived the ordeal, we have gone through a process of healing together and share the same scars.

Walking around the *chakkar* road in Landour, there are times when Ameeta and I see a group of young men loitering by the side of the road, and instinctively we turn back or take another route. We often wonder if any of the faces we pass in town are the men who assaulted us. Even if we don't recognize them, do they recognize us? The idea of a stranger knowing who you are and what he's done to you is more frightening than whatever fragments of memory remain, and it adds to our vulnerability. We have become more alert to possible threats and wary of people we do not know. For each of us it is different, of course. Even after thirty-six years of marriage, I could never begin to understand everything Ameeta feels, how she copes with the frightening memories and the possibility that it might happen again. Though we have decided to remain in Mussoorie, we often speak about leaving, going away to some place where we can feel safe and secure again, moving closer to our children in America, away from the shadows that still haunt us, far away from those dark monsoon mornings when we lie awake listening for a sudden knock at the door.

Ameeta does not share my sentimental attachments to the Himalayas, though she has spent much of her life in Mussoorie and invested a lot in making Oakville our home. An artist and a gardener, she has created a beautiful place for us to live in, preserving the heritage of the property while filling the flowerbeds with colors and bringing light and warmth into each of the rooms. Without her, I could not live here, and she has stayed on mostly for my sake, sacrificing opportunities and interests elsewhere.

One day, about a year after the attack, we were driving up the hill from Dehradun when suddenly Ameeta told me she'd seen one of the intruders, riding on the back of a motorcycle, going past us in the opposite direction. I stopped the jeep and turned around to follow the bike. Though we chased after the riders for a mile or so, they outdistanced us and disappeared. Sometimes, I still wonder what we would have done if we'd caught up with those men on the motorcycle. Afterwards, Ameeta said she couldn't be sure if it was really him or whether she had been mistaken.

For our protection, we hired night guards at Oakville during the first few months following the attack. We also installed an alarm system with panic buttons to alert our neighbors. But our greatest sources of security are the Tibetan mastiffs we got in December 2008. Their imposing presence scares off any trespassers. Unlike the guards, they remain on duty twenty-four hours a day, though much of that time is spent asleep. Our old dog, Maya, was with us at the time of the attack, but her hind legs were crippled and she was dying. When we got word of a litter of four pups at a camp near Corbett National Park, Ameeta and I drove all the way there, eight hours by jeep. Against my protests, she decided that we would take all four pups. Eventually, one of them was adopted by our vet, but the other three remain with us, two sisters and a brother. They have become an important part of the life we've remade for ourselves, guarding us in exchange for two meals a day and our affections.

When the dogs bark, it usually means there are monkeys in the trees around our house, or yellow-throated martens hunting in the underbrush beyond the fence. On a bright spring morning, with irises and peonies in bloom, the rowdy chorus of baying mastiffs sounds a false alarm. Ameeta ignores them as she works in the garden, uprooting larkspur that threaten to overwhelm the other plants, deadheading poppies. She first planted this garden soon after we were married and has brought it back to life after years of neglect. As soon as I come outside from my study, the dogs seem to think they have done us a favor and wait impatiently for a reward. It is a perfect day to be at Oakville. The bitter cold of January and February is behind us and the monsoon is still two months away. Grey-winged blackbirds are singing in the flowering locust trees. Cicadas are buzzing and butterflies sail about like petals floating free on the warm spring air. The monkeys crash away, leaping from one branch to another. Our dogs begin to bark again. But at this moment there is no reason for us to be afraid, and it almost seems as if nothing happened.

෴

A month after the attack, when I was finally able to walk more than a couple of steps, I set myself a goal of climbing a nearby hill, a mile and a half from our home. This forested ridge is called Flag Hill, because the Tibetan community ties prayer flags at the top. From the summit there is a spectacular view of the high Himalayas, snow-covered peaks like Swargarohini and Bandarpunch. Looking eastward, the Gangotri group—Srikantha, Jaonli, Kedarnath, and Chaukhamba—are clearly visible, a crenelated wall of mountains that flank the headwaters of the Ganga. On a clear day, far off to the east, you can see Nanda Devi, a white pyramid silhouetted against the sunrise.

For me, Flag Hill has always been a place where I retreat for solitude and reflection. There are no buildings on the hill except for a deserted watchman's hut near terraces of abandoned fields. Years ago, migrant dairymen kept their cattle on the southern slope, but they are long since gone and all that is left are the ruined foundations of cowsheds overgrown with nettles and other weeds. Most of the property belongs to Vipul Jain, who was a classmate of mine at Woodstock. From the motor road, which passes through a cut in the ridge below Flag Hill, half a dozen trails diverge. The easiest route to the top winds its way gradually up the southwestern face of the hill. Another, steeper, trail goes straight up the spine of the ridge, threading its way between limestone boulders.

As a boy, I associated Flag Hill with all kinds of discoveries. Snakes and scorpions lay under rocks along the path. Stag and rhinoceros beetles clung to the indigo bushes that grew in clumps along a lower trail. Armed with a slingshot or pellet gun, I hunted for green pigeons and hill partridges on these slopes. Almost every time I went to Flag

Hill, I heard the alarm call of a barking deer and often saw these small ungulates with ruddy coats browsing in a clearing. The northern slopes of Flag Hill are part of a reserve forest, where I often go with my binoculars to watch goral, a species of goat-antelope that live on the grass-covered cliffs. Leopards prowl the paths around Flag Hill, and, occasionally, in winter, bears come to feed on acorns. *Rhododendron arboreum* bloom in spring, setting the slopes ablaze with scarlet blossoms. During summer, before the rains, forest fires ignite the pine needles. From mid-June to mid-September, the rain is constant and the hill is clad in ferns and mosses, overgrown with wild ginger and peacock orchids. But autumn is the finest time to climb Flag Hill, when the monsoon mist has finally dispersed and the air is so clear it feels as if you could inhale the sky in a single breath.

There is nothing I would rather do on an October morning than walk from our home to the top of this hill and see the range of snow mountains framed by fluttering strings of prayer flags. Often, I have sat and looked out at those white summits, emptying my mind of errant thoughts and focusing on the sharp profile of the Himalayas, losing myself in silent contemplation. Early in the morning, the only sounds one hears are the distant beating of drums from village temples across the valley, or the shrill cries of whistling thrushes and the cackle of a koklass pheasant.

I had made up my mind that I would walk to the top of Flag Hill before the end of September. Throughout August, I was still shuffling around our house as an invalid. The wounds on my legs were healing, but I was afraid of tearing damaged tissues. The most I could do was walk a short distance along the path that leads from Oakville to a meditation bench my father built, from where he liked to watch the sunrise. Here, a few of the snow peaks can be seen through a lattice of branches. Flag Hill is visible from the bench, its rounded summit like the hump of a bull. Walking down the path, six weeks after leaving the hospital, I needed a cane for support. My legs felt unsteady, as if they would never be able to carry me up or down a mountain again.

By late September, the muscles grew stronger and my confidence increased. The monsoon was lifting, and the leeches had disappeared.

Ferns started to curl up and turn brown. Finally, on the last Sunday before October, I felt brave enough to attempt the short trek. Flag Hill has always been an easy climb, more of a picnic spot than a hike. Though I had done this walk a hundred times before, I felt nervous and uncertain about heading out on my own.

After the first stretch along the motor road, I chose the longer, more gradual route to the top. Instead of scrambling up shortcuts as I usually do, I walked slowly along the main path, pausing to test my legs and make sure I wasn't putting too much strain on my injuries. The week before, I had discarded my cane, but finding a broken branch, I picked it up and stripped off the leaves so I could use it as a staff. When I ascended a natural staircase in the rocks, I could feel a tug of pain in my thigh. My left ankle and calf were numb because of damaged nerves. My hand was still disfigured, the fingers swollen and scabs peeling off the wounds where the stitches had been removed. The knuckles remained stiff, unable to form a fist.

On purpose, I had come alone. Flag Hill has always been a place of solitude for me . . . a private sanctuary. Seldom do I meet anyone along these paths, except an occasional dairyman gathering fodder or firewood. That Sunday, in late September, nobody else was around. As I passed a jumble of boulders that I usually clambered up, I felt suddenly uneasy and afraid. Being by myself in the forest has never troubled me, and I have trekked alone in the Himalayas for days at a stretch. Yet, all at once, I was gripped by a feeling of vulnerability. It was my sixth sense, a primal impulse warning me of danger. Though I had noticed a ropey mass of leopard scat lower down the path, it was human predators that frightened me. The fear was unexpected and overwhelming. I had to resist an urge to turn around and hurry home, even though the trail was familiar. I knew exactly how many switchbacks there were to the top. But at that moment, I was completely terrified, as if confronting a malevolent presence. Every shadow seemed to conceal a threat. Every rustling leaf signaled ambush. I felt as if one of our attackers had followed me to this secluded spot. Any minute now, he would rush from behind and put a knife to my throat.

Another part of me knew there was nothing to fear, despite that first, irrational clutch of terror. I began to whisper to myself, reasoning with my anxieties. I could feel my pulse racing and a cold dampness clung to my skin. Physically, I knew that I could climb the rest of the way to the top, but it was fear that held me back. My legs were still too weak to outrun an assailant, and my injured hand was useless if I needed to defend myself. After several minutes, I began to force my way up the trail again, passing through a cross-hatching of shade under a stand of pines. At every step, the sense of dread grew stronger, and I expected someone to lunge from behind a rock or bush, not a ghost or a demon but a human figure with a knife in his hand.

Five minutes later, I stepped out of the shadows into bright sunlight on the nape of the ridge, where the last few twists in the path led up to a wind-bent deodar tree. From here it was another fifty yards to the highest point, and my fear was ebbing. I was sweating now, as if a fever had broken. The desire to climb Flag Hill was more than just an urge to challenge my injured body. Pushing me forward was another impulsive conviction that, somehow, here on the summit, in the presence of the high Himalayas, I might be healed.

When I reached the top, my anxiety had dissipated. I no longer felt any immediate danger. In front of me lay a panorama of snow-capped mountains. Between the branches of oaks were dozens of prayer flags bearing block-printed images of wind horses, snow lions, conch shells, and other emblems. During the New Year festival of Losar, Tibetan refugees come to Flag Hill. They offer prayers and burn incense in front of the mountains, beyond which lies their homeland. Throughout the day, they worship here, tying fresh flags to the tree limbs, as well as playing cards, drinking chaang beer, and dancing. For these Tibetan exiles, Flag Hill is a place where they can gather and gaze out at the mountains across which their people fled, more than half a century ago.

Their prayers and invocations are printed on the colored flags and relayed on the breeze beyond those far, white summits, toward Mount Kailash. This sacred mountain, also known as Kang Rinpoche, is not visible from Mussoorie, for it lies across the Zanskar Range in Tibet. Kailash is considered the keystone of the Himalayas, the mountain that holds all other mountains in place. For Hindus it is the austere "abode" of Shiva and for Buddhists it is Mount Meru, navel of the universe. Though I could not see Kailash, I was aware of its distant presence, a hidden source of spiritual inspiration that exerts its force throughout the Himalayas.

Finding a flat rock on which to rest, I watched the prayer flags rippling in the moving air. A griffon vulture circled overhead. Though a harbinger of death, the bird was a sign of hope for me, lifting my spirits on its outstretched wings. Northward, the main thrust of the Himalayas rose up in solid grandeur, a reef of ice and snow, where the earth's crust had buckled out of the Tethys Sea millions of years ago. Though I felt a sense of awe, I did not prostrate myself, fold my hands, or pray but simply sat in silent reverence, aware of the far-off ranges but also looking inward. Whatever existed outside of me was also present in my mind, not just an image, but a sense of oneness with the mountains.

Bandarpunch stood directly in front, its twin turrets of ice trimmed with sunlight. Of all the peaks to the north of Mussoorie, it appears the largest and is the easiest to identify. From as long ago as I can remember, I have recognized its shape. My father pointed it out to me when I was a child. Later, I was told the story of Hanuman, the monkey god who flew from the battlefields of Lanka to the high Himalayas in search of a sacred herb, sanjeevani booti, which heals fatal wounds. Hanuman undertakes this mythic journey, determined to challenge death. He saves the life of Lakshmana, one of the heroes of the *Ramayana* who has been critically injured by a demon's arrow. Unable to identify sanjeevani booti among a multitude of Himalayan plants, Hanuman uproots an entire mountain and carries it through the air to his master, Rama, who picks the medicinal herb that heals Lakshmana's fatal wounds. Later in the epic, after setting the demon city on fire, Hanuman returns to the Himalayas and plunges his burning tail in the icy balm of eternal snows. The river that flows from its glaciers is known as the Hanuman Ganga.

These myths have always made the mountains seem more real for me, embellishing the natural splendor of the Himalayas with echoes of an epic imagination. Like the lore and legends of the night sky that bring the stars and constellations into focus, these stories define the mountains with added meaning. Hidden behind Bandarpunch is a third peak that is barely visible, except from certain angles. Known as Black Peak or Kaala Naag (the black cobra), it is the highest summit of the three. Together, the monkey's tail and cobra's hood evoke a mysterious, allegorical landscape that promises answers to eternal riddles and has fascinated me since boyhood.

East of Bandarpunch the mountains concede a valley where the Bhagirathi tributary of the Ganga cuts a passage through the main thrust of the Himalayas. Farther on, the Gangotri group and Kedarnath bulge up in a monumental heap of snow-capped ridges. But the peak that catches my eye is Nanda Devi, punctuating the eastern corner of my vision, faint as a watermark against the sky. This is the highest and farthest mountain I can see. With the sun behind her, she is featureless, a pale silhouette, as delicate as a moth with folded wings. Nanda is the "bliss-giving" goddess. Her blessings dispel all doubt and despair. A dangerous and vindictive deity, she often reveals her violent aspects, but those who worship Nanda are showered with the comforting grace of her benevolence. She is the mountain bride of Lord Shiva, who sits in meditation on Mount Kailash. If I were to ride on the wings of a Himalayan griffon across the mountains, soaring from Bandarpunch to Nanda Devi, then follow a straight line toward Tibet, the trajectory of our flight would take me directly to Kailash, no more than a hundred fifty miles away.

These mountains represent for me three different aspects of the Himalayas. Bandarpunch offers healing and solace, while Nanda Devi promises *ananda* or happiness that releases us from anger, fear, and doubt. And Mount Kailash, beyond my line of sight, marks an elusive threshold of transcendence. Each is linked to the others by a mysterious triangulation of the soul, an inner cartography that maps the routes I must follow. This trinity of sacred peaks signifies the stages of my search for reconciliation and recovery. Tracing their profiles in my mind, I scan the crags and ridgelines for hidden passages through the mountains. Together the three summits pull me toward them, as if through an instinctual force of nature, the same primal impulse that carries a migratory bird across the Himalayas.

Having struggled to reach the top of Flag Hill, I know that some-day I will overcome my injuries and approach those peaks. As I sit here, the last shreds of terror are carried away on the breeze, along with prayers of exile. For a few brief moments, the terrible memories of our attack have left me, those violent figures and threatening voices in my ear. I feel calm and unafraid, at peace with myself and the world around me, released but still connected. Whatever I have lost has been restored, even if it is a transient emotion, an ephemeral touch of deliverance.

What Mountains Mean

Poets and philosophers have always described mountains in human or godlike terms, assigning anthropomorphic traits such as nobility, stoicism, wisdom, and omniscience. The metaphors and similes that mountains acquire through literature, both sacred and profane, compare them to everything from regal elephants to the bosoms of goddesses to celestial thrones upon which kings and creators are seated. The fifth-century Sanskrit poet Kalidasa opens his epic poem *Kumarasambhava* with lines in praise of the Himalayas. He proclaims them a "proud mountain-king!" crowned with a "diadem of snow" in this early translation by British orientalist, Ralph T. H. Griffith, author of *Specimens of Old Indian Poetry*:

> Far in the north Himalaya, lifting high
> His towery summits till they cleave the sky,
> Spans the wide land from east to western sea,
> Lord of the Hills, instinct with Deity.
> For him, when Prithu ruled in days of old
> The rich Earth, teeming with her gems and gold,
> The vassal Hills, and Meru drained her breast,
> And decked Himalaya, for they loved him best,
> While Earth, the mother, gave her store to fill
> With herbs and sparkling ores the royal Hill . . .

Though adjectives applied to mountains sometimes have negative connotations—fearsome, ghastly, treacherous, demonic—more often than not, they suggest positive power and goodness—majestic, magnificent, and even magical. In the past, *sublime* was a word commonly chosen to describe mountains. Current usage, as a gushing superlative, has eroded the original meaning of "the sublime," which nineteenth-century travelers and writers experienced when they confronted mountains, an overwhelming sense of beauty tempered by awestruck fear. Of course, all of this is nothing more than an expression of human sensibilities and attitudes toward the natural world. Poetic renditions of mountains often reflect misperceptions of ourselves, or perhaps our faith in unseen deities whom we imagine to look like us, rather than the geological phenomenon itself. We appreciate mountains largely as a projection of personal dreams and aspirations, objects that render meaning only within the echo chambers of our imaginations.

Similarly, most of our physical encounters with mountains, whether we view them from a distance, circle their slopes, climb their summits, or cross over glaciers and passes, remain limited to a human vantage point. The mountaineer goes up to the top because it makes him appear heroic, strong, and full of perseverance, as if winning a contest against nature. However, as Edmund Hillary reminds us, "It's not the mountain we conquer but ourselves." The pilgrim travels into the Himalayas as a seeker and supplicant, acquiring merit and expressing devotion for the gods or goddesses whose names and mythology have been attached to certain peaks or valleys, in acknowledgement of awe. The scientist who explores high places, collecting specimens of medicinal herbs or recording the behavior of snow leopards, sets off in pursuit of empirical knowledge, to further our human understanding of this environment. He does not try to discover those unfathomable truths that lie beyond the reach of words or formulae.

Even a mendicant who retreats to the mountains may renounce the material world along with his individual identity, but the austerities and penance he performs, living alone in a cave, remain a self-consciously human form of denial. Though his quest is abnegation, he focuses more on himself than the mountain. The truth he pursues seldom emanates from the landscape in which he dwells; it comes largely out of an ego he seeks to suppress.

Instead of defining a mountain in human terms, we must allow ourselves to be defined by mountains. Only then will we begin to comprehend the greater mystery of our tenuous existence. Essentially, we must erase a prevailing bias of separation from the world and move beyond the divisions of perception and reality. This is the message of the Bhagavad Gita, the Upanishads, and other Hindu scriptures. It is also the central teaching of the Buddha and his incarnations. In the Gita, the warrior Arjuna asks his divine charioteer: "Those who in oneness worship thee as God immanent in all; and those who worship the Transcendent, the imperishable—Of these, who are the best Yogis?" Krishna replies: "Those who set their hearts on me and ever in love worship me, and who have unshakable faith, these I hold as the best Yogis. But those who worship the Imperishable, the Infinite, the Transcendent unmanifested; the Omnipresent, the Beyond all thought, the Immutable, the Neverchanging, the Ever One; who have all the powers of their soul in harmony, and the same loving mind for all; who find joy in the good of all beings—they reach in truth my very self." (12:1–4)

Ralph Waldo Emerson understood this when he gave up his parish in New England to seek a transcendent path through the woods. And yet, the most important step toward becoming a mountain is to close the books that others have written and read only those texts imprinted upon rock and ice or in the forests and streams that cascade from above. In *Mountains of the Mind,* climber and historian Robert Macfarlane describes "the great stone book" from which geologists draw conclusions about the origins of our planet—creation myths etched upon the land. Volumes of truth are shelved away in the mountains that reveal mysteries beyond our comprehension. And yet, these high places are linked to us with molecular affinity. The minerals in our bodies, the calcium in our bones, and the iron in our blood share the same substance as the mountains. If we were to break down our bodies into the basic elements out of which we are made, we would understand that we are simply a resurrection of chemicals in the earth we tread. And the ashes that remain after a cremation are no different from ancient carbons in the soil. In turn, those carbons are reconfigured into an organic whole every time a living plant or creature is conceived.

"As beautiful as it is, a mountain cannot have recognition of itself," writes physicist and author Alan Lightman. His novel, *Mr g*, recounts the creation of the universe from a rational, scientific perspective but with a mischievous nod toward the title character. Soon after *Mr g* was published, an essay of Lightman's appeared in *Salon* magazine, titled "Does God Exist?" While asserting his own convictions as a scientist and atheist, he disputes the extreme anti-religious stance of writers like Richard Dawkins. Even if the existence of God cannot be proved, Lightman argues, it is equally true that science cannot disprove the possibility of divine creation.

Suggesting that questions about the origins of our universe are likely to remain unanswered, Lightman writes, "Faith, in its broadest sense, is about far more than belief in the existence of God or the disregard of scientific evidence. Faith is the willingness to give ourselves over, at times, to things we do not fully understand. Faith is the belief in things larger than ourselves. Faith is the ability to honor stillness at some moments and at others to ride the passion and exuberance that is the artistic impulse, the flight of the imagination, the full engagement with this strange and shimmering world."

At the end of his essay, Lightman concludes with a story about ospreys nesting near his summer home on an island off the coast of Maine. He explains that he and his family observed the ospreys for several years, watching the nesting pairs return from their winter migration. One summer, after seeing the eggs hatch and studying the progress of the fledglings, he stood on the deck of his house, witnessing the young birds' first attempts to fly.

> On this particular afternoon, their maiden flight, they did a loop of my house and then headed straight at me with tremendous speed. My immediate impulse was to run for cover, since they could have ripped me apart with their powerful talons. But something held me to my ground. When they were within 20 feet of me, they suddenly veered upward and away. But before that dazzling and frightening vertical climb, for about half a second we made eye contact. Words cannot

convey what was exchanged between us in that instant. It was a look of connectedness, of mutual respect, of recognition that we shared the same land. After they were gone, I found that I was shaking, and in tears. To this day, I cannot explain what happened in that half-second. But it was one of the most profound moments of my life.

What Lightman recounts is an epiphany, a form of *moksha*, that fleeting instant of blinding intensity when we understand everything and nothing all at once.

Alan and I have known each other for close to twenty years, from the time he hired me to teach at MIT. We were colleagues in the Program in Writing and Humanistic Studies and have remained friends ever since. In 2011, Alan and his wife, Jean, visited us in Mussoorie. His essay about God had just appeared in *Salon*, stirring up a minor controversy. Alan was attacked by ardent atheists for conceding that faith and science might be, somehow, compatible. A few weeks earlier, a team of physicists had announced their discovery of the Higgs boson, the so-called God particle, which is partly named after S. N. Bose, one of India's most eminent scientists and thinkers. In the press there was a lot of discussion about science unraveling the mysteries of creation. Though I have no real understanding of physics, Alan and I talked about it around the fireplace at Oakville in the evenings. Both of us are atheists but share the same uncertainty about where to draw the lines between rationality and belief. One of the aphorisms attributed to S. N. Bose, though probably a much older chestnut, sums up my own ambivalence: "Faith is human, doubt divine."

Jean Lightman is an artist who paints exquisite still lifes of peonies, as well as portraits. During their visit to Mussoorie, Jean gave us a copy of one of her paintings, which is a reproduction of a photograph taken by a friend of hers in which a Buddhist monk is silhouetted against the profile of a blue mountain. It is a beautiful work of art, a meditation upon meditation, and we have framed it and keep it on the wall of our bedroom. The title, penciled faintly in the lower margin of the print, reads simply, "Like a mountain."

Our insistence on being different from everything around us is one of the greatest mistakes of mankind. We stubbornly maintain an illusory distinction that sets us apart from rock and ice, water and fire, plant and animal. Both religion and rationality try to explain it through an elaborate vocabulary of separation—soul, atman, spirit, ghosts in the machine, or simply the idea of selfhood. We have dreamed up gods so that we can reassure ourselves that somewhere, someday, somehow, after this life is over, something awaits us: a presence that recognizes who we are. But if we approach a mountain instead, accepting that we are nothing more or less than an integral part of its existence, our ego merges with the nature of the mountain.

In this constant quest for high places, we must erase our desires for meaningless victories or revelations. Rather than conquering a summit, or becoming the first to leave our footprints in the snow, we must absorb the lofty knowledge of a mountain's presence while at the same time allowing ourselves to be absorbed into a greater awareness of what it may or may not represent. Questions and answers should be discarded as we approach the mountain for what it is, free of any preconceptions or beliefs. It is like a story recounted for the first time, in which we are both narrator and subject all in one, as well as the anonymous listener who hears the tale and interprets it, even as he forgets what he has been told. The paradox of mountains lies in the enormity of their stature as well as the invisible space they occupy inside ourselves.

A Buddhist parable, translated by Arthur Waley, relates a story about the eighth-century Dhyana master Wei-k'uan, who lived in the Shaolin Monastery on Mount Sung. He was asked by one of the monks: "What is the Way?" Wei-k'uan answered: "This is a nice mountain, isn't it?" "But I was asking you about the Way, not about the mountain," protested the monk. "The mountain is something you understand," said the Dhyana master. "The Way is not."

❧

Aldo Leopold coined the phrase "think like a mountain," which is the title of a short chapter in his memoir *A Sand County Almanac.*

He was writing about the extermination of wolves in the American southwest, and recounts an episode from his youth when he hunted these predators in the mountains of New Mexico. He describes how he and his companions fired rifles upon a family of wolves, killing the mother and wounding her pups.

> We reached the old wolf in time to watch a fierce green fire dying in her eyes. I realized then, and have known ever since, that there was something new to me in those eyes—something known only to her and to the mountain. I was young then, and full of trigger-itch; I thought that because fewer wolves meant more deer, that no wolves would mean hunters' paradise. But after seeing the green fire die, I sensed that neither the wolf nor the mountain agreed with such a view.

Leopold uses this tragedy as an allegory for the vital relationships that exist between different species in an ecosystem, explaining how, with the disappearance of wolves, an increasing deer population would destroy the mountain environment through overgrazing. He argues that the ranchers who offered a bounty on wolves because they killed their sheep and cattle did not understand the precarious checks and balances in the natural food web. The extinction of one species sets off a chain reaction that environmental biologists describe as a "trophic cascade," one of those felicitous expressions from science that verge on poetry. The cowboys and sheepmen of the American West failed to understand that by eradicating wolves, they would ultimately turn their pastures into dust. Leopold believes that the ranchers had "not learned to think like a mountain."

↶

Years ago, in 1980, Ameeta and I were trekking through Ladakh, soon after that part of the Himalayas had reopened to foreigners. We were camped just below a broad pass, entering the Zanskar valley, before motor roads penetrated this region. To carry some of our gear and supplies, we had hired a horse, owned by a man named Nabi. In the middle of the night, I was awakened by a frightened neighing and clamor of hooves. I went outside our tent and switched on my flashlight. In the beam of light, I could see the white horse rearing up on its hind legs in a panic and straining against the tether. At first, I could not tell what had frightened the horse, but when I shone the flashlight around, I spotted the eyes of a wolf standing at the edge of our camp, the green glint of its gaze reflecting the electric sheen of my light. For several long seconds, he stared at me from a distance of forty or fifty feet before disappearing into the night. Even today, more than thirty years later, I can still see the glimmer of his eyes watching me in the darkness.

To become a mountain—not just to think like one—we must commit these moments to memory. Switching off the flashlight that night, I was aware of the wolf's presence but also the myriad eyes of stars looking down on us from above and the dark silhouettes of the ridges on either side of the pass. At times like this, a feeling comes over us that we are entirely part of this world, connected to every-thing and anything that surrounds us. Just as the wolf and the horse are part of the mountain, so are we inseparably bound to this place, held here by a power much stronger than gravity. The wolf did not return that night, and Nabi was finally able to calm his horse down so that we could sleep. The next morning, I followed the paw prints in the dust to where they trailed away into the rocks and up the ridge.

Near our camp was a small stream that fed into the Zanskar River. While most of the mountains were bare and dry, this spring irrigated narrow margins of grass and wild herbs along its banks—chives, cara-way, and thyme, which were blooming in the short Ladakhi summer. The place felt as close to wilderness as anywhere I've been in the Himalayas, though today it is probably nothing more than a bend in the road, with jeeps and trucks rumbling by. Recalling the eyes of the wolf and the rampant horse, as well as the sprig of fragrant thyme pinched between my fingers, I can think only of Dylan Thomas's line, "the force that through the green fuse drives the flower/Drives my green age." I was twenty-four years old at the time, and about to become a father.

Gretel Ehrlich, one of America's most perceptive and eloquent nature writers, explores the meaning of mountains in a slender volume titled *Questions of Heaven*. It opens with verses by the Japanese poet, Nanao Sakaki:

> Why climb a mountain?
> Look! a mountain there.
> I don't climb mountain.
> Mountain climbs me.
> Mountain is myself.
> I climb on myself.
>
> There is no mountain
> nor myself.
> Something
> moves up and down
> in the air.

Ehrlich explains that after viewing an exhibition of scroll paintings at the Metropolitan Museum of Art in New York, she set off for China to visit the sacred mountains depicted by those painters. She was entranced by the fluid lines and brush strokes that show crags and hilltops draped in mist, with waterfalls and hermits' huts and staircases ascending the rocks beneath crooked pines. As a student of Buddhist teaching, Ehrlich seeks the sacred truths in these landscapes and their healing message. Her first destination is Mount Emei, in the foothills of the Eastern Himalayas, described by ancient poets as "the most beautiful mountain in the world." What she discovers is the whole-sale corruption of natural beauty beginning with the "Stalinesque" architecture of the buildings in the town below, marauding monkeys, shrines to gods of greed, and rat-infested hotels. Her final ascent is by tram instead of on foot where the summit has been flattened into a concrete arcade of tea stalls and gaudy souvenir shops blaring Chinese pop music. Protected by guardrails at the mountain's edge, tourists wait to see the rings of light that twelfth-century poet Fan Che'eng-ta described as "Buddha's halo," which consume the observer, making him one with the mountain. But the swarming tourists are disappointed by clouds that close off the sunset.

Though the book ends with notes of redemption, played on flutes by Naxi musicians, most of Ehrlich's story is about disillusionment and the impositions of a modern industrial society on the once pristine face of Emei Shan. It is a cautionary tale for anyone who believes that mountains are immutable. Yet Ehrlich holds onto the potency of her earliest encounters with the scroll paintings and the mystical connection between artists and the landscape:

> To make a painting of a mountain was to engage in meditation in action. The *chi* of the mountain entered the heart of the painter. Its unbound energy moved ink and brush, but the artist first had to understand the mountain, to have swallowed it whole. To view the finished scroll of a sacred mountain was thought to be the same as traveling there: it represented spiritual progress and altered the life of the viewer, just as walking up its steep slopes changed the consciousness of the pilgrim making the ascent.

Gretel Ehrlich visited Mussoorie as part of a literary festival I organized. We had never met before, but I had read most of her books. On the second day of her visit, I led Gretel and a group of other writers to the top of Flag Hill so that we could see the snow peaks arranged to the north. Climbing the hill, she asked about our attack, and I remember telling her in detail about the men who stabbed us and the fact that I felt no pain as the blades cut into my flesh. Between pointing out the birds and trees on the hill, I kept recounting those events, probably more than anyone wanted to hear, as if the story was enmeshed with this place. Afterwards, she said, "You might as well write a book about it." In her memoir *The Solace of Open Spaces*, Ehrlich escapes the trauma and loss of a lover and companion by going off to Wyoming and finding redemption in the wild, vast spaces of the American West, herding sheep and attending Native American festivals and ceremonies. But more than anything it is the landscape that consoles her and gives her the strength to move on. At one point, she writes, "Everything in nature continually invites us to be what we are." Those words could easily be turned around to say, "Everything we are continually invites us to become one with nature."

Gretel owns a home in Wyoming under the slopes of the Wind River Mountains, south of Jackson Hole. When I stopped by for a visit the summer after she came to Mussoorie, it struck me that she'd found the perfect place. Instead of the sacred mountains of China, or the ice floes of the Arctic where she has spent whole seasons accompanying Inuit hunters, here was her own "home on the range" with pronghorn antelope roaming nearby and the late afternoon sun painting the mountains with brushstrokes of light.

〜

Mamang Dai, a writer from Arunachal Pradesh, in the northeastern corner of India where the Himalayas taper away toward Burma, has written a poem titled "The Voice of the Mountain." The poet's point of view and the "I" of the mountain merge in these verses, so that in the closing lines it is impossible to say who is speaking:

> I am the breath that opens the mouth of the canyon,
> the sunlight on the tips of trees;
> There, where the narrow gorge hastens the wind
> I am the place where memory escapes
> the myth of time,
> I am the sleep in the mind of the mountain.

A mountain can be a state of mind but only if it replaces all of the expectations, fears, and sorrows that occupy our thoughts. Meditating upon a mountain is a traditional technique of freeing the mind endorsed by mystics from almost every tradition. Tibetan mandalas depict a ring of mountains that focus our thoughts on idyllic realms within. Whether it be the ziggurats of Mesopotamia or the tiered pyramids of the Aztecs, Hindu temples, Christian and Muslim domes, or Buddhist chortens, the architecture of faith attempts to replicate a mountain so that devotees enter its depths and worship at its core.

Those of us who are nonbelievers can only approach the mountain itself. We take *darshan* of its presence through the concentration of our senses, bodies, and minds, which prehistoric hunters experienced before any of the current gods were recognized. Like the Himalayan hunter etched upon the surface of a rock in Ladakh, aiming his arrow at an ibex thirty thousand years ago, we must enter a trance that dissolves the barriers between our species and the rest of nature. Like indelible petroglyphs that become part of the stone, we must learn to trace our profile on the mountain.

A primal sense of spiritual longing draws us toward the mountains, just as skeins of geese and other migratory birds are guided by magnetic forces emanating from the earth. Even the most pragmatic climbers speak at times of mysterious forces they encounter at great heights. More than any other range on earth, the Himalayas contain a rarified atmosphere of sanctity. Most seekers are content to find their gods on the lower slopes and passes as well as in the valleys below these peaks. But some believe that they must ascend into the snowy heights in order to achieve transcendence. An extreme example was Tulshuk Lingpa, a Tibetan shaman who led a devoted band of followers across Sikkim and onto the slopes of Kanchenjunga, promising that he would open a portal to the "promised land," a *beyul* or valley of immortality that Tibetans believe exists beneath the surface of the landscape. Claiming supernatural powers of navigation, Tulshuk Lingpa interpreted events following the Dalai Lama's exile as an auspicious moment when the gates of the promised land would open for those who believed. In October 1962, he set off with three hundred true believers to find this hidden paradise. Thomas Shor has written an account of their ill-fated journey, *A Step Away from Paradise*. The conclusion of this quest leaves open the question of whether Tulshuk Lingpa achieved his goal, even as the mountain opened up and drew him in.

Equally passionate and irrational was the bizarre story of Maurice Wilson, a quixotic Yorkshireman who flew his single engine plane to India in 1934 and sneaked into Tibet, following in the footsteps of the first British Everest expeditions. He believed that the true path to God lay up the highest mountain in the world and, if he could reach the top, he would be lifted into heaven. Disguising himself as a pilgrim, Wilson reached the Rongbuk Glacier accompanied by a band of porters who finally abandoned him below the North Col. Wade Davis tells this tale in *Into the Silence*, a tragic history of the early expeditions to Everest. With barely any equipment and no experience of mountaineering, Wilson made a remarkable effort to achieve his spiritual goal. His frozen corpse was discovered the next year by British climbers above the glacier at an altitude of 21,000 feet. Earlier, while pioneering the same route, George Mallory achieved a form of immortality when he and Sandy Irvine disappeared beneath the summit of Everest, their fate a cause for eloquent obituaries suggesting they became one with the mountain, part of an imperial dream, and a fatal catharsis following the devastation of World War I.

These myths and legends portray the mountains as pure and pristine landscapes through which human beings enter a kind of mental and physical rapture. While the truth of the mountains can be harsh and brutal, faith and poetry ignore these facts, transforming the cold and exposure into tests of physical and spiritual fortitude, which saints and knights take on in pursuit of higher goals. In many ways, the mountains become epics in which multiple narratives collide and cascade together, suggesting dreams of heaven.

Among all of its muscular and esoteric contortions, Yoga includes the *tadasana*, or mountain stance. It is one of the simplest of all physical postures, in which a person stands erect with his or her feet firmly planted on the ground, arms held at the sides, palms facing inward. The chest is pushed out and the chin raised, no different than a sentry standing at attention. In this way, an adept practitioner of yoga takes on the mountain's lofty demeanor, its resilience and dominating stature. Breathing is controlled, and eyes are closed. Sinews and skeleton, nerves and blood vessels, mucous and bile, every gland and organ becomes an integral part of a somatic metaphor while the practitioner focuses on a mental image of a perfect mountain, unattainable yet fully realized in mind and body.

"When the sage climbs the heights of Yoga," the Bhagavad Gita explains, "he follows the path of work; but when he reaches the heights of Yoga, he is in the land of peace" (6:3).

The Katha Upanishad echoes these thoughts with the exhortation: "Awake, arise! Strive for the Highest, and be in the Light! Sages say the path is narrow and difficult to tread, narrow as the edge of a razor."

Challenging his followers to engage in a physical and spiritual renaissance, Swami Vivekananda, the great Hindu reformer who helped introduce Hinduism to the West, has written: "You will understand the Gita better with your biceps, your muscles, a little stronger. You will understand the Upanishads better and the glory of the *Atman* when your body stands firm upon your feet and you will feel yourselves as men."

Arjuna's dilemma in the Gita is how to reconcile his duty as a warrior with the battle he must fight against his kinsmen. Through their discourse on the field of war, Krishna, his divine charioteer, reveals the higher purpose of Arjuna's actions and the illusory nature of life and death, which leads to the final annihilation and absorption of the soul, the atman, becoming one with the cosmic whole, with brahman.

Emerson paraphrases lines from the Gita in his poem "Brahma":

> If the red slayer think he slays,
> Or if the slain think he is slain,
> They know not well the subtle ways
> I keep, and pass, and turn again.

These verses were originally published in the *Atlantic Monthly* in 1857, a year in which India saw its first rebellion against British rule and plenty of redcoats were killed, after which they retaliated with vengeful slaughter. The same lines, as translated by Juan Mascaró in 1962, offer a somewhat different gloss. "If any man think he slays, and if another thinks he is slain, neither knows the ways of truth. The Eternal in man cannot kill: the Eternal in man cannot die" (2:19). Profoundly ambiguous, these lines resurface, word for word, in the Katha Upanishad, translated by Swami Prabhavananda and Frederick Manchester: "If the slayer think that he slays, if the slain think that he is slain, neither of them knows the truth. The Self slays not, nor is he slain."

After our attack, I read these words again and again, trying to decipher the meaning of the original Sanskrit as reiterated in English. The lines remain a riddle that confused Emerson's Yankee readers to the point of ridicule. After "Brahma" appeared in the *Atlantic Monthly*, several parodies were composed that mocked his Eastern wisdom. But though the verses remain opaque, steeped in enigma and paradox, I find them strangely comforting.

～

Like Aldo Leopold, I hunted when I was a boy, setting off into the mountains with a shotgun or rifle cradled in the crook of my arm, walking for miles up and down the hills near Mussoorie. It was a youthful passion that verged on addiction. Sometimes I followed village paths or game trails. At other times, I made my way through the forest without any clear sense of direction, letting my instincts guide me, scrambling up grass slopes and through tangled underbrush. Aside from pheasants and partridges, the two animals I hunted most were kakad (barking deer) and goral. Both of them are shy creatures, and the best approach to hunting in Mussoorie was to find a spot overlooking the slope of a mountain across the valley, then sit and wait for the animals to appear. Usually, I hunted with one or two friends, but often I would be by myself. When I turned sixteen, my father let me take his rifle, a bolt action .30-06, into the jungles alone. It was a rite of passage, and I felt as if I had assumed adult responsibilities and left my boyhood behind.

The valleys near our home were steep and thickly wooded. Before the first light of dawn, I would descend along a familiar route, often without a flashlight. My feet knew the way, and my eyes adjusted to the dark. By the time I reached whatever spot I'd chosen for that day, the sky was brightening and I could begin to see the profiles of the ridges around me, the layered shadows of surrounding mountains. By now a dawn chorus of bird calls had begun: the burbling whistle of green pigeons and the cackle of laughing thrushes, the single, plaintive note of a hill partridge, and the wailing of barbets. At no other time of day do the mountains seem so alive, so full of sounds and smells, the sour-sweet odor of moldering oak leaves and the resinous scent of pines. The air at daybreak seems as if it has never been breathed before and the light is young, full of unseen possibilities. Sitting on a grassy knoll, huddled in my canvas jacket against the cold, I listened and waited, alert and silent.

Below me in the valley, I could hear the murmuring whisper of a stream falling over rocks. In the sky, the last few stars were burning out and the moon was sliding beyond the ridge behind me. Grass was brittle with frost, and I could see my breath condensing in the air. Across from me, the opposite side of the valley rose up a hundred yards away at its closest point, extending high above me to the ridge-line. I was acutely aware of the smallest things: the itch of wool against my arms, the perspiration from walking, cold and damp along the collar of my shirt, the bitter aftertaste of instant coffee that I'd swallowed before setting out. Gradually, shapes began to coalesce—oaks and rhododendron trees forming out of the darkness. The day was brightening far above me, but the valley had still to emerge from the night. The air was hardly moving, though it carried my scent up the ridge and I knew that animals would be aware of my presence, even as I sat as still as possible.

Every part of me was attuned to the mountain. While my mind may have drifted off, recalling incidents from school, the mundane anxieties of adolescence, another part of me was completely focused on the forest and slope across from where I sat. I listened for the snap of a twig or a pebble dislodged on the cliffs, any sound that might signal movement.

In his monumental study of the Alaskan wilderness, *Arctic Dreams,* Barry Lopez writes:

Hunting in my experience—and by hunting I simply mean being out on the land—is a state of mind. All of one's faculties are brought to bear in an effort to become fully incorporated into the landscape. It is more than listening for animals or watching for hoofprints or a shift in the weather. It is more than an analysis of what one *senses*. To hunt means to have the land around you like clothing. To engage in a wordless dialogue with it, one so absorbing that you cease to talk with your human companions. It means to release yourself from rational images of what something 'means' and to be concerned with what it 'is.' And then to recognize that things exist only insofar as they can be related to other things. These relationships— fresh drops of moisture on top of rocks at a river crossing and a raven's distant voice—become patterns. . . . The mind we know in dreaming, a nonrational, nonlinear comprehension of events in which slips in time and space are normal, is, I believe, the conscious working mind of an aboriginal hunter. It is a frame of mind that redefines patience, endurance, and expectation.

For that boy seated alone on the ridge, a rifle across his knees, none of these thoughts would have made much sense at the time, for I was there to hunt, not to ruminate on the meaning of my actions. And yet, I suppose, in an unconscious way there was a primitive awareness in me, knowing that I was taking part in some kind of prehistoric ritual or ancestral rite. Whether it was wrong or right, I didn't care. There was no other place I would rather have been at that moment than seated there on that mountainside.

By now, the first bands of sunlight had touched the top of the ridge, lighting up the feathery pines and promising a warm walk back up the hill. If I were carrying an animal, its hooves tied together to make a rucksack, the steep trek home would take a couple of hours. My mind flowed forward and back as I waited. Everything around me seemed alive. Far off down the valley, I could hear a dog barking outside a village, the bells of cows and mules. Sounds carry in the mountains. An insect was crawling up my shoe, but I did not brush it away, keeping as motionless as the rocks around me. My eyes scanned the opposite ridge as my fingers tightened around the cold gunmetal and wooden stock. The stillness at dawn is like a meditative trance. It holds us in perfect stasis, as if time has stopped, and breathing slows, while the current of blood in our veins is no longer seething but moves without a pulse. I felt totally connected to the mountain, transfixed within its vastness, as well as in the immediacy of this particular spot, the moist earth, and dead grass beneath my feet.

And then, I saw the slightest movement across from me, as if a single leaf had turned over on the breeze. A shadow seemed to rustle within the foliage, the indistinct form of an animal still hidden from view. My eyes strained to confirm its presence even as I began to lift the rifle—slowly. It was there and not there. I saw patterns shifting, and, a moment later, a goral stepped into view, its gray coat nothing but a smudged blur in the half-light, with a faint white patch on its throat. The animal's ears flicked nervously as it looked across at me. In that moment, we were each alone in ourselves, yet one with the mountain.

NANDA DEVI

Chasing Bliss

My god is the god of walkers.
If you walk hard enough, you probably
don't need any other god.

Bruce Chatwin

Approaching the Goddess

Several months after my father's death and my first attempt to climb Bandarpunch, I turned my attention toward Nanda Devi. Though I knew that I could never reach the summit of this mountain or enter the natural sanctuary surrounding the peak, my objective was to approach Nanda Devi from different directions and take darshan of the mountain.

Darshan is a Hindu concept that involves little more than being in the presence of a deity, saint, or teacher, sometimes even a natural phenomenon. It does not require formal worship or prayer, though darshan can involve personal rituals according to an individual's inclination—the offering of flowers, for instance, or prostrating oneself on the ground. But in its purest form darshan simply means approaching an object of reverence and accepting whatever blessing is bestowed. Diana Eck, who has written extensively on Hindu practice and beliefs, translates darshan as "auspicious sight" and "sacred perception." Most idols in Hindu temples, even those that are not given a recognizably human form, have prominent eyes that are painted or carved, wide open and staring straight ahead. The devotee who enters a shrine confronts this unblinking vision, and by meeting the gaze darshan is received. Divinity lies in the eye of the beholder. For some, darshan can be a powerful experience that changes a person's life; for others, a daily routine performed out of habit as much as faith.

Nanda Devi is often translated as the "bliss-giving goddess," though the Sanskrit word *ananda* at the root of her name is better understood as "contentment." Bliss and joy are forms of happiness that suggest the kind of ecstatic faith that often borders on insanity. However, the darshan I seek releases me from discontentment rather than evoking euphoria. Most importantly, darshan does not require the intercession of a priest, which is why it appeals to me. The act of darshan is unencumbered by liturgies, pious rhetoric, or moralizing. As an atheist, I can appreciate the spiritual experiences others claim through darshan without accepting the theology and dogma.

Throughout my life, I have taken darshan at temples and shrines across India, as well as religious sites around the world, including the ancient monuments at Luxor and the mosque of Ibn Tulun in Cairo, one of the most peaceful places on earth. Standing on volcanic cliffs in Hawaii where the goddess Pele presides over her island paradise, I received a form of darshan, just as I did at the ruins of Athena's sanctuaries in Greece and Cyprus. At the British Museum I have taken darshan of the Elgin Marbles and the Rosetta Stone. At the Lahore Museum I have looked into the eyes of the starving Buddha, his emaciated figure carved out of gray schist. At the Duomo in Milan I have approached the statue of Saint Bartholomew, who was flayed alive and carries his skin draped over one arm like a cloak—a monument to suffering even more alarming than the cross. And on a midsummer morning in the gardens of the Cathedral of Saint John the Divine in New York City, I received darshan from a snow-white peacock that appeared out of nowhere like a bird from a fairy tale. But aside from man-made sites, it is more often in nature that I have sought darshan, at places such as the tip of Sinai, where coral gardens bloom beneath the unwavering surface of the Red Sea. Submerging myself amid clouds of colored fish, I met their gaze through goggled eyes. Or in the autumn forests of New England, where shimmering leaves of gold made me feel I was hallucinating, dazzled by the fiery blaze of dying foliage.

Approaching Nanda Devi, the darshan I seek is more from the mountain than the goddess, though the two are inseparable. Topography and myth converge in a mysterious, multilayered landscape of narratives where nature takes on many different forms, such as rock and ice, lichens and moss, air and sunlight, just as the gods assume their various permutations—Shiva, Bhairava, Rudra, and Mahasu—consorting with feminine aspects of Uma, Maya, Parvati, or Nanda, all of them being one and the same.

High Places

My search for Nanda Devi begins at the Kuari Pass, where the Curzon Trail crosses over into the Dhauliganga valley above Joshimath. At an altitude of 12,500 feet, the pass is relatively low by Himalayan standards, but it opens onto a spectacular panorama of snow peaks, which rise almost twice that height. The challenge of Kuari Pass is to reach there as early in the day as possible. Clouds often gather by mid-morning, and soon there is nothing to be seen.

Leaving camp before dawn, my companion, Mukesh, and I move as quickly as we can up the steep path overshadowed by oaks. At first light, we are above the tree line and arrive at the pass by 9:00 a.m. It is the first week of November, and all of the streams we cross are rimmed with ice. Yesterday we met a party of trekkers, but today there is nobody else along this route, except for a red fox that crosses below us, the white tip of his tail like frost on the grass.

Kuari Pass overlooks the inner core of the Garhwal Himalayas, which form an arc of 180 degrees, from Chaukhamba, the four-pillared mountain, across to Nilkanth, Mana, and Kamet. Directly in front of us are Ghori and Hathi Parbat, the horse and elephant peaks, caparisoned with fresh saddles of snow. And, farther east, Dunagiri's white pyramid cleaves the sky. Seated next to a cairn that marks the pass, I feel as close to the mountains as I can be without actually setting foot on their slopes. The only disappointment is that Nanda Devi is hidden behind the Pangarchula ridge. We will have to wait until we descend 2,000 feet below the pass before the goddess reveals herself.

A few weeks later, seeing a photograph of me seated on the pass, a friend exclaims, "You look so happy!" Her comment takes me by surprise, for in my notebook, on that date, I have written: "Today, I see the mountains through my father's eyes, even as my own vision blurs with tears." Throughout my trek, I am intensely conscious that I can no longer share this experience with him when I return home.

The traditional approach to Nanda Devi, before motor roads cut their way through the valleys of Kumaon and Garhwal, was to walk from Ranikhet or Almora, across the foothills and over the Kuari Pass to Lata, which is the last village before the Nanda Devi Sanctuary. Most of this route is referred to as the Curzon Trail because it was prepared for the viceroy of India in 1900. As Queen Victoria's representative, Lord Curzon was intent on getting a firsthand look at British dominions in the Himalayas. This was the period of "the Great Game," when England and Russia were competing for influence and power on the roof of the world. In the end, however, Curzon never made his intended journey to the Himalayas, though his trail has served many pilgrims, shepherds, and mountaineers.

In his memoir, *Upon That Mountain*, Eric Shipton extols the pleasures of the Curzon Trail, which he and Tilman followed on their way to Nanda Devi in 1934.

> Fatigue and stiffness left us; feet were no longer sore; having left behind the filth of semi-civilisation we could drink freely from frequent springs; we marched in the cool of the morning and lazed in the shade of the oak and pine woods during the heat of the day; we became fit and gloriously alive. The weather was perfect, the country magnificent. Our way led over ridge after ridge of forest-clad hills; not the oppressive rain forest of the Eastern Himalayas, but gentle wooded slopes interspersed with grassy glades, moss and bracken and splashing streams. The rhododendrons were in bloom, and many kinds of Alpine flowers. Above were the sparkling white peaks of Trisul and Nanda Ghunti. The soft music of running water, the murmur of a light breeze in the trees, the summer note of the cuckoo, these were the sounds we awoke to each morning. With such a small party, we could camp far from the dusty villages, wherever we chose. We rarely bothered to pitch a tent, but lay, instead, on a luxurious bed of deep grass, beside a huge log fire. We lived with a sense of perfect freedom and deep physical and mental well-being. We wanted nothing.

The broad path appears and disappears as we descend across grass-covered slopes below the pass, circling the ruins of shepherds' huts and a stone corral. There seems to be no sign of life, and the only movement is dry grass whisked by the wind that has already pulled a veil of clouds over the mountains to the west. Last night, I lay awake in my tent, listening to a flying squirrel calling in a spruce above our campsite, an insistent chirring sound. Though I recognized its cry, there was something eerie and unnerving about the noise, like someone spinning a top on a gravestone. I left the warmth of my sleeping bag to investigate. In the white beam of my headlamp, I saw its gleaming eyes looking down at me, then heard a faint whisper as the squirrel glided from its perch into the darkness beyond.

Just before we drop back down below the tree line, a lammergeier takes flight with wings that eclipse the valley for a second, a feathered shadow detaching itself from the rocks and soaring out to meet the clouds. I feel a sudden sense of loneliness and exposure above the trees and am glad to enter the forest, though we have been warned of bears. Lower down is a temple dedicated to Pandya Devta, a local deity worshipped by shepherds and woodsmen. Peering into the shadowy chamber of the shrine, I take darshan of this jungle demigod. The shrine is caged off with steel bars and contains a variety of sacred implements. An image of the deity is wrapped in embroidered cloth. It is a crude stone structure encircled by oaks draped with angel hair moss. The flagstone courtyard is decorated with dozens of brass bells and strips of vermillion cloth tied to wooden beams. Shepherds offer sacrifices to this guardian spirit for protection from the dangers of the mountains and surrounding jungle. Mukesh tells me that one man who neglected to perform the rituals was attacked "by a wild beast like a tiger" and sixty of his goats were killed.

Two hours after leaving Kuari Pass we come to a clearing, where a pair of Hanuman langurs are foraging for the last few edible plants of the season. Their silver coats and long tails stand out against the tawny grass. Nearby is a shallow pond that mirrors the ridges on either side. Squatting on their haunches and plucking leaves with agile fingers, the monkeys look half-human. I wonder if, like their namesake, they are searching for the herb of immortality. The langurs watch us come out of the trees, then scramble up the slope, wary of our presence.

At Chitrakantha, which means "picturesque point," we finally catch sight of Nanda Devi emerging above the ring of peaks that guard her sanctuary. The steepled summit is like a vast cathedral that has taken millions of years to carve, buttressed by eroded ridges and corniced with ice. By this time clouds obscure all of the other mountains, and only Nanda Devi is visible. In the sky above her floats a gibbous moon so faint that I mistake it for a scrap of cirrus. The same color as the peak, pale white and blue, it looks as if it has chipped off the mountain and is now orbiting her sacred summit.

Uncertain Altitudes

Until 1808, when the Great Trigonometric Survey of India was conducted under the direction of Sir George Everest, Nanda Devi was considered the highest peak in the world. Today, at a carefully measured 25,643 feet above sea level, her rank has been reduced to twenty-third in elevation, though Nanda Devi has never surrendered her stature or sacred prominence. This beautiful yet forbidding mountain remains the highest peak inside the borders of India. Her perpendicular faces of rock and ice have been calculated as one of the steepest ascents. When asked which mountain he considered most difficult, after having just climbed Everest, Tenzing Norgay identified the eastern summit of Nanda Devi.

The goddess Nanda who inhabits this mountain is both benevolent and terrifying, the divine personification of nature's creative and destructive forces. Hymns in praise of Nanda are sung throughout Uttarakhand, celebrating her maternal power and cosmic passion. Both the mountain and the goddess have fascinated me since childhood, the mythology and lore of the hidden sanctuary out of which she rises. But in the aftermath of our attack, the significance of this mountain has taken on a deeper resonance as I seek refuge and strength in the mountains. While the snow peaks of Garhwal have always been an inspiration for me, they now provide some sense of reassurance and redemption.

Despite her violent aspects, Nanda Devi is known for her beneficence, a mother who fiercely protects her children. This mountain has captured the imagination and claimed the lives of many who scaled her slopes. Yet, for me, Nanda Devi is neither a deity nor a challenge but simply a wild and beautiful place that represents the uncorrupted face of nature, the essential and eternal goodness of the world into which we are born.

Approaching Nanda Devi on foot, following different valleys and ridgelines, I find that I am drawn toward her through an instinctual urge of pilgrimage but also a personal need to escape the shadows that haunt my mind. As Peter Matthiessen wrote in his book *The Snow Leopard*, "We climb onward, toward the sky, and with every step my spirits rise. As I walk along, my stave striking the ground, I leave the tragic sense of things behind; I begin to smile, infused with a sense of my own foolishness, with an acceptance of the failures of this journey as well as of its wonders. . . . I know that this transcendence will be fleeting, but while it lasts, I spring along the path as if set free."

The Eye of Creation

Taking darshan of Nanda Devi as the last rays of sunlight set the mountain aglow, I trace her familiar profile, which I have seen so often from Mussoorie. But here on the slopes below Kuari Pass, she appears much closer, no longer the faint mirage far off in the distance, but a giant shard of rock and ice, pushing up from the fault line of the Himalayas, where India collides with the rest of Asia. Her features are clearly visible: the broad shoulder to the west, with epaulets of snow. The main peak rises abruptly in a steep, unrelenting rock face that only eases near the summit before plunging again more than three thousand feet to the east. From this angle, her second summit is not visible, nor is the coxcomb ridge that early expeditions scaled. She looks impossible to climb, inaccessible, inviolate. I study her visage, the fluted snowfields and couloirs of ice scoured by avalanches. Horizontal bands of rock curve downward, as if bearing the weight of the sky. Her summit is like a fulcrum on which the heavens lean, balancing the setting sun and rising moon.

From where I stand, I can imagine a mountaineer trying to map new routes to the top, seeking the ideal access for a solo ascent. Alpinists speak of perfect lines the way physicists speak of elegant equations—those paths they follow to the top that nobody else has dared attempt. Taking darshan of the mountain, a climber measures each pitch with his eyes and identifies fissures in the rock that will give him purchase on the cliffs, ledges on which to rest. He places pitons and fixes ropes like a musician composing a score in his mind, each camp marked out along the route, rising to a crescendo. It begins as an abstraction, like notes of music waiting to be plucked from a string. A climber's hands can feel the rocks long before he touches the mountain.

Just as I share the mountaineer's vision, charting invisible lines, I find myself observing Nanda Devi through a pilgrim's eyes. The clouds and snow spume that drift about her summit are said to be the smoke from sacred fires of mystics who sit atop the mountain performing rites of worship for the goddess. (One Englishman referred to it as Nanda's kitchen.) This mountain stands out from the rest, not only because of her altitude but through a natural symmetry that suggests perfection. Daubed with vermillion at sunset, she is an uncarved image, the raw shape in stone that a sculptor sees before chiselling her face, the hidden idol awaiting discovery beneath the surface of a rock. In one of the more playful Hindu myths, Shiva and his bride, the mountain goddess, are cavorting in the Himalayas. Teasing her omnipotent lover, the goddess sneaks up behind him and innocently covers his eyes with her hands. Suddenly, the world disappears into a void of darkness. As creator, Shiva's vision brings the universe into being. When his all-seeing eyes are closed, nothing exists. The light is extinguished, and we plunge into darkness. Alarmed, the goddess removes her hands and restores the world as we know it.

Penetrating the Sanctuary

One of Nanda's most persistent devotees is my friend, mentor, and neighbor, Bill Aitken. As a young man straight out of Scotland, he hitchhiked across Turkey, Iran, and Afghanistan in 1959, eventually ending up in the foothills of the Himalayas. He has stayed here ever since, becoming a citizen of India and a worshipper of mountains. But unlike most world travelers and hippies of the generation that followed, he retains a sharp and critical eye toward religious chicanery and false prophesies. In his book *The Nanda Devi Affair*, Bill writes that he arrived in the hill town of Kausani and encountered his guru and his mountain on the same day. Aitken's fascination with Nanda Devi grew from that first moment he saw her, rising above the lower ranges of Kumaon. Over a period of twenty years, he pursued the goddess, an infatuation that was both physical and spiritual. After several arduous treks, he was finally able to enter the sanctuary of Nanda Devi, nearly slipping to his death on the Rhamani slabs, an exposed rockface that bars the way. Eventually, he scrambled up the crags with the help of sure-footed Garhwali porters. Arriving in the monsoon, Aitken found the mountain hidden behind clouds. Building a small shrine in which he placed an image of Nandi, Shiva's sacred bull, he waited for the goddess to reveal herself. Eventually, she consented to give him darshan.

As I sat on the cave roof facing the black ramparts across the echoing river, the shredded mist higher up the mountain suddenly revealed a patch of blue. It was the first hopeful sign in five days of wet marching that the weather might clear. Contented, I sat back to breathe in the pleasure of the moment and as I idly stretched in the warming air the great moment happened. The top layer of cloud began to thin and tantalisingly the outline of the main peak began to flicker into recognition. I couldn't believe my eyes. Unknown to me I had built the temple to Nandi exactly facing the Goddess. It seemed a minor miracle that the sun should choose this moment to reward my labours. As the reluctant beauty of the mountain strove to outwit the parting cloud cover I was aware almost painfully of the strong erotic pull this peak of passion had on me. It was almost as if a spiritual striptease was being performed. I could only gape as the revelation neared its climax. The sun climbed to disperse the upper band of mist and lo! the full breathtaking face of the mountain coyly floated into focus. Only her peak was revealed, as lovely a portrait in ermine as any queen could wish for. She sailed majestically against the brief blue of eternity and I could not take my eyes off this stunning apparition. Everything I desired had come to fruition. There was a feeling of utter fulfillment and a song of thankfulness welled up from that core of contentment that follows the union of heaven and earth; the perfect end to all our striving.

Even today, thirty-five years after that moment, Bill continues to describe his darshan of the mountain as "a supreme moment of cosmic consciousness." He believes that Nanda Devi told him to write, inspiring the book about his quest for the goddess as well as several other travel memoirs about his experiences in India. Though Bill writes with spiritual flourish and passion, he remains a totally grounded mystic with a dry sense of humor.

In the final paragraph of *The Nanda Devi Affair*, Aitken sums up his search for the goddess and her mountain.

The conviction that the outer and inner, the spirit and flesh are no different may be the ultimate discovery of he who seeks to know the essential nature of his mountain Goddess. But equally important I discovered is the prayer that implores the beloved never to withdraw her favours. For the few who spurn the static state of oneness and prefer to place themselves between the pull of the magnet and the lodestone there can be no peace. Only the dulcitude of desire.

Illusions of Conquest

Eric Shipton described the first ascent of Nanda Devi, in 1936, by Bill Tilman and Noel Odell as "the finest mountaineering achievement ever performed in the Himalayas." Two years earlier, Shipton and Tilman, along with Angtharkay, Pasang, and Kusang, were the first men to find a route up the Rishi Ganga gorge into the natural sanctuary at the foot of this mountain, a bowl-like valley that is all but inaccessible.

During the early years of Himalayan exploration, Nanda Devi remained an elusive summit, frustrating the skills and determination of the best mountaineers of that generation, including Dr. Tom Longstaff and his Italian guides, the Brocherel brothers. Virtually unapproachable, Nanda Devi and her sanctuary are protected by a chain of peaks over twenty thousand feet that guard the innermost sanctum of her domain.

When Nanda Devi was first climbed, her summit represented the highest altitude that mountaineers had ever reached. One of the climbers in this 1936 Anglo-American expedition was a young navy doctor from New York City named Charlie Houston. According to his biographer, Bernadette McDonald, he was included in the expedition as much for his medical skills as his accomplishments as a climber. Houston was particularly interested in the effects of altitude and oxygen deprivation on the human body, and he studied the causes of pulmonary and cerebral edema. In the end, however, it wasn't altitude sickness that ruined Charlie Houston's chance to climb Nanda Devi, but a spoiled tin of meat. Less than a thousand feet from the summit, with complete confidence that they would reach the top the next day, Houston and Odell celebrated their impending success by opening a can of corned beef for dinner. Odell scooped out the meat from the top of the tin while Houston finished off the bottom, which he didn't realize had been punctured and contaminated. Two hours later, he came down with a severe case of food poisoning and Tilman had to take his place in the summit party. As a consolation, however, Houston, Tilman, and Pasang Kikuli completed an epic crossing of Longstaff Col, a near vertical route out of the sanctuary, which brought them into the Gauri Ganga valley.

Severe floods in Garhwal and Kumaon in 1936 coincided with Tilman and Odell's successful climb. Many believed that the conquest of Nanda Devi provoked the wrath of the goddess. Whether it was the tin of corned beef or those first bootprints on the summit, climbing Nanda Devi amounted to a form of sacrilege in the minds of many Hindus who believe that the upper reaches of the Himalayas are sacrosanct, the domain of deities, not human beings.

The first ascent of Nanda Devi was remarkable because it represents an early example of "light" climbing, rather than the usual "siege tactics" that most expeditions employed. After his successful climb, H. W. Tilman wrote: "To some the Himalayas may be only a name associated perhaps with a mountain called Everest; to geologists they provide a vast field for the starting and running of new hares; to other learned men, glaciologists, ethnologists, or geographers, the Himalaya are a fruitful source of debate in which there is no common ground, not even the pronunciation of the name; while to the mountaineer they furnish fresh evidence, if such were needed, of the wise dispensation of a bountiful Providence."

The western approach that Tilman, Houston, and Odell ascended is no longer accessible to climbers. Following the creation of Nanda Devi National Park in 1981, mountaineers have been refused access to the sanctuary. Now that entry up the Rishi Ganga gorge is forbidden, recent expeditions have focused on Nanda Devi East, which stands about 1,300 feet lower than the western summit and is accessible from the Milam valley and Longstaff Col. Nanda Devi East was first climbed by a Polish team in 1939.

In 1993 a joint expedition of the Indian Army Corps of Engineers and naturalists from the Wildlife Institute of India undertook an environmental survey of the sanctuary and removed more than a ton of garbage from the area near base camp. Several members of this team also successfully reached the summit. Following their report of widespread pollution, poaching, and destruction of juniper, yew, and birch forests, the sanctuary remains closed to trekkers, mountaineers, and shepherds.

Braided together like the multiple strands of a climbing rope to which an alpinist harnesses himself and entrusts his survival, the many stories of Nanda Devi anchor us to this mountain. Even if we are not mountaineers, we can understand what James Ramsey Ullman meant when he wrote: "The climbing of earth's heights, in itself, means little. That men want and try to climb them means everything. For it is the ultimate wisdom of the mountains that man is never so much a man as when he is striving for what is beyond his grasp, and that there is no battle worth the winning save that against his own ignorance and fear."

Pathfinding Hero

Nobody alive today has more firsthand experience of Nanda Devi than Dorjee Lhatoo, who has climbed the mountain on three occasions and reached both summits—east and west. His first encounter was during the Indo-French expedition in 1975 when he stood on top of Nanda Devi East along with Yves Pollet-Villard and Walter Cecchinel. The following year, he returned to the mountain with an Indo-Japanese expedition, in which two Japanese team members successfully climbed both summits and completed a traverse of the connecting ridge. Lhatoo supported the Japanese climbers by ascending from the west and replenishing their oxygen and other supplies. Bad weather intervened to stop him from attempting a traverse in the opposite direction. His third and final encounter with Nanda Devi was in 1981, when he participated in the joint Indian men's and women's expedition. One of the country's most distinguished mountaineers and a member of the elite community of Sherpa climbers in Darjeeling, Lhatoo summited Everest in 1984, and successfully ascended a number of other major Himalayan peaks.

Despite his many excursions, today Lhatoo is reluctant to leave his home in Darjeeling, where he was an instructor at the Himalayan Mountaineering Institute (HMI) from 1962 to 2000. A dignified, soft-spoken man in his seventies with a trim, athletic build, Lhatoo looks as if he could still climb a mountain with ease. His manner is casual but cultured, almost courtly, as he pours a glass of HIT beer, an extra-strong brew from Sikkim that lives up to its name. His living room contains climbing mementoes and pictures on the walls, including one of himself as a young man, standing between his mentors, Tenzing Norgay (the first man to climb Everest) and Nawang Gombu, (the first man to climb it twice). Lhatoo is taller than both, with a rakish hairstyle that makes him look a little like Elvis Presley.

On the opposite wall is a large photograph of the snow peaks one can see from Darjeeling: a dramatic panorama with Everest and Lhotse to the west and Kanchenjunga massif in the center. The panorama extends eastward to Chomolhari, a 24,000 foot peak on the border of Bhutan and Tibet, which Lhatoo climbed in 1970.

This mountain has special significance for him because it overlooks the Chumbi Valley, his ancestral home. A narrow corridor
between Sikkim and Bhutan, this strip of land is part of Tibet, one
of the many anomalies of Himalayan cartography, where borders
never follow a straight or predictable line. Until Nepal opened up,
the Chumbi Valley was the only route to Everest, traveled by George
Mallory and other climbers in the 1920s and 1930s. Lhatoo was born
in Yatung, a small settlement along the caravan road from Gangtok to
Lhasa. His father was caretaker for the Himalayan Club dak bunga-
lows on this route. When Spencer Chapman led the first successful
expedition to Chomolhari in 1936, he stayed with Lhatoo's family.

"Chomolhari is considered a sacred mountain by the Bhutanese,"
he explains. "In Thimpu, before we set off, the king gave us an ornate
copper pot called a yangu, and asked us to place it on the summit. It
was very beautiful and contained all of the different minerals known
to man, including gold and diamonds. I put it in my backpack and
carried it to the top. All along our route, villagers came out to see
who was carrying the yangu and they pressed their foreheads to my
pack as I walked by."

Lhatoo smiles hesitantly. "I'm not a religious person. In fact, I
don't believe in rituals . . . a lot of humbug. But I do not disrespect
religion, either. Having been asked to carry the yangu, I was determined to fulfill my responsibility, whether I believed in it or not."

Like Nanda Devi, Chomolhari is named after a goddess who
is both protective and full of wrath, a paradox that symbolizes the
unpredictable and ever-changing elements of Himalayan mountaineering, where disaster often follows in the footsteps of success.
Though Lhatoo and another Indian climber reached the summit,
their second team vanished completely.

Five years later, Lhatoo made his first ascent of Nanda Devi East
as part of an Indo-French expedition attempting a traverse. That year
there was a lot of snow at lower altitudes, which made the difficult
entry into the sanctuary even more treacherous than usual. "In retro-
spect it may seem like a great experience, but while you are climbing
in and out of the sanctuary it is very difficult, very exposed, with

rocks falling from above, and then, below you . . ." Lhatoo gestures to indicate a fall of several thousand feet or more.

Concerned about the safety of their porters, the French team fixed ropes all the way from Dharali into the Rishi Ganga gorge. The Indian team leader, Colonel Balwant Sandhu, organized helicopter drops of supplies from Joshimath, which reduced the need for porters.

Lhatoo explains how the Indian team provided food up to base camp, after which French cuisine took over. The army arranged for "meat on the hoof," which meant a flock of goats and sheep that accompanied the party, to be butchered along the way.

"By the time the goats had walked all the way it into the sanctuary, there wasn't any meat left on them, just skin and bones," he recalls.

As a contingency plan, Colonel Sandhu had brought two hunting rifles with him. They had heard stories about wild sheep and other game with which they hoped to supplement their diet. "But we didn't see any animals," said Lhatoo, "except for some ibex that were far out of range." Though Tilman and Shipton had described a peaceable kingdom within the sanctuary where herds of bharal grazed near their tents like tame livestock, by the 1970s, poachers and shepherds had made inroads into the sanctuary, destroying the high meadows and birch forests and decimating the herds of wild animals.

Just as Lhatoo rejects spiritual and religious associations with a mountain, he has little time for nationalistic interests. "When you are climbing a mountain, you do not think of yourself as an Indian, or an Englishman, American, Japanese, or French. There are no borders in the mountains," he says. "It's only when you come back down to Delhi that the flag waving begins and the country lays claim to your achievements."

As he describes the twin summits of Nanda Devi, Lhatoo holds up his left hand with the two middle fingers folded down and the index finger and little finger raised to suggest a profile of the mountain. With his other hand he traces the route of the traverse, showing how they climbed up one side and descended from another. His voice is matter-of-fact, almost expressionless in its careful, methodical recitation of events. The words allow for little exaggeration. "Very exposed," is the strongest phrase he uses to describe what must have appeared to be an impassable wall of ice. And when he tells of lives lost on the mountain, he doesn't embellish the tragedy. The expression he chooses most often to describe a climber's death is that he "disappeared on the mountain," a gentle, respectful euphemism for the bone shattering tumble down unyielding rock and ice.

I ask him how he deals with fear on the mountain. Sitting back in his chair, his thinks a moment before replying. "When you are afraid, you think of the immediate danger, but also what lies ahead. The only way to deal with fear is to focus on what must be done right now, the task at hand—find the rope, clip on, make your way down. You cannot let what might happen next overwhelm you," he says, then adds after a pause: "Our will to live helps us overcome fear."

Once, he almost lost his life while rock climbing, falling a hundred feet and slamming into the side of a cliff while his rope and harness held him. The other near-fatal accident occurred when he was driving a motorcycle up the road from Siliguri to Darjeeling during the monsoon. While passing a truck, he collided with a car and was thrown down the side of the hill.

"Both times, I remember thinking *this is it*," he says. "And then I felt myself hit the rocks. There was no pain at that moment. It was the same with the motorcycle accident. I remember hitting the car, that's all, then later being dragged up the hill."

He broke both arms, several ribs, and his femur as well as cracking a couple of vertebrae.

"But there was no pain at first . . . maybe later in the hospital, but when it happened . . . nothing." He smiles and shrugs, suggesting that death doesn't hurt. The painful part is survival.

Being a refugee from Tibet, Lhatoo expresses ambivalence toward the experience of exile. India is very much his home, yet he has vivid memories of what lies beyond the ranges. A few years ago he accompanied a Canadian film crew to Everest base camp in Tibet. They had hoped to enter the Chumbi Valley but at the last minute permission was refused by the Chinese authorities.

"I was disappointed," Lhatoo says. "I have clear memories of our home in Yatung, and I wanted to see it again."

At the same time, he has few illusions about the past. "Of course, I am opposed to the Chinese takeover of Tibet, but when young people today talk romantically about Tibet, I tell them that my memory is of a cold, dusty, dark place. We often didn't know where our next meal was coming from. I left Tibet when I was seven, and I saw my first water faucet in Gangtok."

One of Lhatoo's earliest memories is of watching disassembled motorcycles and motorcars being carried on the backs of porters all the way from India to Lhasa, where they were put back together again. "Just so the lamas could take joy rides around the Potala Palace. The cars were Dodge, I think, and they had to carry all of the petrol too!"

When Lhatoo returned to Nanda Devi in 1976 with the Indo-Japanese expedition, he was stranded at Lata village for three weeks with mounds of gear and supplies that needed to be transported into the sanctuary. A shortage of porters and political wrangling among the Garhwalis made it difficult to get the baggage up to base camp.

Despite early setbacks, the Japanese were able to achieve what the French had not accomplished: a true traverse of the mountain. Climbing the eastern summit first, they descended to the intervening ridge and crossed the mile and a half between the twin peaks.

"The ridge has been described as 'knife-edged,' but we could see the two Japanese almost running across. They were excellent climbers. Much more difficult than the traverse was the final ascent to the western summit. We met them and gave them oxygen, which helped them keep on going to the top. After they crossed, we were planning to repeat the traverse in the opposite direction but had to abandon this plan because of bad weather."

Lhatoo's final experience on Nanda Devi was in the summer of 1981, with an Indian expedition that succeeded in putting the first women on the summit: Chandraprabha Aitwal, Harshwanthi Bisht, and Rekha Sharma. Following an extended stay in the sanctuary to acclimate, they moved up the mountain to Camp 4. The men and women were paired off and roped together. After having been stranded at high altitude for four days because of high winds and severe cold, the team set off at 4:00 a.m. Lhatoo was climbing with Rekha Sharma, and they were the last to leave camp. With so many recent expeditions on the mountain, "there were ropes fixed all the way up Nanda Devi, like telephone lines," he recalls. Yet, progress was slow. Lhatoo and Rekha finally reached the top at 5:30 p.m. Ordinarily, the climbers would have turned back well before, but they knew this was the only opportunity they would have.

"By the time all of us reached the summit, it was completely dark," he remembers, "but there was a moon and we began to descend by its light." As a precaution, Lhatoo cut a rope of about thirty feet, measuring it out with his arms. He anchored this at the top so they could rappel down the steepest part of the rock face. This was accomplished, and the six climbers slowly made their way down by moonlight. It was exhausting work, and they had been climbing since early that morning. A thousand feet above Camp 4, there was near disaster.

"Suddenly, I went blind," Lhatoo recalls. "I had been concentrating so much on getting us down safely, but then, I couldn't see anything at all. It wasn't snow blindness, just exhaustion and altitude. Fortunately, Rekha was able to locate the fixed rope and we clipped on. After that, I felt more confident that we would get down safely."

Inch by inch, Lhatoo felt his way down, hitching and unhitching himself to the ice-clotted ropes until they finally reached their tent at 5:00 a.m., after climbing for twenty-five hours.

"When I lay down, I collapsed completely. Just as I was falling asleep, I remember worrying about what would happen the next day. Being blind, it would be impossible for me to get off the mountain safely." He smiles ruefully, considering the consequences for himself and his teammates. "Fortunately, when I finally woke up and opened my eyes, I could see again."

With his sight restored, Lhatoo was able to lead the team off the mountain, though he remembers that those who followed were not as fortunate. An Indian Army paratroop expedition was on its way up Nanda Devi as they were coming down. One of the climbers was a former student of Lhatoo's from HMI, an officer named Lakha Singh.

"Sandhu told us to leave our fixed ropes behind for the paratroopers, as well as our tents and extra supplies of fuel and food. They would bring the equipment down for us after they finished. But Lakha didn't like Sandhu, and he insisted that they would fix their own ropes."

The paratroopers seemed overconfident on the mountain. If three "girls" had climbed Nanda Devi, they believed it would be easy enough for them. Caught in a storm on his descent from the summit, Lakha died of exposure. Another paratrooper was killed while rappeling down the rope that Lhatoo had fixed just below the summit.

"There was no knot at the end, nothing to stop him. He came down jumping, the way they teach them in the army, though the Sherpas warned him to be careful. When he reached the end of the rope, he just kept going. . . ."

Maternal Hymns

> Victory to Nanda!
> Victory to the Great Goddess . . .
> Victory to the Mother of the World!

Songs in praise of Nanda Devi are part of the sacred repertoire of priests and balladeers throughout Garhwal and Kumaon. The mythology of this region recognizes Nanda as the chaste daughter of the mountains who is given in marriage to Lord Shiva, the supreme ascetic and master of the universe. Nanda lives most of the year with her husband in his remote and inhospitable home on Mount Kailash, but she longs to return to the familiar comforts of her natal village in Uttarakhand. Pilgrimages like the Raj Jaat Yatra reenact the ritual journey of the bride leaving her parents' home and being carried away in marriage. Pilgrims literally and figuratively "escort" the goddess with songs and prayers. Her leaving is accompanied by sadness and mourning, while her return is greeted with joy and thanksgiving.

The geography of the Himalayas merges with the fertile cosmogony of the goddess, symbolizing an ongoing struggle between male and female aspects in nature. Nanda Devi is an incarnation of the primal mother, Maya, who created the universe including Shiva, her consort. In one of her most violent avatars, the goddess sacrifices herself in order to overcome the taboo of incest so that she can have sexual intercourse with Shiva. This gruesome and erotic fertility myth involves a dance with seven knifes, which leaves her violated and dismembered. She kills herself in order to resolve conflicting gender roles on a cosmic level. Her self-sacrifice, symbolized by her menstrual blood and dramatized in the dance with seven knives, is all part of what folklorist William Sax in his book *Mountain Goddess* describes as "the separation and reunion of a primordial whole . . . her self-destruction introduces duality into her being. Nanda Devi's myth, and especially her pilgrimages, can be understood as attempts to reunite that primordial whole," not unlike the collision of continents out of which the Himalayas were born.

Numerous episodes converge within this story, including a version of the myth that Sax translates, in which Nanda adopts a buffalo calf. Ignoring Shiva's warnings,

> Devi cuts her little finger,
> and the milk comes flowing out.
> Shiva says, 'Why should I raise him?'
> Devi cuts her little finger,
> puts it in the young calf's mouth.
> Devi says, 'How fine he is!
> What a lovely, loyal child.
> He's drinking milk. Be off, my swami! (meaning Shiva).
> From my little finger, milk is flowing!'

When the male buffalo matures, he turns into a monstrous demon, Mekhasur, who threatens to rape and kill Nanda Devi. At first she flees from the demon, then she finally fights with him and cuts him with her blades. But every drop of the buffalo's blood brings another demon to life. Ultimately, the only way she can destroy him is to drink his blood before it touches the ground. These narratives assert taboos of incest and depict the goddess in her most ferocious form. They also justify animal sacrifices made in her honor. Though these

practices are discouraged, the blood of male buffalos and other animals, including rams and goats, is offered to Nanda at many of her
shrines.

Daughter of the Mountain

In 1948 two young Americans who had recently survived the war
against Hitler stood by the side of US Route 66 in Los Angeles, heading east. They carried rucksacks, ropes, ice axes, and a cardboard sign
that read: SWISS ALPS. What they didn't tell anyone as they hitchhiked
across the United States, then caught a freighter to Europe, was their
real destination—the Himalayas. Willi Unsoeld and his companion
had summited most of the major peaks in the Pacific Northwest, but
they were determined to gain entry into the competitive fraternity of
international mountaineering.

After kicking around Switzerland for a couple of months and
scaling peaks like Jungfrau and the Matterhorn, they ran out of
money. Undeterred, the first postwar American Himalayan Expedition headed to Gothenburg, Sweden, where they got jobs in an
iron foundry to pay for their passage to India. Eventually, working
as deckhands, riding third-class trains from Bombay to Delhi and on
to Dehradun, swapping stories for meals, they reached their ultimate
destination: Nilkanth, a 21,640 foot peak in the Garhwal Himalayas
that stands near the Tibetan frontier. Edmund Hilary tried to climb it
once but gave up, claiming it was "too bloody steep for me!"

Bad weather and dysentery kept Unsoeld from reaching the summit, but standing on Nilkanth, he looked across to see what he would
call "the most beautiful mountain in the world—Nanda Devi, two
spires of rock and snow that remained an obsession for the rest of his
life. Though Unsoeld failed on Nilkanth, he returned to the Himalayas several times and became one of the first Americans to reach the
top of Everest in 1963, pioneering a first ascent of the difficult West
Ridge. This expedition almost cost him his life, as he and three other
climbers were forced to spend a night huddled together at close to
28,000 feet without sleeping bags or tents. Unsoeld sacrificed eight

of his toes to frostbite on Everest. Settling in Oregon, he went on to become an advocate of wilderness preservation and adventure learning, a guru of the outdoors, whose passion for the mountains echoed a spiritual quest. When his wife, Jolene, gave birth to a daughter, Willi Unsoeld named her Nanda Devi after his favorite mountain and the bliss-giving goddess who watches over her slopes.

In 1976, Unsoeld returned to the Garhwal Himalayas, leading an Indo-American expedition, intent on climbing Nanda Devi. Willi had recently turned fifty. Arthritic hips and missing toes made it unlikely that he would reach the summit, but he had ambitions for his daughter, who was a member of the team. Nanda Devi Unsoeld was clear about the significance of this climb: "I feel a very close relationship with Nanda Devi. I can't describe it, but there is something within me about this mountain, ever since I was born."

Though the lead climbers, including John Roskelley, made it to the summit, the Unsoelds' obsession with Nanda Devi ended in tragedy. Trapped in a blizzard at 24,000 feet, Devi developed acute abdominal pain complicated by altitude sickness. Unable to carry her down from the mountain, Willi and others desperately fought to save her life, giving her mouth-to-mouth resuscitation until "her lips turned cold." In an article for the *American Alpine Journal*, Unsoeld recounts the moments after his daughter's death:

> As our faculties gradually returned to us, we discussed what was to be done. We agreed that it would be most fitting for Devi's body to be committed to the snows of the mountain for which she had come to feel such a deep attachment. Andy, Peter and I knelt in a circle in the snow and grasped hands while each chanted a broken farewell to the comrade who had so recently filled such a vivid place in our lives. My final prayer was one of thanksgiving for a world filled with the sublimity of the high places, for the sheer beauty of the mountains and for the surpassing miracle that we should be so formed as to respond with ecstasy to such beauty, and for the constant element of danger without which the mountain experience would not exercise such a grip on our sensibilities. We then

laid the body to rest in its icy tomb, at rest on the breast of the Bliss-Giving Goddess Nanda.

Devi's death and the strained relationship between Roskelley and Unsoeld flared into controversy. Roskelley's book, *Nanda Devi: The Tragic Expedition*, describes an acrimonious team, and he accuses his fellow climbers of being undisciplined and irresponsible. Reflecting on his daughter's death, Unsoeld recounted part of this experience in a lecture to outdoor educators: "In the face of reality, it's difficult to know what to say. Upon our return to Delhi I was asked at the news conference, 'Do you have any regrets?' and my answer was startled out of me—'No!' And then I wondered, 'How can I say that?'" Later, Unsoeld became more philosophical. "[T]his experience has opened my life to the reality of death and I can never look at it in quite the same way. Intellectually, I feel I've handled it. But emotionally, how does one handle the death of such a surpassing human being? And my answer is—you don't. It handles you. It rubs your nose in the reality of your mortality. We are helpless before death's onslaught and I guess therein lies a very great lesson that's difficult for us control-types to learn. We're not in charge in the face of reality and nature, and in the final analysis, I wouldn't have it any other way."

Three years later, Willi Unsoeld was killed in an avalanche on Mount Ranier.

Near base camp in the Nanda Devi Sanctuary, Indian climbers have erected a memorial to the American girl who died on the mountain for which she was named. The inscription is taken from her diary and speaks of a personal moment of communion: "I stand upon a wind-swept ridge at night with the stars bright above and I am no longer alone but I waver and merge with all the shadows that surround me. I am part of the whole and am content."

Desecration

The idea of planting a nuclear powered sensor on the summit of Nanda Devi to keep a watchful eye on China's atomic weapons tests in Tibet illustrates the extreme paranoia of the Cold War, while echoing romantic yodels of the Great Game. Elevating espionage to 24,000 feet above sea level requires a high degree of mountaineering skill and commitment, as well as complete secrecy and cooperation. During the height of superpower rivalry in the 1950s and 1960s, America and India looked at each other with a certain degree of distrust. A brief but devastating border war between India and China in 1962 changed the political landscape so that New Delhi and Washington were finally able to find common cause.

According to M. S. Kohli and Kenneth Conboy's book, *Spies in the Himalayas,* the clandestine expedition to Nanda Devi began at a cocktail party in Washington. Speaking with US Air Force Chief of Staff, General Curtis Lemay, Barry Bishop, a *National Geographic* photographer and climber who took part in the first American ascent of Everest, is said to have proposed the idea of putting an early warning device atop a Himalayan summit. Initially, Kanchenjunga was proposed, but Nanda Devi was ultimately chosen as a more viable option.

Several Everest veterans, including M. S. Kohli and Lute Jerstad, were teamed together in the Nanda Devi expedition of 1968, combining adventure with patriotism. Unlike most other climbs, the joint CIA–Intelligence Bureau effort used helicopters to enter the sanctuary and establish their base camp. While the summit was their goal, the primary purpose was not to conquer the mountain but to defeat Communism and secure India's northern borders. The goddess Nanda did not look kindly on this expedition, and the climbers were eventually pushed back by severe storms. Leaving the listening device at Camp 4, at about 24,000 feet, they decided to come back the next year and complete their mission.

When Kohli and the Americans returned to Nanda Devi the following summer, they discovered that the sensor, as well as its plutonium power source, had disappeared. Apparently, an avalanche had carried them away into a glacier several thousand feet below. Desperate efforts were made to locate the debris, with agents rappelling into crevasses, but no trace of radioactivity was found. The only successful footnote to the second expedition occurred when Robert Schaller, one of the CIA climbers, secretly soloed the summit without telling the others in his team. When news of the lost sensor reached India's Parliament more than a decade later, it caused political uproar, partly because of cooperation with the Americans but also because of fears that the plutonium would pollute the headwaters of the Ganga.

I met Captain Kohli at the Legend Inn, a guesthouse he owns in a residential colony of Delhi called East of Kailash. The inn is decorated with climbing memorabilia and photographs of Kohli posing with eminent mountaineers like Edmund Hilary and Reinhold Messner. Each room in the Legend Inn is named for a mountain, including Nanda Devi.

Though the covert operations were so secret that even Parliament was not apprised of details, most of the story has come out now, including Captain Kohli's published account. A dignified man with a white beard and a dark blue turban, he has no hesitation talking about the expedition, though at times his eyes are guarded. The spymasters who set the plot in motion, B. N. Mullik and R. N. Kao, are no longer alive. Tucker Gougelmann, the CIA's station chief in Delhi and a paramilitary expert in Vietnam, is long gone. So is Barry Bishop, whom Kohli once disguised in a turban, pretending he was the Maharaja of Patiala, while they chatted up girls at a bar in Anchorage, Alaska. Lute Jerstad, Harish Rawat, and Sonam Gyatso are also dead. By some accounts, several of the Sherpas who carried plutonium up the mountain died of cancer caused by radiation. M. S. Kohli is one of the last survivors of the Nanda Devi mission and he tells the story with relish.

"We had just come back from climbing Everest," he explains, referring to the first successful Indian expedition he led in 1964. "Within a few weeks, Mullick told me to assemble a team and head off to America, where we were taught how to set up surveillance devices on Mount McKinley."

After their training sessions, the Indian climbers did some sightseeing, including a visit to the New York World's Fair. Kohli says that he initially opposed the plan to plant a listening device on Nanda Devi because it was a difficult peak to climb. He suggested Nanda Kot instead. After the first sensor was lost, the Americans finally took his advice and Kohli successfully planted another sensor on Nanda Kot, a peak he'd already climbed on one of his first Himalayan expeditions. Though commissioned as a naval officer, Kohli was deputed to the newly formed Indo-Tibetan Border Police, a paramilitary force that guards India's Himalayan frontier.

"A year after it was installed, the device on Nanda Kot stopped working, and we had to go back up," he recalls. "It was buried under snow, but because of the plutonium power source, the ice around it had melted, forming a cave." He describes the weird scene they discovered as if it were a miraculous phenomenon: a radioactive totem enshrined in a cavern of ice.

While he has written many books, Captain Kohli says that one of his most popular publications is a small monograph on the power of prayer, or *ardaas* as it is known in the Sikh tradition. This book, written in Punjabi, explains how he took strength from his faith, which protected him in the Himalayas.

In an effortless segue from espionage to religion, he tells me how he was camped high up on a mountain. In the middle of the night he heard the sound of horse's hooves and saw a vision of Guru Govind Singh, the martial saint of Sikhism, riding a white stallion.

"Immediately, energy flowed into me," he says. "I woke up my men and told them, chai banao! (make tea), and then I put on my crampons and set off, kicking steps in the ice, making my way up the mountain."

Eventually, when I steer our conversation back to Nanda Devi, he rings a call bell for his assistant and asks him to fetch a file folder from his office. When it arrives, Kolhi opens it for me to see. Inside are clippings about the covert expedition, telegrams, and cyclostyled circulars with TOP SECRET stamped in the margins. The press reports and classified documents are all preserved, a tale of national intrigue and high altitude heroics sustained by the power of prayer.

Sacraments

Coming down from Kuari Pass, on my first approach to Nanda Devi, we spend the night at a small guesthouse near Auli, built within a field of boulders, remnants of an earthquake that wrenched the mountains apart hundreds of years ago. A scrubby orchard of apple trees has been planted on the few patches of soil between these giant rocks. Yellow-billed blue magpies scavenge amid the fallen fruit, eating worms and insects that have burrowed into rotting apples. The leaves on the trees have turned brown, and most of the branches are bare. Autumn colors are reflected in the evening light that tints the slopes of Nanda Devi.

Next morning, Mukesh and I drive to Lata village, along a road that carries on to Niti Pass. Tibet is only fifteen miles ahead. The Indo-Tibetan Border Police maintain a checkpoint beyond Lata, turning back civilians, especially foreigners like me. This is the Inner Line, a buffer zone that runs parallel to India's Himalayan frontier. Before reaching Lata, we cross a bridge over the confluence of the Rishi and Dhauli Gangas, both rivers flowing out of forbidden gorges, their sources inaccessible because of political and environmental boundaries.

Lata used to be the starting point for all of the Nanda Devi expeditions, as well as climbs to Dunagiri and Changabang. Several generations of high-altitude porters from this village ferried loads up the Rishi Ganga gorge, accompanying some of the greatest mountaineers of the twentieth century. Today, those climbs have ceased, and the watershed of the Rishi Ganga lies within the core area of the Nanda Devi Biosphere Reserve, a national park that has been closed to visitors since 1981. Even the shepherds of Lata and other villages nearby are forbidden to take their flocks to the high pastures inside the sanctuary.

As we scramble up a landslide, where the main path to Lata has washed away, Mukesh explains there are two sections of the village, less than a mile apart. The upper homes are occupied in summer, but as soon as it snows the villagers move down to their lower quarters. The residents of Lata are preparing for winter. Red chilies, kidney beans, and apricot pits are spread on the rooftops to dry, where TV antennae and solar panels have been rigged up, amid sheaves of harvested amaranth and buckwheat. Women with their heads covered in shawls of rough spun wool are carrying firewood down from the forest above. An old man is plowing his fields with a pair of oxen. He tells us that he is planting winter wheat, which will sprout only after the snow melts in spring. The slate-roofed houses are built close together with staircases and narrow lanes leading from one courtyard to another. In each of the households, women are threshing grain and grinding it in stone mortars.

We have come to meet Dhan Singh Rana, one of the directors of Mountain Shepherds, an organization that employs Mukesh. Set up to train young men like him as trekking guides, Mountain Shepherds is a grassroots effort to tap into Uttarakhand's ecotourism industry. They have organized my trek to Kuari Pass. Dhan Singh is a short, wiry man with a weathered face and a mustache that droops over a cautious smile. He wears a black Garhwali cap and a blue Patagonia jacket. Smoking a bidi, he holds it by habit in his cupped hand, as if protecting it from the wind. Our arrival coincides with a visit from the local forest guard. Dhan Singh takes this opportunity to berate the government for closing off the Nanda Devi Sanctuary and destroying Lata's economy by putting an end to mountaineering expeditions and the grazing of flocks in the Rishi Ganga valley. The forest guard looks at me with a chastened smile as Dhan Singh rants while his nephew serves us tea.

Somewhere below us, drums are beating. After sending the forest guard on his way with more abuse, Dhan Singh leads me up to the Nanda Devi temple at the center of the village. A straggling procession of men is working its way up a steep flight of stairs between the village homes, leading a young ram with yellow ribbons tied to its horns. The drummers maintain a steady rhythm as they climb toward the temple.

Dhan Singh tells me that Lata gets its name from Latu, the mountain deity who is often described as the bodyguard or herald of the goddess. He is also known as the "path-finding hero" of Nanda Devi. During pilgrimages and other ceremonies, village oracles become possessed by Latu's spirit and lead the procession, brandishing sacred staves or spears. Bill Aitken describes Latu as a "spiritual artful dodger who always produced dramatic results." During my visit there are no oracles, but one of the drummers rolls his head and looks at me with a crazed expression, as if he were entering a trance. The ram is led into the courtyard of the temple and tied to a wooden stake.

Nanda Devi's temple at Lata reflects the iconic shape of Mount Kailash, a tiered dome rising above a square stone platform. The door of the temple is locked. Next to it is Latu's shrine, positioned at right angles, almost like a sentry box. At the far side of the courtyard stands a stone cistern filled by a spring that used to be the main source of drinking water for the village until the government provided a pipeline. Carved fragments of granite and broken columns lie about. Dhan Singh explains that these are the remains of earlier temples felled by earthquakes.

We can hear more drums approaching, and soon a second procession arrives. A much larger ram, with red ribbons tied to his spiral horns, comes up the narrow passage into the temple complex. One of the bystanders mutters his approval. "Cut this one first," he says. Both animals will be sacrificed, then butchered, their flesh divided among priests and celebrants. As we watch the drummers competing with each other, a young girl approaches, carrying a brass tray filled with buckwheat dumplings and a glutinous mound of muddy green dough. "Prasad," Dhan Singh tells me, sacred food. *Phaapad* is the name he uses for buckwheat. We take a pinch of raw dough and a dumpling each. The strong, wild flavor with a bitter aftertaste reminds me of millet.

Listening to the drums, Dhan Singh falls silent. One of the men is sharpening the curved blade of a *pathal*, or cleaver, on the stones. The priest is yet to arrive. Straight above us lies the steep ascent to Nanda Devi, which is closed beyond Dharansi. The path-finding heroes of Lata, high-altitude porters who accompanied scores of mountaineers up the treacherous Rhamani slabs and across the raging waters of the Rishi Ganga, no longer have access to the natural sanctum of their goddess. I can picture a line of porters, years ago, making their obeisance at this temple before shouldering their loads and filing out of the village. Every year when the climbing season began, they threaded their way up the slope above us, weighed down with tents, ropes, and mountaineering gear. How many expeditions made offerings at this temple for a safe return? Nanda Devi Unsoeld and her father stopped here and took darshan of the goddess before setting out for the summit, as did Shipton, Tilman, Houston, and Odell.

Dhan Singh Rana invites me to stay for the sacrifice and attend the feast that follows, but I excuse myself, saying that I have a long drive home to Mussoorie. Having seen enough animals being slaughtered by the swift blow of a pathal's blade over the years, I have no desire to witness this sacrifice and watch their blood flow onto the flagstones. The bitter taste of buckwheat remains on my tongue as I watch the two rams chewing straw and butting heads, blissfully unaware of their fate.

Slaughter Road

I travel into these mountains searching for what I have lost. Among the things I find are objects I never possessed, ideas and images unknown to me, experiences I can never reclaim for myself alone. What was lost, in the first place, was never forgotten but was transformed into something else—discoveries and observations that opened up new ways of looking at the world. A friend of mine has said that when his house burned down, and all of his belongings reduced to cinders and ash, he felt an immediate sense of sorrow, followed by cathartic release. To lose something, or everything, sharpens our vision and gives us an acute awareness of what remains.

Every time I set off on a trek, I go through a simple ritual of removing my wristwatch and leaving it behind in one of the pigeon-holes of my desk. This is the only watch I have ever owned; I've had it since 1982, when I first started teaching. Before then, I prided myself on being punctual without wearing a watch, though a regular schedule of classes required more than instinct and guesswork. I bought my HMT Quartz in New Delhi, at a shop in Connaught Circus. It has a stainless steel case and a rectangular window on its face displaying the date and day of the week. By turning a knob, I can change the display from English to Hindi whenever I wish. Other than that, there is nothing special about my watch— a sturdy, utilitarian timepiece that has served me well. Over the years, I have changed the metal strap five times, and the battery has been replaced on seven or eight occasions. Soon after I bought my watch, I can't remember when exactly, I made a decision that I would keep it for the rest of my life. To own only one watch seemed a wise and frugal choice, but more than that, it symbolized a resistance to change that appealed to my conservative nature.

But in 2003, I lost my watch. We were living in Reading, Massachusetts, and I was teaching at MIT. Every day, I would walk our dog, Maya, in a forest known as Kurchian Woods, which was across the street from our home. I'm not sure what happened that day. The leash may have brushed against the clasp as I was setting the dog loose, and the watch slipped unnoticed from my wrist. Only when we returned home did I discover that it was gone.

By then, I had owned the watch for twenty years and I was bereft. Here was something that mattered to me, not because of its material value or any sentiments attached, but because it represented a promise I had made to myself, as well as the illusion of permanence that was suddenly gone. I went back into the woods immediately, and retraced my steps, hoping to recover the watch, but soon it grew dark and I had to give up.

This happened in early spring, when patches of snow still lay on the ground and the maples and oaks were as bare as the bent tines on a rake. After a long New England winter, the leaf litter was compressed and skunk cabbages were just beginning to send up green finials out of the black wetland ooze. These woods were protected as the breeding grounds for a rare species of salamander that crawled out of layers of dead leaves only to be crushed under the tires of passing cars on the streets that bordered the forest. Kurchian Woods covers about forty acres of conservation land with a gas line running through the middle. Very few people walked in the forest, perhaps out of fear of deer ticks, which carry Lyme disease. Maya and I were the only regular intruders on this patch of suburban wilderness. The paths were poorly maintained, and high school students occasionally partied in the woods, leaving behind fairy circles of broken beer bottles and cigarette stubs.

At one place, on a small hillock, lay the ruined foundations of a hermit's hut. I used to imagine him as an early twentieth century Thoreau living near a marsh instead of a pond. The hermit was long gone, and the only signs of human habitation in the forest were the stone walls from a century ago, when this land was still farmed. An abandoned plow lay near the hermit's hut, a rusting relic that intrigued me as a reminder of an ancient, unmotorized age. Nearby was an old well, which had been filled up by conscientious boy scouts, so that nobody would fall in. There were also the remains of a cart road that dated back to the eighteenth century when Yankee settlers moved north out of Boston and Salem. According to Reading's historical records, this track was known as Slaughter Road because pigs were once driven along its rutted path into town, where they were killed and processed into bacon and ham.

Every day, for almost ten years, Maya and I walked along Slaughter Road and the intersecting paths that digressed through Kurchian Woods. Deer lived in the forest, as well as raccoons and coyotes, wild turkeys, and all kinds of other birds, insects, and reptiles. One time I was walking across a narrow boardwalk of planks, which had been laid out to cover a stretch of marshland near the entrance to Kurchian Woods. Glancing down to my left, I saw something camouflaged in the dead leaves. The shape suggested a bird, but the perfect blend of foliage and feathers made me wonder if I was imagining things. Yet, there in the mottled mosaic of decaying leaves was a woodcock, its distinctive beak like the long stem of a hickory leaf and its seed-like eye fixed on me.

Only a few weeks earlier, heading out to lunch with my editor in New York, we had found a dead woodcock on the sidewalk near Madison Square Park. Its variegated plumage was iridescent against the gray concrete. Migrating through the city, the woodcock must have struck one of the plate glass windows on the floors above. But here in Kurchian Woods this bird was alive, though almost invisible in the leaves. I had seen it by accident and could have easily walked by without noticing its hidden presence.

For at least two weeks after losing my watch, I kept returning to the woods with Maya, searching again and again, scouring the paths for a telltale glint of stainless steel. I even made a small poster that I tacked to a tree near the entrance to the woods, offering a reward to anyone who found and returned my watch. Maya seemed to sense my loss and sniffed about with the urgency of a bloodhound, though she never found it.

While I had no success in locating what I'd lost, there were many other things I noticed now, which I had never seen before. Because I was focused on the ground near the trail, I discovered bottle caps and chewing gum wrappers, as well as shards of colored glass, bright as uncut jewels. There were also hoof prints of deer and pellets of dung, the exploded hulls of hickory nuts, a knotted tangle of dry ferns. On one of these walks, I found an oak twig shaped like a one-armed crucifix, and I've kept it ever since. The six-inch piece of wood sits on my desk today, a totem of my loss. The watch had vanished, but as my eyes scanned the ground I saw so much else. It was early spring, and the woods seemed dead or dormant, but as I walked along those paths, I was aware of the first signs of life emerging from the ground, leafbuds on the blueberry bushes along the gas line, acorns cracking open, an early cardinal taking flight, its red feathers disappearing amid a scribble of twigs and tree limbs.

Beyond the tangible objects in my path, I was also aware of temporal changes, each day a little brighter and longer than the last. Maya and I had shared these walks since she was a puppy. Like most dogs, she had an inner clock that told her when it was time for us to set out, at which point she began nudging my elbow with her nose or scratching the door. Without my watch, I was attuned to a different kind of clockwork that exists within the synaptic impulses of our brain. Instead of the quartz crystals vibrating at my wrist, it was the ticking of nerves and the pulse of my heartbeat that marked each passing second, slowing down or quickening when I walked.

All of these things came to me because of what I no longer possessed. Gradually, I also gained an acceptance of my loss and was reconciled to giving it up. By the end of the first week, I was willing to concede that my watch would never be found. Someone may have picked it up and kept it as salvaged treasure from the woods. I wondered what they would make of the day and date in Devanagari script.

About three weeks later, when I was about to tear down the signs I'd posted, and several heavy spring downpours made me think my watch could never have survived, I came back home from work to find it lying on the steps of our house. My HMT Quartz had been placed there carefully by someone, I don't know who. It was working perfectly, the second hand circling like a spider weaving its web, the scratched crystal intact. Someone had returned it to me, an anonymous neighbor who did not want to claim the reward or answer questions. As I put the watch back on my wrist, snapping the clasp securely, I felt a sense of elation but also a twinge of remorse. The next day, when we went back into the woods, following the familiar contours of Slaughter Road, I no longer needed to search the ground near my feet. Unlike the dog, who nosed about with persistent curiosity, picking up scents along the trail, I could let my mind wander free in all directions, without a narrowed focus.

Since then, I've often made a point, when walking in a forest or trekking in the mountains, of imagining that my watch has fallen off my wrist again and that I am searching for it along the trail. This has become a form of meditation, distilling my senses so that I can perceive not only what is lost but what lies beyond the objects we try to call our own.

Lake of Sorrows

Seeking Nanda's darshan, I follow another path, east of Kuari Pass. This trek begins along the Curzon Trail but leads in a different direction, toward a small, high-altitude lake called Roopkund. Unlike my trek in November, when the panorama of snow peaks was clear and close at hand, this journey takes place during the monsoon, nine months later, when the mountains are covered by clouds.

Few places in the Himalayas have aroused as much speculation, dispute, and exaggerated expectations as Roopkund, a glacial pond at 16,500 feet above sea level that remains frozen most of the year and only melts between July and September. During these few weeks, when the ice and snow recede, hundreds of human bones are revealed in the shallow, green waters of the lake and along its rocky shoreline. The presence of skeletal remains is a mystery. Nobody knows for sure why they are there.

Carbon dating suggests that the bones are at least five hundred years old. According to popular lore they can be traced back to the fourteenth century. The most plausible explanation is that a cataclysmic storm or avalanche killed a party of pilgrims who were trying to cross Junargali, the pass of death, directly above the lake. This pilgrimage, which reenacts the bridal procession of the goddess, is the longest and most arduous ritual journey in Uttarakhand, beginning at Nanda's natal home in the village of Nauti, then circling through the watershed of the Pindar and Nandakini Rivers. Roopkund is the penultimate stage of this pilgrimage, beyond which the goddess in her palanquin crosses Junargali and descends into Shila Samudra, the ocean of rock, a seemingly endless expanse of glacial moraine at the foot of Trishul.

Nanda Devi's procession is led by a four-horned ram and an oracle possessed by the demigod Latu, her bodyguard and "path-finding hero." Unlike the staid and relatively comfortable pilgrimages to shrines at the primary sources of the Ganga, which attract pilgrims from all across India, the Raj Jaat Yatra is held only once every twelve years, and the participants are primarily from this region. Many devotees complete the 175 miles barefoot, protected from sun and rain by parasols of split bamboo or birch bark. The Raj Jaat Yatra takes place at the end of the monsoon, when the mountains are obscured by mist and trails washed out by landslides. The culmination of the yatra is the source of the Nandakini river, a tributary of the Ganga that flows out of Shila Samudra. Differing accounts suggest that the four-horned ram is either sacrificed to honor and appease the goddess, or released into the crags and glaciers of Trishul, the trident peaks, associated with Shiva, Nanda's bridegroom. In either case, the ram does not return.

I had heard about Roopkund for many years and read several accounts of the pilgrimage, particularly William Sax's *Mountain Goddess*, an anthropologist's chronicle of the Raj Jaat Yatra of 1987. A photographer and friend, Gurmeet Thukral, had trekked to Roopkund in the eighties and showed me pictures of bones and skulls encased in ice. The lore and legends were provocative, though most of them seemed to overstretch the limits of credibility. One of the wilder theories suggests that the skeletons are the remains of an army led by the Dogra General Zorawar Singh, who attacked Tibet in the nineteenth century, though it is clear he invaded by a different route and his grave lies on the outskirts of Taklakot, near Mount Kailash. More than gruesome riddles and mysterious remains, what drew me to Roopkund was the mythology of Nanda Devi. The pilgrimage retraces her bridal journey but also reenacts the violent myth of her battles with the buffalo demon who pursues her relentlessly through the mountains.

～

On earlier monsoon treks, during the months of July and August, I have remained wet for days on end, soaked through by constant showers, until it is impossible to tell the difference between per-spiration and precipitation. Nothing stays dry and my sleeping bag becomes a clammy cocoon. With each cloudburst, paths turn into rivers and you find yourself wading upstream or down, over slick boulders or through channels of mud. No matter how many layers of plastic, nylon, or Gore-Tex you wear, the enveloping dampness seeps into your skin. Walking through mist, the air becomes so saturated with moisture, it seems almost too thick to breathe.

But when it clears, as it always does, after a few hours, a day or a week, the brilliant green of the forests and mountains is so vivid, it feels as if everything is alive, even the soil and rocks beneath your feet. On our way to Roopkund, we set off from Lohajang, a village whose name means "battle of iron," though it is a quiet wayside settlement with no evidence of military history. The night we arrive, however, a violent thunderstorm echoes with the sounds of warfare—the clang-ing of giant swords and booming of cannons.

By dawn the sky is bright and still. Above us, we can see the snow-blanched face of Nanda Ghunti, the veil of the goddess, one of the many peaks that hide Nanda Devi from view. The mountain is like a wedge of ice driven into the upper end of the forested valley. Our destination lies close to the foot of Nanda Ghunti, amid cliffs and snow. From Lohajang the broad *chey-footia* (six-foot-wide) trail descends into a forest of oak and rhododendron, our path festooned with peacock orchids and wild begonias. Though it isn't raining, my boots are soon soaked by flowing streams that follow our route. Groups of schoolchildren, dressed in neat uniforms of blue and white, are coming up the path from nearby farms. Some of them carry their shoes so they won't get wet. Book bags are heavy with homework. One of the girls warns us about a landslide that blocks the way on ahead, though she has made it across.

In the first hour, we drop a thousand feet. The opposite slope of the mountain grows steeper as the valley narrows, and it is obvious that we will soon be forced to regain altitude. Below us, hidden from view by a canopy of foliage, the Bedni Ganga roars in the depths of its gorge. Descending into one of the side valleys, we cross a bridge over a lesser stream that falls in a torrent between banks of bamboo and tree ferns that rise above our heads. The arched branches on either side of the bridge are draped with polypods and moss.

The landslide turns out to be less of an obstacle than we imagined. Scrambling across gray mud and shale, we come to a series of abandoned terraces, overgrown with weeds. The path disappears as we bushwhack through thickets of marijuana ten feet tall, resinous florets dangling over us like limp green tassels. Soon after we have battled our way through this fragrant jungle, the foliage turns to stinging nettle, and we are forced to retreat and take a detour through another field. Eventually, after vaulting over a stone wall, we rejoin something that looks like a path. A hundred yards ahead is another stream, where the bridge has washed away and we will have to wade across.

As soon as I begin to unlace my shoes, I realize that my feet and ankles are covered in leeches. They look like black stitches coming undone, fastening and unfastening themselves to my skin. No matter how quickly I pick them off, others appear. They cling to my fingers as I try to flick them into the stream. After counting at least twenty-five, I lose track of numbers. Fortunately, because the bridge is washed out, we have been forced to stop and remove our shoes before crossing the stream, otherwise our feet would have become sieves of blood. Several leeches have already gorged themselves and fallen off. Welts on my calves and between my toes are oozing red. In one episode of Nanda Devi's myth, as she is trying to escape the buffalo demon, the goddess is attacked by a plague of leeches that fall from the sky like rain.

While planning this trek, I debated whether I would go alone, which I prefer, or employ porters to carry my gear. This region of Garhwal is unfamiliar, a twelve-hour drive from home. In the end, I have compromised by hiring two young men from Mussoorie to accompany me, though I carry my own tent and most of my equipment. One of my companions, Titu, has worked as a trekking guide and completed the basic and advanced courses at the Nehru Institute of Mountaineering. I have hiked with him before and know that he is a strong walker and resourceful when it comes to setting up camp.

More to keep him company and allow me to be alone whenever I choose, I have also hired a friend of his, Akshay, who has little trekking experience but seems eager for the adventure.

Though I crave the solitude of trekking alone, there is still a residual fear from our attack, an uncertain, uncomfortable feeling of being vulnerable and exposed, unable to defend myself. Having Titu and Akshay with me is reassuring. They help lighten my load and will be there if we face an emergency.

Soon after we ford the stream our path crosses a bridge over the Bedni Ganga and the climb begins. From here to Roopkund is a steady ascent of 10,000 feet. Over the course of three days we pass through every variety of Himalayan botany, from semi-tropical foliage full of liverworts and mosses, ground orchids and ferns, through various bands of deciduous forest marked by different species of oaks—banj, moru, and kharsu. Each of these trees provides fodder for cattle at different times of the year, as the dairymen move their herds up and down the slopes during spring and fall. The conifers change too with altitude, chir pines giving way to cypress and cedar, then spruce and fir, and finally thuner, the Himalayan yew, a hardy tree with delicate needles and papery bark. An experienced naturalist can gauge the elevation without an altimeter simply by marking the presence of different species. Once you climb above the tree line at about 10,000 feet, *bugyal* meadows provide a lush zone of grass and wildflowers, layered between forest and crags. These summer pastures attract herdsmen with their cows, buffalos, goats, and horses. For trekkers, the bugyals provide a brief respite from the relentless climb, their rolling slopes less steep and strenuous, before the final ascent into rock and snow.

The mythology of the goddess reflects the ecology of this region. As she escapes from the buffalo demon and takes refuge in the forest, Nanda curses the turmeric and potato plants that offer no protective shade, banishing them underground. When she trips on the stubble of a wheat field, her tears of sorrow and anger leave the soil barren. Nanda also curses the pines, because their needles fail to hide her from the demon. Their branches will never regenerate themselves after they are cut. However, as consolation, she grants the pine a boon to serve as the flagpole at her shrines. After finally hiding behind a kunju shrub, a thorny bush with dense foliage, Nanda blesses this plant, saying that it will never lose its leaves: no goats or cattle will eat kunju for fodder, and men will not cut it for fuel or timber.

As we start up the path to Didana, which is the last village along this route, we meet two women and a man. The women are carrying loads, while the man seems content to let them bear the supplies they have bought at Lohajang. Four hundred yards ahead, a second man latches on and begins to quiz me as we climb together. Soon, I realize that he is simpleminded, an adult with the intelligence of a ten-year-old child. His questions are as unrelenting as the gradient. Where have we come from? What are we carrying? Do I have a mobile phone? Do I have cookies to share with him? Do I smoke? Could he have a cigarette? How much money do I have? Will I give him a hundred rupees? What medicines am I carrying in my pack? What time is it? Why aren't I wearing a watch?

Every time I stop, he stops and the inquisition grows more persistent. When I try to walk faster and outpace him, he quickens his stride. "You're an old man with white hair, but you walk too fast," he complains. He speaks a dialect of Garhwali that is difficult to follow. Why is my skin white? Am I married? How many children? Have I had a vasectomy?

"What kind of question is that?" I ask, losing my patience.

But he isn't fazed. "I've had a vasectomy," he says. "I'm a poor man. After five children, I can't afford any more." Then, in the same breath, he demands chocolate.

Though I want to get away from him, there is no escape. We have to share the trail and no other path presents itself. After a while, I stop answering his questions. Only when we reach Didana, an hour and a half later, am I finally able to shake him off by giving him some antibiotic ointment for his mother, who he claims has injured herself while cutting leaves. He demands painkillers for her as well, but I am afraid that he will swallow them all himself.

We have reached Didana sooner than expected. It is too early for us to camp, and the weather remains clear. After lunch, we decide to carry on toward Ali Bugyal, another six miles uphill. Though we could stay a night in Didana, the idea of spending the rest of the afternoon being questioned by my friend makes me eager to escape. At the same time, I know it is foolish to attempt a double-march on the first day of our trek. When we ask directions from a villager who is rebuilding a stone wall surrounding his house, he points us straight up a path through the forest. There is a longer route that circles around the mountain but the man urges us to take the shorter path, which zigzags into the trees.

The climb grows more and more precipitous, until we are scrambling up a ladder of tree roots along the spine of the ridge. The oaks cast plenty of shade but it is hard work and sweat pours down my face. Too late, I realize that I have made the mistake of not drinking enough water before leaving Didana. Halfway up the ridge, my legs begin to cramp. Though I swallow half a bottle of water, it doesn't help and I know that we must stop. Somewhere to our left, I can hear the sound of a stream, but it lies beyond dense thickets of ringal bamboo. The ravine looks even more precipitous than the ridge. Fortunately, Titu is able to scout for a campsite, and after exploring in the direction of the water, he finds enough flat ground for us to pitch our tents. Though I am not particularly tired, my legs continue to cramp. Frustrated and discouraged, I drink a liter of water and lie down to rest.

Before long, clouds sweep in and it begins to rain. It was fortunate that we stopped here, because the storm would have caught up with us on ahead. Impatience is a walker's downfall, and I wish I hadn't forced our pace. There is no real urgency driving us on, and my body has signaled its resistance. Though I know that the cramps will be gone by nightfall, I wonder whether I will be able to complete the trek. After a bright beginning we spend the first evening in a sober mood, the mossy limbs of trees dripping onto our tents and thunder bellowing above the bugyals.

Next morning, when I test my legs, they feel much stronger. Breaking camp after breakfast, all three of us are in a better mood. Blundering through the bamboo, I locate our path and start slowly up the trail. With each step, I keep expecting my calves and thighs to knot up, but the muscles have regained their elasticity. Despite the climb, I am able to appreciate the forest again. The ground is covered with mushrooms and other kinds of fungus, including a bright orange variety as large as dinner plates. Another species that grows out of a tree stump has the appearance and color of scrambled eggs.

After half an hour, I stop to rest, waiting for Titu and Akshay to catch up. Minutes later, I hear children's voices and three young girls come up the trail. They are ten or twelve years old, each of them carrying baskets woven out of split bamboo. Seeing me sitting on a fallen tree, they stop abruptly, as if confronted by a demon. Greeting them, I try to reassure the girls that I am not dangerous, though they leave the trail and skirt around me cautiously. Only when they are a safe distance up the path, do they ask where I am going.

As we keep passing each other over the course of the morning, stopping at different points to rest, the girls and I carry on a fragmented conversation. They are headed to their *chaan*, a summer shelter where goats and cattle are kept at pasture. The girls are from Didana, and their family chaans lie at one end of Ali Bugyal. When I ask if they attend school, the eldest says they study at the temple because the nearest school is five miles away, and they have work to do at home. All three walk steadily up the slope with purposeful maturity. Learning that I am going to Bedni Bugyal and Roopkund, they want to know if I am going to make an offering to the goddess. Unlike the man who followed me the day before, their questions are carefully asked and they consider my answers with thoughtful expressions. While he was an adult with the mind of a child, these are children who seem much older than their years. They do not ask for anything and seem completely self-reliant. The baskets they carry contain bags of rice and flour, as well as steel *darantis* (small sickles) for cutting firewood and fodder.

When we finally reach the tree line where my path continues up the hill and theirs cuts across the lower edges of the meadow, the youngest girl points toward a plume of wood smoke rising from their huts. Smiling with anticipation, she tells me, "Chaan pey bhaat

banayenge—When we reach our chaan, we're going to cook rice."
The simple satisfaction in her statement makes me appreciate the
hardship and deprivation these girls endure, as well as the false pretense of self-sufficiency that I carry on my back. Compared to theirs,
my life seems far too complicated and full of dubious privileges.

⁓

Ali Bugyal is one of the largest alpine meadows in Uttarakhand, rolling fields of grass that spread for hundreds of acres across the upper
flanks of a broad ridge that leads onto Bedni farther up. Thin curtains
of mist begin to drift across the meadows as we wade knee-deep
through fields of anemones, potentilla, and lousewort. Wild salvia and
thistles grow along our path, which converges with dozens of other
trails, trod out of the meadow by cattle and sheep. Animals are grazing all around us, appearing and disappearing in the mist. During the
monsoon, bugyal meadows are peaceable, plentiful pastures where
the mountains provide an abundance of food until they are covered
by snow in winter. At one place, half a dozen horses seem to race
the retreating mist. Two of them are foals testing young limbs as they
chase their mothers. We can hear cowbells as we walk, a gentle, clang-
ing sound from somewhere in the clouds. These meadows are the
summer gardens of the goddess, a symbol of her fertility.

The looming black bulk of a buffalo appears, shaking its head
as we pass. Though harmless, it is easy enough to see how someone
might confuse this creature for a demon, with its heavy, ungainly
shape, wild eyes, flared nostrils, and dangerous-looking horns. Male
buffalos serve little purpose for villagers in the mountains and are
often killed soon after birth or starved to death. When sacrificed to
the goddess, buffalos become scapegoats for all of the evil and mis-
fortune of this world.

One bell seems to follow us. When I look back, I am surprised to
see a black dog. Someone has tied a dented brass cowbell around his
neck, which gives him a foolish demeanor. He trails us for the rest
of the day, even when a swift downpour drenches us before we can

unpack rain jackets or umbrellas. Watching from the slopes above the path is a flock of several hundred sheep. A sullen shepherd does not return our greeting as he crouches beneath an overhanging rock. His animals are dripping wet, their wool caked with mud. I look to see if any four-horned rams are among the herd.

Bedni, where we spend the night, is one of the primary halts on the Raj Jaat Yatra. Here we join the main pilgrimage route that comes up from a village called Wan, which has a large temple dedicated to Latu, Nanda's bodyguard. For most of the year, above this point, the path is covered with snow and ice. The bugyals at Bedni have plenty of water. An artificial lake has been created with the help of a concrete dike, converting a marshy wetland into a sacred pond. Trekkers' huts and a makeshift teashop stand nearby, along with a Forest Department outpost. These haphazard structures and mangled strands of barbed wire mar the natural sanctity of the bugyal. Yet, Bedni has an eerie beauty, particularly after a storm. We arrive in the rain and take shelter in a trekker's hut, a domed structure made of fiberglass and tin, with a wooden floor. By early evening the clouds begin to disperse. I watch as they slough off the cliffs, spilling across high ridges like milk boiling over the rim of a pan.

A few minutes later, I can just make out the shape of a snow peak emerging from the mist. Its silhouette is barely visible at first but gradually takes shape before my eyes, until I recognize the scalloped summit of Trisul. Villagers in this region often refer to this mountain as Kailash, where Nanda Devi lives with her consort, Shiva. Trisul's three summits are considered the three points of his trident. Mount Kailash actually lies 150 miles northeast of here, at the edge of the Tibetan Plateau, but within the shifting matrix of Hindu mythology almost any mountain can represent Kailash. From Bedni the three points of the trident are not clearly evident, but there is no mistaking Trisul's towering crest that rises 23,360 feet above sea level. Eventually, the entire mountain is revealed, though the clouds keep it wrapped in shadow, while the sunset picks out more distant ranges to the west. Far off, beyond a fretwork of ridges, I recognize Chaukhamba glinting in the waning daylight.

Near the lake at Bedni stands a small Nanda Devi temple, as well as a shrine for Latu. Made entirely of rock, no mortar holds the stones in place, though moss has grown between the crevices. The central niche of Nanda's shrine houses two small idols of the goddess, carved from stone. Next to these is a single conch shell, white as a lump of snow. No coins or offerings have been left at the shrine, except for a fresh bunch of wildflowers. Tucked into the open alcove beside the idols are a few ritual implements, including a crude iron knife and a rusty ladle.

According to one version of the Nanda Devi epic, it was here in the wetlands at Bedni that the goddess tried to escape the demon by submerging herself in the shallow pond beside the temple. Her tormenter, the giant buffalo Mekhasur, full of lust for his adoptive mother, plunged into the water and gored the mud with his horns. For this reason, it is said the pond remains murky to this day. At another point Nanda takes shelter behind a bush nearby, but a flock of goats eat the leaves, revealing her hiding place. Finally, the goddess can no longer bear the demon's insolence and malevolent desires. Taking on her most fearsome aspect, as Mahakali, the eight-armed goddess who has sixty-four incarnations, the Devi confronts the buffalo, retaliating with all her fury. The peaceful meadows become a raging field of battle. All but invincible, Mekhasur is endowed with horrific powers of regeneration. Eventually, the goddess destroys her son by drinking his blood before it falls to the ground and becomes another demon. This myth is similar to other narratives from different parts of India, but here at Bedni the story has been localized and the goddess Nanda is worshipped as the chaste daughter of the Himalayas, a bride and mother who maintains her purity by annihilating evil.

When pilgrims carry the goddess from their village temples to Bedni, she rides in brocade palanquins, accompanied by a cacophony of drums, bagpipes, and horns, as well as songs that extol her virtues. The annual pilgrimage, often called the "small pilgrimage" ends here on the meadows where the demon was killed. In the aftermath of battle, the Devi's idols are bathed in the pond and devotees are cleansed by submerging themselves in its cold, spring-fed waters. Her images are worshipped at this shrine, which serves as a transitional shelter during the Raj Jaat Yatra, the "big pilgrimage" that occurs every twelve years, when the goddess is carried on to Roopkund and Shila Samudra glacier.

Without the ceremonies and crowds of pilgrims, the temple looks like an ordinary cairn of stones. A single flagpole made from the trunk of a small pine is rigged up like a mast with tattered pennants. On the one hand, it seems a disappointing structure bereft of carving or inscriptions, but the rude solidity of the rocks, piled one upon the other, speaks to the mute secrets of these meadows and an awe-inspiring presence that requires no man-made monuments, only the quiet grandeur of nature.

&

The break in the weather has been short-lived, and we wake up to a wet morning with mist so thick we can barely see two steps ahead of us. Waiting until the rain eases for a few minutes, we set out. There is no escaping the monsoon. After a few wrong turns while crossing the meadow, we reach the main pilgrim trail, which is easy to follow. Chunks of slate are placed vertically as rough cobblestones, creating a path that doesn't get mired in mud or dung. With the next Raj Jaat Yatra only a year away, work has started on improving the trail, and I can see where fresh sections of stones have been laid.

Our climb grows steadily steeper as we follow the contours of the ridge. Trishul remains hidden behind clouds. All I can see are precipitous slopes of grass falling away from the side of the trail and disappearing into the mist. Along this part of the trek, we meet no cattle or herdsmen, though I hear two gunshots somewhere below us in the clouds. It must be a poacher, or a farmer guarding his fields with a muzzle-loading musket. Eventually, we reach a place called Paathar Nachuni, where the exposed rocks look like the ruins of a giant amphitheater.

The legends and lore of Nanda Devi's pilgrimage are almost as rich and layered as the myths of the goddess herself. Walking these trails, we follow in the footsteps of those who have gone before us, retracing a collective journey, of which we become a part. Just as the strata of botanical species change as we go upward, so do the stories. According to one legend, the raja of Kannauj, an ancient city on the plains of North India, undertook the Raj Jaat Yatra many years ago. He is said to have brought with him a retinue of household servants and courtiers, accompanied by all of the luxuries and indulgences to which a raja is accustomed, including his dancing girls. Different renditions of the story have evolved, but we are told that here on these boulders, against a dramatic backdrop of snow peaks, the raja ordered his nautch girls to dance for his amusement. Judgmental versions of the legend suggest that this performance was an affront to the modesty of the goddess, who turned the dancers into stones and later inflicted retribution on the king and his party by striking them down with hailstones of iron. The bones at Roopkund are said to be their remains, the result of improprieties committed along the trail. Until recently, women were forbidden to accompany Nanda's pilgrimage, for her priests believe that she is a jealous deity who refuses to let her territory be polluted by the menstrual blood of others. Similar injunctions exist against non-Hindus and untouchables, not to mention foreigners like me, though these have been diluted over time.

⁓

Climbing steadily, we pass several shrines. One of these lies at a pass called Kelu Vinayaka, where a new stone structure has been built containing an image of Ganesh with his elephantine features and human body. As the eldest child of Shiva and Parvati, Ganesh is revered throughout India. He is considered a threshold deity, and the pass at Kelu Vinayaka marks a point where steep grasslands merge into the uppermost margins of rock and ice. Here, too, another trail comes up the opposite side of the ridge from the village of Sutol, an alternate route for pilgrims. Cloaked in mist, the wayside shrine seems less a portal to another world than a forgotten milestone in the clouds. The benign image of Ganesh, securely seated on his rugged perch, looks like a helpful mountaineer, ready to belay us with his trunk.

After we cross the pass, the rain increases, even as the clouds begin to lift, revealing more of the landscape. The upturned stones beneath our feet are painfully rough but nothing compared to the rockfalls that cover the slopes ahead. The face of the mountain has been quarried by erosion, exposed slabs of stone cracked and fissured by the freezing and melting of ice. Glaciers and avalanches have dragged the rocks and scattered them like the flattened ruins of a vast citadel devastated by an earthquake. Walking through frayed curtains of mist, it feels as if we are the first to arrive in the aftermath of a natural disaster, with no survivors left to rescue.

Our camp for the night is Bhugubasa. We reach there in the early afternoon, but the sky is so dark it feels as if the sun is about to set. Amid the rocks, I can see wild rhubarb and sedum, but my attention is focused on locating a level place to pitch our tents. We reject an abandoned cave with rough stone walls enclosing its entrance, a temporary shelter for shepherds or mendicants, as uninviting as a yeti's den. Just beyond, we find a sorry-looking cluster of broken walls and collapsed slate roofs, the abandoned remains of a pilgrim shelter. The stone floors inside two ruined huts offer the only level ground that we can see. As the rain continues to fall, I quickly erect my tent amid the ruins at Bhugubasa, while Titu and Akshay head off to search for drinking water.

By some accounts *Bhugubasa* means "God's campsite," while others say it denotes the home of the sacred *bagh* or tiger on which the goddess rides. Yet there is nothing about this place to suggest an aura of divinity. In the shrouded light, the stones are colorless and gray. We are above 14,000 feet and a sharp wind cuts across the slope, invisible blades of air whetted by glaciers above. Just before I crawl into my tent, the mist parts for a few seconds and I can see a cluster of huts ahead, but we have already chosen our place for the night. While the lower stretches of our trek have been marked by constantly changing belts of foliage, and even the slopes below Kelu Vinayaka are covered with dark blue gentians, buttercups, and edelweiss, at this point we seem to have entered an altitudinal zone of near desolation.

෴

In another episode of the legends surrounding Roopkund, the king of Kannauj camps here at Bhugubasa along with his pregnant wife, who is a sister of Nanda. Earlier, the goddess had visited them in Kannauj, but they offended her by refusing appropriate hospitality. Now, the royal couple are trying to make amends by undertaking the Raj Jaat Yatra. Before the king and his wife can reach the lake and cross over to the other side, a terrible storm erupts and the queen of Kannauj becomes so frightened that she goes into labor, giving birth to a daughter. Enraged by her sister's presence and the "unclean" amniotic fluids and afterbirth, which are washed into the Nandakini River, the goddess kills the hapless pilgrims in a ferocious hailstorm, leaving their bones strewn on the shores of Roopkund.

The vengeance of the goddess is equal to her blissful beneficence, reflecting the contrasting moods of the mountain. A story is told of G. W. Traill, the first British commissioner of Kumaon who was a mountaineer and explored much of this region in the 1830s. A pass above Pindari glacier bears his name. When Traill ordered the shifting of Nanda's temple in Almora, he was warned of the goddess's wrath. Soon afterwards, while climbing in the mountains, he suffered a severe attack of snow blindness, which was interpreted as divine retribution.

৩

The rain, which started before dawn, continues for twenty-four hours. At times it lessens to a fine drizzle, but mostly it falls in steady sheets, shredded by the wind. Having seen little on our walk to elevate our spirits, I feel a depressing loneliness, as if the ghosts of long-dead pilgrims are watching us through crevices in the ruined walls. Though the flagstone floor provides a flat surface for my tent, there are few places where I can drive in pegs or tie off ropes. The seams of the outer fly are awkwardly aligned and sections begin to sag, collecting water. Lying inside, I watch streams trickling down the opaque fabric and forming lakes above my head, until they overflow and spill onto the rocks beneath.

Titu is able to improvise a small kitchen under the only portion of the rock shelter that hasn't collapsed, a precarious-looking corner overhung with heavy shingles of slate. Most of the wooden beams and timbers have been scavenged for firewood. Crouched beneath umbrellas, we prepare a meal of rice and lentils boiled together as *khichdi*, enough to fill our stomachs. For dessert I pick a few stems of wild rhubarb, peeling them and chewing the inner flesh, though it is much too sour and I spit it out immediately. After that, we slink back into our tents and lie awake to the drumming of rain. I had hoped it would stop before nightfall, but there is no sign of it clearing. When I wake up in the middle of the night, thunder is rumbling and the wind has become a gale. Even within the shelter of rock walls, my tent is buffeted about, and it feels as if the outer fly will soon be torn away. Pulling on rain gear in the dark, I crawl outside and try as best I can to secure the ropes. Rain lashes at me as I struggle to lay rocks on top of the few pegs that hold my tent in place. By the time I crawl back inside, I am soaked and shivering.

Unable to sleep for the next six hours, I make up my mind not to spend another night at Bhugubasa, even if the weather clears. The altitude doesn't bother me, but I have an uncomfortable premonition about this place. Lightning illuminates the synthetic membrane of my tent in weird white flashes, and the thunder sounds as if someone is dynamiting the cliffs above and rolling boulders down the slopes. Despite its name, Bhugubasa seems more demonic than divine. Having secured my tent, I feel somewhat safer, but there is a lingering sense of dread until the first light of dawn begins to seep through the clouds and the rain finally ceases.

When we emerge from our tents, the clouds are low overhead, but most of the gloom has been washed away. Below our camp, I see a broad, green valley veined with streams, and, far off in the distance, a herd of sheep huddle inside a corral of rocks. Choughs are calling and, at first, I mistake their cries for the whistling of marmots. The breeze is cold, but the mist has evaporated and there is a clarity to the air, as if the storm has polished the atmosphere into a perfect lens that magnifies everything in sight. What startles me most of all are the greenish white blossoms of the brahmakamal flower, which grows in profusion. I can't believe I didn't notice them the day before. Known as Brahma's lotus, they are considered a sacred bloom. Dried brahmakamal are often suspended above the doors of temples in Garhwal. The flowers look more like giant poppies than lotus, though the crepe-like petals are cupped together in the shape of a supplicant's folded hands.

Brahmakamal grows above 13,000 feet, one of the last plants found on any Himalayan climb. Most times I have seen no more than a dozen scattered among the rocks, but at Bhugubasa thousands of brahmakamal cover the slopes, as if they have all burst forth in the aftermath of the storm. Their pale, luminous shapes are as delicate as Chinese lanterns, fields upon fields of blossoms that seem to have appeared overnight, a spontaneous miracle of nature.

Titu and I decide that we will take advantage of the break in the rain and make a dash for Roopkund before the storm resumes. Leaving Akshay to keep an eye on our tents and gear, we set off up the trail unburdened. The distance from Bhugubasa to the lake is three miles. For the first section, the trail seems clear enough, though I can't figure out exactly where it is headed. Above us lie nothing but cliffs, impassable precipices of shale and ice. Unlike the Raj Jaat pilgrims, we have no path-finding hero to guide us.

Eventually, we come to a crumbling staircase of stones that brings us to a loose rockfall, where I can see traces of a path. Scrambling up this slope, I keep my eyes on the ground in front of me, to avoid looking at the drop below. A short distance on ahead, the rocks turn to gravel as we traverse an unstable stretch that looks more like a landslide than a passable trail. Just as I begin to wonder if we have taken a wrong turn, we crest the rise and there below us lies Roopkund, not more than forty feet long and twenty feet across. Ice-scarred rocks form a natural chalice beneath the cliffs, and its jade waters have a poisonous tint. A dense ceiling of clouds hangs above us, obscuring all but the closest crags. To our right lies a glacier of dirty ice, worming its way through a notch in the ridge. Westward, the lower slopes of Nanda Ghunti are streaked with snow, though most of the mountain remains hidden. Only below us is an unobstructed view of the rain-scoured valley extending to Bhugubasa and beyond.

A small shrine of rocks, about the size of a postbox, overlooks the lake. Inside is a framed picture of Shiva and his bride, the kind of conventional calendar art that adorns every teashop on the plains. The goddess looks thoroughly domesticated, sitting sidesaddle on her tiger like a middle-class housewife riding pillion on a scooter. Here amid the harsh tumult of rocks and ice, the picture seems incongruous and absurd. The *Shakti*, or feminine power of Nanda Devi, is far more dangerous than demure.

A few feet away from the shrine is a stack of bones. A group of trekkers from a year ago have left a small plaque beside it, on which are engraved the words: "Himalaya Enjoyment Association." Someone who followed after them has broken the plaque in half, perhaps out of irritation or disapproval of this gruesome altar, on top of which sits a human skull. Their desecration of the site seems far worse than priestly injunctions against shedding menstrual blood or giving birth to a female child. The idea that these trekkers, whose plaque suggests they came from Kolkata, should find enjoyment in the Himalayas by stacking up a grotesque pyramid of human femurs, tibia, vertebrae, and ribs, gives the place an unsettling, sacrilegious aura.

Descending to the lake, a short glissade down steep funnels of debris, we carefully avoid the mud, which is a morbid gray color, contrasting with the green water. Most accounts of Roopkund describe hundreds of skeletons, though it is hard to imagine how anyone could have counted the bones, which are scattered and mixed together like a conglomerated bed of fossils. I estimate no more than thirty to forty victims of whatever catastrophe occurred, though it's possible that members of the Himalaya Enjoyment Association, and other visitors like them, have carried off grim souvenirs.

Only a dark rind of ice remains at one end of the lake, from which a trickle of water spills through the rocks. The cliffs above are fiercely toothed and wreathed in fog. It is an unhappy, sterile site, overshadowed by archaic taboos. The thought of royal pilgrims being felled by hailstones of iron seems too cruel a fate for these unfortunate souls. Many of the rocks have a rusty hue, but it is difficult to imagine cannonballs dropping out of the clouds. A few of the bones, which are frozen most of the year, appear to have adhering scraps of flesh or skin. Like the mummified remains of prehistoric hunters and mountaineers that emerge from alpine glaciers centuries after their deaths, these skeletons seem to be a tragic tableau from the past, reenacting a sacrificial drama of the goddess so that we might contemplate our own mortality, as well as the fatal consequences of pilgrimage and faith.

One theory that has been put forward, though it cannot be proved with any more certainty than the others, is that pilgrims who came to this place sacrificed themselves to the goddess by leaping from the cliffs of Junargali, above the lake. Other religious sites in Garhwal have similar stories, including Kedarnath, where a cliff nearby is known as Bhairav Jhamp. Pilgrims in the past have ended their lives in a ritual plunge onto the rocks below, releasing their souls from future suffering and becoming martyrs to the mountain.

For all its mysterious legends and lore, Roopkund inspires no cathartic feelings of empathy or elation. I have no desire to loiter in this joyless place. There is no darshan of the goddess, only a premonition of foreboding. After arriving here, I feel no need to sit and contemplate the suffering and deaths of pilgrims, mendicants, warriors, or shepherds—whatever their story—who perished by this pond so many years ago.

Climbing back up to the rim above the lake, I brace myself for a slippery, unstable descent to Bhugubasa, but a flash of blue on the cusp of the ridge catches my eye. At first, when I kneel down on the mossy soil stitched with white strands of lichens, I think this plant is a species of aconite, poisonous monkshood, which grows at these altitudes and seems suited to the deathly surroundings of Roopkund. But on closer inspection, it turns out to be *Delphinium*, a much more cheerful flower. Clustered above the lake, like a last flourish of life, the fragile blue petals redeem my sense of the place, a tenuous burst of color and beauty amid this dismal patch of frost and stone.

Writing with My Feet

Strings of verses kiting on the wind.
Prayers of penance and devotion.
Om.

We climb toward Taktsang, the Tiger's Nest, in Bhutan, nine months after my trek to Roopkund. Here, I am digressing from my search for Nanda, though separate paths in the mountains have a way of converging on the truth. This cliff-top monastery is built around a cave where Guru Padmasambhava meditated, after flying here from Tibet. His consort turned herself into an airborne tigress so that she could transport him over the Himalayas. Prayer flags are draped across a precipice, fluttering scraps of sacred texts that mark the trajectory of the guru's flight.

If I were to design prayer flags of my own, they would ask for nothing and praise only these Himalayan hemlocks with their tiny, compact cones and paintbrush needles; or the white-collared blackbird that alights in front of me, as reverend as a Christian cleric with a bleached band around his throat. I would commit the syntax of my footsteps to squares of colored fabric, inked words impressed on cotton gauze, to be suspended across the valley—white, blue, yellow, green, and red—a deconstructed rainbow, cross-referenced by the breeze.

Instead of snow lions and conch shells, wind horses and bodhisattvas, my prayer flags will bear the emblems that I see around me: a nutcracker pecking beetles out of the bark of a dying spruce; three pebbles stacked as a miniature cairn in a wayside cave; the five white petals on a musk rose growing along the path. An oriental turtle dove—its name suggesting untold myths—watches me from a nearby branch.

My flags won't pray for a better life next time around or forgiveness for sins I don't regret—evil thoughts, perhaps, but not the daily transgressions that I'm supposed to confess. On the ridge across from us, I see the other kind of prayer flags, narrow lengths of cloth draped from long poles and grouped together like the grieving ghosts of trees. These flags are colorless. Their entreaties seem to be for the dead, mourning the tallest pine struck by lightning, or an oak whose time has passed, its lifeless roots still clinging to the mountain soil, dry branches draped with angel hair moss. The poles are topped by metal finials, like spears. They cluster together on the ridge, and the frayed strips of fabric could be mistaken for unraveling clouds.

I prefer colorful prayers, the invocation of a yellow primula growing out of the mud, the intercession of scarlet rhododendrons still in bloom at the end of May, the benediction of a blue aster wilting amid a field of green.

For close to fifty years, I haven't prayed. Others have performed the task on my behalf. But on this walk the wind and trees seem to tug words from my soul. At Taktsang, I watch a Bhutanese family prostrating themselves in front of the guru's image. A girl of four or five mimics her parents, flattening herself to the floor, as if doing calisthenics. The teenaged monk who unlocks the sanctuary for us trickles holy water into my palm from a silver vessel adorned with peacock feathers. I baptize my face and head, wondering what these rituals mean.

We are told that having climbed up here to the Tiger's Nest, we can pray for anything we desire and it will be granted. Suddenly, I don't know what to ask for—Enlightenment? Healing? Solace? . . . No, I don't believe in this, any more than I believe in wishing upon a star or trusting my fate to the hollow snap of a chicken bone.

Outside the temple, flags stream across the gorge, framing a waterfall that cascades down the rocks. The fluttering prayers blur my vision, and I imagine a winged tigress soaring through the air with a hermit meditating on her back . . . too late I realize what I should have prayed for.

Unmask this landscape, and reveal the myth!

⌘

Whenever I fly over the Himalayas, as I did when coming to Bhutan, I am overawed by the vast expanse of snow-caked ridges and summits, extending from one horizon to the next. These mountains stretch beyond the limits of history and human imagining. The formation of the Himalayas is one of the greatest creation myths ever told. Fragments of Pangea disintegrate and coalesce through continental drift until India collides with Asia in a tectonic moment of coitus, out of which the Himalayas were born. These mountains rise up along the line of impact, forming the highest elevations on earth. Geologists tell us how it happened in primordial slow motion, Gaia's dance displacing oceans, a process that continues even today, the mountains eternally reaching up to meet the sky. Even the gods could not have conceived an epic of these proportions.

The Himalayas seem as infinite as an ocean, frozen at the climax of a storm. Tsunamis of ice and rock rear up beneath the wings of our thunder dragon—a Druk Air jet, the national carrier of Bhutan. Cruising at 30,000 feet above sea level, we have surpassed the highest altitudes on earth. The atmosphere is a smooth meniscus over which we glide, untroubled by turbulent terrain below. Lower slopes of the mountains are engulfed in clouds, like foaming surf washing over the arid beachheads of the Tibetan Plateau. And yet, for all the staggering enormity of the Himalayas, this airborne encounter leaves me dissatisfied and unfulfilled, as if I have not earned this view. For me, the only meaningful way to experience mountains is on foot.

⌘

His Majesty the King of Bhutan has decreed that Gross National Happiness is the primary objective of his Himalayan state. Visiting the country, I try to understand the portent of this royal edict, an arbitrary idealism that only a monarch could impose. As Bhutan attempts to turn itself into a modern Shangri-La, a mountainous Eden that excludes all forms of discontentment and banishes sorrow, I wonder whether it is possible to find genuine happiness in a place where authority dictates its own cheerful benevolence.

The happiness I seek is not euphoric joy or spiritual bliss, but the simple contentment that frees us from terror, anguish, and anxiety. More than something that possesses us, it is the absence of sadness, a release from melancholy.

Happiness isn't truth—too absolute a noun. Nor is it faith, which seems to me a charade of the human psyche. Peace might serve as a suitable synonym, though it leads in far too many directions. Happiness is a transient emotion that can arise out of discipline and meditation but, more often, surprises us at moments when we least expect it. Suddenly, the dark clouds of anger or distress, and the opaque mists of depression, lift to reveal a sublime panorama of mountains that reduce our human travails to insignificant proportions. We understand that terrible things happen in beautiful places just as beautiful things happen in terrible places. Yet, we are alive and grateful to be here.

Ultimately, my search for happiness leads me to Taktsang. Setting out soon after daybreak, we have the trail to ourselves. Four hundred yards from the roadhead, I come to a shrine built over a stream that flows from the mountain. Nearby is a large rock painted with an image of the guru, water pooling at his feet. In the lee of this rock is a cluster of conical objects made of clay mixed with funereal ashes. On a moss-covered boulder near the stream, someone has carved a raised inscription, a single line of words embossed upon the rough surface of the stone. Neither the shrine nor the painted rock intrudes on the natural beauty of the stream or the quiet sanctity of this place. The only sounds are the music of falling water accompanying birdsong.

Walking together, my companions and I talk and laugh, but another part of me is striding up the trail in a meditative trance. I could just as easily have come alone, though I am grateful for their company. On my own, I might have raced up this path in half the time, impatient to reach the top. But pausing every fifteen steps allows me to appreciate the walk at a slower pace.

Four dogs have attached themselves to us as we climb the steep switchbacks. They follow at our heels and lie down to rest whenever we stop, eager for a handout. One of them is a Tibetan mastiff. Her undercoat is blowing out after the winter, shedding matted clumps of fur. They walk with us for an hour, until we reach a giant prayer wheel on the ridge, from where the Tiger's Nest comes into view once more. Looking down at the valley, I can see that we have climbed almost a thousand feet but Taktsang hardly seems any closer. A Bhutanese man rotates the prayer wheel, which is as large as a cement mixer. His chanting is a steady rumble, like an engine, as he turns the wheel with one hand, moving around and around, in slow stages, a walk that takes him nowhere.

Nearby, discreetly removed from the main path, is a rest stop and cafeteria with a view of the monastery above. Thermos flasks full of tea and coffee have been prepared. We are the first visitors to serve ourselves. I am struck by the simplicity and uncluttered ambience of this place. In other parts of the Himalayas, many pilgrimage routes have been covered over with concrete, and, at every turn of the path, somebody sets up a tea shack selling soft drinks, instant noodles, and cigarettes. Here, the trail is a dirt track, carefully maintained but deliberately unpaved. Despite the hundreds of pilgrims who make this journey every week, the approach to Taktsang remains unspoiled.

This is the mountain refuge of the guru who came to this place before anything was built, carried through the air on the wings of his consort. While the guru entered his cave and immersed himself in contemplation, seeking inner paths to enlightenment, the tigress assumed her human form. She attended to his material needs, even as she protected him with the ferocity of her animal self. In essence, it could easily be the story of Shiva and Nanda, or Parvati, whose *vahana*, or sacred vehicle, is the tiger. In this way Buddhist and Hindu myths of ascetic masculinity and dangerous female partners echo each other across the Himalayas.

The sun is still hidden behind the ridge and won't touch the gilded roof of the temple until late afternoon, though Taktsang seems to glow with a light of its own. Its presence dominates the rocks and crags, yet seems to be an integral part of the mountain. A few of the outer buildings are tucked into rocky crags, and a sloping carpet of grass lies at the foot of the final staircase, overshadowed by a tall cypress with drooping limbs.

Near the foot of the waterfall, which burst from the rocks when the guru's consort flung his prayer beads at the cliffs during a domestic spat, hundreds of swallowtail butterflies swarm and flit amid wild roses and other flowers. They never alight, even for a second, a constant agitation that frustrates any attempt to photograph them.

At a guardhouse just below the temple, I am disarmed of my camera and asked to produce my passport. The policeman who frisks me is chanting Buddhist prayers, a sonorous mumble, as his hands move over my pockets and belt. I notice a rack of fire extinguishers nearby. The monastery burned down in 1998. Many of the scriptures and thangka paintings were lost, the precious idols damaged. During the reconstruction, a cable car was erected to transport material for the restoration, a process that lasted seven years. In 2005, after the Tiger's Nest was rebuilt, the cable car was dismantled so that pilgrims can approach only on foot or by horse.

We climb the steep flight of steps to the main doors of the shrine. A cloud of incense envelops us, and the smell of smoldering juniper needles mingles with sweeter, synthetic perfumes. I visit each of the sanctuaries and see the guru's cave, framed with gold leaf and decorated with plastic lotus and hydrangeas. The faces on the idols express a divine happiness that none of us will ever achieve. Two life-size figures are locked in tantric coitus, arms and legs entwined. I imagine the guru making love to his tigress after the waterfall has sprung into being and all is forgiven. Near the top of the temple complex, a faded photograph of a white tiger confronts me, with an arrow pointing into a cleft in the rocks. Climbing into this cave, I can just make out a precarious staircase of weathered planks that ends in a void, light filtering up through a vacant funnel in the cliffs. I decide to explore no further.

Sacred places have a way of quickly losing their sanctity, particularly when shrines, temples, and teashops are constructed near a popular site. Over the years, I have found the most moving and inspirational places in the Himalayas remain unmarked and often unnamed. A ridge above Uprikot where I saw a flowering tree in winter, or the hillock below Patreni, where an iron flail lies rusting in the grass. The Bhyundar Valley in Garhwal, which contains no man-made structures beyond a few cairns, the foundations of a demolished rest house, and the ruins of herdsman's huts, conveys a far greater spiritual aura than the multitiered clutter of temples at Badrinath. The shrine of Surkanda Devi near my home has grown from a simple, slate-roofed sanctuary into a three-story eyesore of reinforced concrete. Taktsang, however, contradicts my conviction that most religious buildings are best unbuilt. The inner chapels of the Tiger's Nest, with their idols and ritual accoutrements, do not stir me beyond an appreciation for the workmanship and artistry. But the external architecture is as powerful as the place itself. These buildings complement the sculpted face of nature, eroded cliffs and waterfalls, trees taking root on a vertical plane. Whatever caves the guru inhabited with his feline lover have been covered over by stone walls and sloping roofs. Yet, the monastery and its temples express an innate reverence for the natural contours of the rock.

Beyond these shrines, however, there is something older that draws us in, a powerful presence of which I feel a part, the hollow force of gravity within a cave. To be here is all that matters. To arrive and enter. I don't need to understand the myths or murals. Those stories are incidental to the place. More important is the walk that brought me here, the dirt trail that winds up the mountain. When I reach Taktsang, there are no blinding lights or crashing cymbals, but as I brush a hand over the rough stone walls and feel the cold texture of granite boulders under my feet, it seems as if the mountain has admitted us into a secret chamber where human desires merge with natural phenomena to amplify our dreams.

I feel no sudden tumult of ecstasy or spiritual vertigo despite the dizzying heights, only a comforting sense of negative space. In this moment, happiness is neither gross nor nationalistic, but omnipresent and immeasurable. I am overcome by a sense of clarity and understanding that has nothing to do with any doctrine or philosophy that I can name. While others are present, I am alone in myself, as if the world around me has been erased.

Though the experience is deeply moving, I feel no compulsion to stay. In fact, as soon as I enter the Tiger's Nest, I am prepared to leave. It makes no difference how long I am here, whether I wait for a minute or an hour. I remember illustrations from a children's edition of John Bunyan's *The Pilgrim's Progress*, which my grandmother gave me when I was seven or eight years old. Toward the end of the story, a burden drops from the traveler's shoulders and disappears into a bottomless chasm. In the pious allegory, this is the weight of sin and suffering. But for me, the image suggests something far less certain, a loss that releases me from anger, fear, and sadness, while entering into a tenuous state of emotional equanimity.

⌘

Henry David Thoreau's essay "Walking" was first delivered as a lecture at the Concord Lyceum and ultimately published in the *Atlantic Monthly* after his death in 1862. More than a century and a half later, his distinctive voice is clearly audible, at times wry and mischievous, often strident or cranky, yet rising to a passionate pitch of eloquence. In many ways, "Walking" is as much a sermon as an essay, exhorting us to get outdoors and discover our place in nature.

Thoreau rails against sedentary men, merchants, and scholars, who spend their lives indoors. He speaks of spiritual epiphanies and redemption that await us along woodland trails. For him, walking is a sacred mission. "For every walk is a sort of crusade, preached by some Peter the Hermit in us, to go forth and reconquer this Holy Land from the hands of Infidels." He admits it is a healthy pursuit but points to a higher goal: "the walking of which I speak has nothing in it akin to taking exercise, as it is called, as the sick take medicines . . . but is itself the enterprise and adventure of the day."

An inveterate wanderer, Thoreau urges us to leave the highways and well-beaten paths in search of untrodden wilderness. "Life consists with wildness. The most alive is the wildest. Not yet subdued to man, its presence refreshes him. One who pressed forward incessantly and never rested from his labors, who grew fast and made infinite demands on life, would always find himself in a new country or wilderness, and surrounded by the raw material of life."

Giving us the example of the poet Wordsworth, whose library was inside his house, "but his study out of doors," Thoreau makes a case for literature that explores new paths in nature. "A truly good book is something as natural, and as unexpectedly and unaccountably fair and perfect, as a wild-flower discovered on the prairies of the West or in the jungles of the East."

Transcendentalist preacher that he was, Thoreau invokes his calling as a writer: "Where is the literature which gives expression to Nature? He would be a poet who could impress the winds and streams into his service, to speak for him . . . who derived his words as often as he used them—transplanted them to his page with earth adhering to their roots; whose words were so true and fresh and natural that they would appear to expand like the buds at the approach of spring, though they lay half smothered between two musty leaves in a library—aye, to bloom and bear fruit there, after their kind, annually, for the faithful reader, in sympathy with surrounding Nature."

And finally, at the end of his essay, after rambling digressions and detours, Thoreau returns to the theme of a pilgrimage and crusade. "So we saunter toward the Holy Land, till one day the sun shall shine more brightly than ever he has done, shall perchance shine into our minds and hearts, and light up our whole lives with a great awakening light, as warm and serene and golden as on a bankside in autumn."

꿍

As a child, I didn't take easily to walking. Whenever my parents suggested we go for a walk, the idea never excited me, and I would make up excuses to stay behind. Walking, simply for the sake of walking, was something that older people did because they sat around all day, working at their desks or reading or doing housework. I walked to school and back, often with reluctance, but always knowing that I must not be late for the bell. I also walked into town, driven by the motive of seeing a movie, eating at a sweet shop, or buying firecrackers. Growing up in Mussoorie, there was no way to avoid walking, and most of the time we were going uphill or down, seldom on the level. It was something we took for granted, a physical activity that occurred of its own volition rather than out of any conscious choice we made.

Only when I started hunting did I begin to appreciate the greater pleasure and purpose of walking. My father was not an obsessive *shikari*, but he enjoyed hunting mostly because it gave him a reason to get outdoors and tramp about in the forest, seeking the companionship of others who shared his love of nature. The shooting of a bird or animal was secondary, though we hunted for the pot and ate everything we killed.

Accompanying my father on *shikar*, I enjoyed the adventure and exertion of these trips because they had a clear purpose at the end. We would bring back meat for the household, and if we didn't, there were always stories of what got away. The predatory impulse behind our walks sharpened my senses and taught me to observe the forest and learn its language.

During our winter holidays, which corresponded to hunting season in North India, I spent four or five days every week stalking game in the jungles around Mussoorie. Pari Tibba, Flag Hill, and the ridges above Kimoin were some of the places I hunted. But mostly I went to Patreni, a village about three miles from Mussoorie, where a hunter named Dil Das was my mentor and companion. Each day, I must have walked between ten or twelve miles, climbing and descending more than three thousand feet between dawn and dusk. Most of the time I came home empty-handed. During high school, this was my main source of distraction from the pangs of growing up, and I explored every path and game trail within twenty miles of our home.

Soon after I turned twenty-two, I gave up hunting. The last animal I shot was a kakad. Our cook, Prem, was celebrating his eldest daughter's wedding, and he asked me to get him some meat to serve his guests. Taking my father's rifle into the forest beyond Jabberkhet, I went alone and killed a kakad, then carried it home. These barking deer are about the size of a small goat. I tied the hooves together and hoisted it onto my back like a knapsack. Climbing the steep trail to the top of the ridge as the sun went down and the night closed in around me, I remember thinking that I had outgrown my need to take a rifle into the forest or bear the weight of another animal on my shoulders.

Around this time, hunting was banned in India and I lost interest in shikar, though I was now addicted to walking. While I have no regrets about giving up hunting, whenever I set foot in the forest, even today, a part of me still calls up those predatory instincts, alert to the sounds of birds and animals, scanning the slopes and clearings for any sign of movement, measuring distances with my eyes. If I spot an animal, adrenalin releases a safety catch in my nerves.

Carl von Essen, a medical doctor and avid outdoorsman, wrote in his book, *The Hunter's Trance*, about the mystical experience of observing nature through a hunter's eye, particularly in that eternal instant when an arrow is aimed at its target and the bowstring pulled taut. Von Essen compares the concentration and primal impulse of the hunter to the meditative state of a spiritual seeker intent on comprehending the divine. He quotes the biologist E. O. Wilson from his book *Biophilia*:

> I walked into the forest, struck as always by the coolness of the shade beneath the tropical vegetation, and continued until I came to a small glade that opened onto the sandy path. I narrowed the world down to a few meters. Again I tried to compose the mental set—call it the naturalist's trance, the hunter's trance—by which biologists locate more elusive organisms. . . . The effect was strangely calming. Breathing and heartbeat diminished, concentration intensified. It seemed to me that something extraordinary in the forest was very close to where I stood, moving to the surface and to discovery.

This trance-like state is familiar to anyone who has observed nature closely, not only the hunter drawing a bead on his prey but also the lepidopterist readying his net to catch a butterfly. Peter Smetacek, who grew up in the foothills of Kumaon, a hundred miles east of Mussoorie, has described in his memoir, *Butterflies on the Roof of the World*, a lifetime spent in pursuit of rare insects. The opening chapter recounts a trek above Nainital in search of a Golden Sapphire, which has a suitably immortal Latin name: *Heliophorus brahma.* Scrambling toward the summit of a forested peak in search of this small butterfly, Smetacek found himself stranded on a ledge of slippery shale, overhanging a drop of two thousand feet. Under these precarious circumstances, he confronted his own mortality, wondering if anyone would hear him scream when he fell to his death: "Here, reality was the waving grass, the breeze, the crumbling ledge and the ever circling butterfly, tripping along the edge and being lifted over to safety on the shoulders of the breeze. After the instant of agony, would I, too, be lifted by the breeze?"

Conservationist George Schaller experienced a similar moment of epiphany, which he describes in *Stones of Silence.* Pursuing a snow leopard in the mountains of Pakistan, he climbs a barren ridge in winter, crawling up a slope of scree and snow, hoping to find this elusive predator. After a long and difficult ascent, he is rewarded.

> Then I saw the snow leopard, a hundred and fifty feet away, peering at me from the spur, her body so well molded into the contours of the boulders that she seemed a part of them. Her smoky-gray coat sprinkled with black rosettes perfectly complemented the rocks and snow wastes, and her pale eyes conveyed an image of immense solitude. As we watched each other the clouds descended once more, entombing us and bringing more snow. Perhaps sensing that I meant her no harm, she sat up. Though snow soon capped her head and shoulders, she remained, silent and still, seemingly impervious to the elements. Wisps of clouds swirled around, transforming her into a ghost creature, part myth and part reality. Balanced precariously on a ledge and bitterly cold, I too stayed, unwilling to disrupt the moment. One often has empathy with animals, but rarely and unexpectedly one attains a state beyond the subjective and fleetingly almost seems to become what one beholds; here, in this snowbound valley of the Hindu Kush, I briefly achieved such intimacy. Then the snow fell more thickly, and, dreamlike, the cat slipped away as if she had never been.

Each of these writers express profound yet passing moments of transcendence that we discover in nature. Though it is an experience of stillness, these mystical encounters often occur in the course of a walk or a climb, the physical process of ambulation interrupted by a vision that transports us beyond ourselves.

The act of walking itself can be a form of meditation. Gautama Buddha urged his disciples to wander, shedding all material possessions, seeking trails that led them away from desire and suffering. At the same time he cautioned: "You cannot travel on the path until you have become the Path itself."

The *Aitareya Brahmana*, an ancient Hindu text, contains Lord Indra's advice:

> There is no happiness for him who does not travel, Rohita!
> Thus we have heard.
> Living in the society of men, the best of men becomes a sinner.
> Therefore wander!
> The feet of the wanderer are like the flower, his soul is growing
> and reaping the fruit;
> And all his sins are destroyed by his fatigues in wandering.
> Therefore wander!
> The fortune of him who is sitting, sits; rises when he rises;
> It sleeps when he sleeps; it moves when he moves.
> Therefore wander!

Lung-gom, often translated as "trance walking," is a meditative exercise practiced by Tibetan mystics, both Buddhist and Bonpo. An early explorer and scholar of Tibetan culture, Alexandra David-Neel described her first encounter with a trance walker:

> He proceeded at an unusual gait and especially with an extraordinary swiftness. . . . I could see his perfectly calm impassive face and wide-open eyes with their gaze fixed on some invisible far-distant object situated somewhere high up in space. The man did not run. He seemed to lift himself from the ground, proceeding by leaps. It looked as if he had been

endowed with the elasticity of a ball and rebounded each time his feet touched the ground. His steps had the regularity of a pendulum.

Lama Anagarika Govinda, in *The Way of the White Clouds*, quotes David-Neel and goes on to recount his own personal experience with trance walking along the shores of Pangong Lake in Ladakh.

> Beginners in the art of *lung-gom* are often advised to fix their mind not only on a mentally visualized object, namely the aim towards which they want to move, but to keep their eyes fixed on a particular star, which in some cases seems to produce a hypnotic effect. Even in this detail I had unwittingly conformed to the rules, and I clearly reached a condition in which the weight of the body is no more felt and in which the feet seem to be endowed with an instinct of their own, avoiding invisible obstacles and finding footholds, which only a clairvoyant consciousness could have detected in the speed of such a movement and in the darkness of the night.

෨

For years I have experienced a recurring dream of walking or running in the mountains along a narrow trail through a pine forest. A carpet of needles cushions the ground beneath my feet. The forest has little undergrowth, and the mountain falls away in steep, grass-covered slopes. Inevitably, at some point in the dream, I always leave the path and step out into the air. It seems so natural and simple, as easy as taking a breath. Instead of turning a corner, I launch myself into empty space, like one of the lung-gom monks. It feels as if I can fly, though my legs continue to propel me forward and my arms swing loosely at my waist. Nobody is chasing me but there is a feeling of escape, defying gravity, my feet gaining traction on the wind. This dream always ends while I am still striding through the air, weightless. And when I wake up, a sense of disappointment overwhelms me, finding myself flat on a bed, firmly fastened to the earth.

My dream repeats itself with unpredictable regularity. I know exactly where it takes place—near a forest bungalow called Nali where we used to go on hunting trips when I was a boy. Nali is ten miles east of Mussoorie, and the ridges, fringed with pine, are visible from Oakville. In the late sixties and early seventies, Nali was a shooting block, which my father would book for a couple of weeks. We could drive by jeep partway, though the final approach to the bungalow was along a forested trail. It was an easy hike, and we loaded up our pack boards with sleeping bags and other gear. The ridge near the bungalow is covered in long needle pines, a species planted by the Forest Department both for timber and for resin tapped from these trees. Known as chir, it allows few other species to survive beneath a thick mulch of needles. The reticulated bark always makes me think of giraffes because of the patterns on the trunk. In my dream, I walk alone along the trail from Nali bungalow through a forest of pines. Approaching a bend in the path, I break into a run and leave the earth behind.

Every walk in the forest becomes a prayer. Instead of kneeling and folding our hands, or bowing down before whatever deity demands our obeisance, we set out with a measured stride, our inner compass fixed on invisible coordinates that lead us farther than the path itself. In the mountains our trail is never straight. Each corner reveals a different vista, framed by trees that align themselves to the contours of the ridge, growing vertically despite the rugged terrain. At times the trail is level with their limbs, so that we can easily step out onto a branch, the trees providing detours from the path.

Wandering in the mountains, our senses are attuned to other species that surround us, each of them a strand of life, woven into a web of eternity. We recall the names of plants and birds, or give them new names from our imagination, a personal taxonomy both whimsical and precise. Each species is a god, a living image of creative forces that invite devotion but never dictate faith. The sounds we hear need no translation; they speak to us at a deeper level than human language or words of scripture. Walking is a ritual that recognizes the divinity in nature, what animists have known forever, the undefinable footfalls of being.

✍

Somewhere along the extended timeline of our evolutionary journey, probably in the late Pliocene epoch, about 1.8 million years ago, our hominid ancestors stood up on their hind legs and started to walk like the creatures we are today. At that moment, a change came over us, both physical and psychological. No longer were we forced to move about with our faces lowered to the ground or crane our necks upward for brief glimpses of the sky. Instead, we could pivot on our heels and survey 360 degrees of the world around us, as well as gaze up and down, from the soil beneath our toes to the highest branches of the trees. Moving from a horizontal plane to the vertical, we became a different species altogether, and the stories we told took on a new perspective. As Peter Matthiessen in *The Snow Leopard* quotes Ovid: "All other creatures look down toward the earth, but man was given a face so that he might turn his eyes toward the stars and his gaze upon the sky." Our skeletons and muscles adjusted but also our minds, adopting an open, forward-looking stance. Much more had changed than just our center of gravity. No longer crouched on all four limbs, we gained a freedom of movement that was as liberating as flight must have been for the first birds when they took to the air. At the same time, it reorganized our senses and made us more alert to danger, as well as opportunity. Our hands became instruments of survival and creativity. Being hunters, we etched images of the chase on boulders or painted figures like ourselves on the walls of caves, erect and poised, one leg cocked in front of the other, holding our bows ready, aiming at wild deer and mountain goats.

Our bodies have been constructed to provide mobility, particularly forward motion. At a very basic level, walking fulfills the purpose for which we have been created, whether in the likeness of God, as some would argue, or through the patient craftsmanship of our genes. Placing one foot in front of the other gives meaning to our lives, directing us to what lies ahead. It is as fundamental to human nature as opposable thumbs or the pleasure we feel at the moment of orgasm. Regardless of all of the speculation and shoe-marketing jargon about collapsed arches and over-pronation, Homo sapiens are designed for walking. Loping, strolling, sauntering, stepping out, or ambling along, we owe much more than our survival as a species to the act of walking.

Being hunter-gatherers required our ancestors to cover long distances following migratory prey. This was better achieved on two feet rather than four, leaving our hands free to use weapons and tools. Over time, as hunters became herdsman, we continued walking, shepherding animals from one pasture to another. In *The Solace of Open Spaces*, Gretel Ehrlich writes: "To herd sheep is to discover a new human gear somewhere between second and reverse—a slow, steady trot of keenness with no speed. . . . But the constant movement of sheep from water hole to water hole, from camp to camp, becomes a form of longing. But for what?"

～

Early Greek geographers and historians who visited India following Alexander's campaigns describe "fabulous races" of men living in the mountains, whose feet are turned around in the wrong direction. In *Historia Naturalis,* Pliny writes with some skepticism about these "antipodes." He reports: "According to Megasthenes, on a mountain called Nulo, there live men whose feet are turned backward and who have eight toes on each foot; while on many of the mountains there lives a race of men having heads like those of dogs, who are clothed with skins of wild beasts, whose speech is barking, and who, being armed with claws, live by hunting and fowling."

Stories of demons, vampires, and witches whose feet are reversed have always been part of the folklore of India. In most cases, the purpose of this aberration is to fool whoever tries to track the demon down. Those who attempt to follow their footprints end up going in the wrong direction where, unsuspecting, they fall victim to an ambush. This inversion of anatomy is a frightening, twisted, even monstrous image. Nevertheless, some evolutionary biologists suggest that our feet may have evolved from the flippers on an aquatic

ancestor and turned backwards at the ankles so that our distant forefathers could paddle through the water.

It is difficult to imagine how anyone might be able to walk if their
toes were pointed in a direction opposite to their face. The added riddle is whether these mythological creatures actually move forward or
backwards. It reminds me of villagers in the mangrove jungles of the
Sundarbans who wear masks on the backs of their heads in order to
confuse marauding tigers, who prefer to attack from behind. In his
autobiography, *Tiger of the Snows*, Tenzing Norgay recalls how folklore in western Nepal describes the yeti as having its feet pointing
backwards. Mountaineers who find the footprints of an abominable
snowman on a glacier must wonder whether the beast is coming or
going. For human beings, whose sense of direction and balance is
based on the way in which our anatomy has evolved, there is something deeply unsettling, almost perverse, about footprints that lead in
the wrong direction.

Megasthenes's *Indica*, one of the first travelogues ever written,
exists only in fragments—quoted, paraphrased, or plagiarized by later
authors who repeated many of his remarkable and exotic assertions.
In addition to describing men whose feet are turned the wrong way
around, he writes about gold-digging ants and people who sleep
inside their own ears. One of the strangest myths that Megasthenes
relates is about a Himalayan race of men without mouths "who live
near the source of the Ganges, who requiring nothing in the shape
of food, subsist on the odor of wild apples, and when they go on a
long journey they carry these with them for safety of their life, which
they can support by inhaling their perfume. Should they inhale very
foul air, death is inevitable." Plutarch picks up on this reference when
he writes, "For how could one find growing there that Indian root
which Megasthenes says a race of men who neither eat nor drink,
and in fact have not even mouths, set on fire and burn like incense,
in order to sustain their existence with its odorous fumes, unless it
received moisture from the moon?"

Bruce Chatwin, in *The Songlines*, proposes a theory of journeys suggesting that our urge to migrate is ingrained in us from the age we begin to crawl away from our parents. As we mature, he believes this innate wanderlust becomes one of the primary motives of human existence. With more than just a hint of self-reflection, he proposes that we are happiest when traveling away from home. Using the example of aboriginal storytellers in Australia, whose songlines mark the course of ancestral journeys that describe natural phenomena and creation myths, Chatwin proposes that the narratives we recount are itineraries of the soul, mapping out both memory and imagination, as well as retracing our origins. Like the dreamsongs of wandering hunters in the Australian outback or the folklore of Himalayan Sherpas, something powerful roams beyond the limits of logic and proof.

The architecture of our bodies is as fabulous as any of the imaginary races of man that early Greek tourists reported in India. Our feet, our ankles, knees, and hips are all aligned to make us move efficiently and comfortably along a trail. Our limbs are oriented to the future. The grotesque reversal of this marvelous feat of anatomical engineering suggests a distortion that we reject as evil or demonic. As we walk forward, stepping on heels or toes, each of us sets off on journeys short or long. Our mobility is what keeps us alive. It is the verb in the sentence, the wick inside the flame, the pulse in the vein.

The symbolic act of walking as a political statement has been employed by countless revolutionaries and freedom fighters, from Jesus to Chairman Mao, just as parades and goosesteps give fascism its relentless momentum. When Gandhi protested British Rule in India, he led a *padyatra* or march to the sea, where salt was extracted to defy taxation. At weddings, celebrants walk down an aisle or around a fire, enacting a physical ritual of affirmation. Walking is a fundamental part of countless ceremonies, from coronations and commencement exercises to funeral processions.

When I walk regularly, I feel healthier and less hungry for the kind of food and drink that poisons my body. My mind expels the stress and anxiety that builds up during the day. On a walk, I seldom think in any constructive or methodical manner, allowing my brain to react to the sensory experiences along the way rather than trying to solve a problem or compose a story. This helps ease the tension of work and frees my thoughts to dwell on happier things than debts or deadlines.

Whenever I find myself depressed, pinned down by that terrible sense of immobility that makes everything seem hopeless, I force myself to go for a walk. Most times, this helps lift the oppressive burden of doubt and despair. At first, when I start walking to escape that relentless sadness, I feel like a creature with my feet turned backwards, not wanting to move, possessed by demonic forces. But gradually my footsteps straighten, and I find myself proceeding in the same direction as my senses and my thoughts. Chatwin quotes the poet Rimbaud, who suffered melancholia and turned to walking as a cure. "I was forced to travel, to ward off the apparitions assembled in my brain," he exclaimed, walking several hours a day. His fellow poet Verlaine described him as "the man with footsoles of wind."

As we have evolved into a sedentary species, the urge to migrate, to hunt and gather, has been suppressed by the impediments of modern life. Like other instincts that civilization denies us, this often leads to discontentment and depression. The hunter in me struggles to break free of monotonous routines and, worse than that, the unhappy state of killing time. Denied the impulsive need to roam in search of prey, I feel constricted and ill at ease in the company of others. I want to stalk in silence, separating myself from conflicted relationships and responsibilities, becoming one with the wild.

Ennui, boredom, lassitude—all of which contribute to the unhappy malaise that drags us into depression—are the result of inaction. Walking outdoors relieves the claustrophobic darkness of our thoughts. Once when I was in high school, I became miserably depressed and angry for some reason that I can no longer recall. Returning home from school, I said nothing to my parents but picked up a 20-gauge shotgun and half a dozen shells, setting off into the forest on my own. Walking until it grew dark, I improvised a bivouac for the night, under a grove of wild cinnamon trees in the valley near a stream. I remember clearly how upset I was, the helpless misery bordering on the suicidal that comes out of adolescence. But I had taken the shotgun more out of habit than because I considered shooting myself. In fact, I did not even fire the gun, though several pheasant flew up in front of me. I had no matches to light a fire and no way of cooking the birds. This was late spring, warm and dry enough, so I needed no tent. Sitting alone on a sandy patch of ground near a shallow stream, beneath the branches of the cinnamon trees, I stayed awake all night. By this time the walk had settled my mind, and I felt much better for being alone in the forest. At some point, an owl began to call, the only creature sharing my solitude. For a while, the moon came out and its pale aura filtered through the trees, but it soon gave way to darkness again. I had no watch with me, nor any kind of flashlight.

Hours later, when the first light of another day began to outline the ridges to the east, I climbed into one of the trees and peeled some of the cinnamon bark before scrambling out of the valley. By the time I got back home, breakfast was on the table. My parents must have been worried but somehow they understood and did not press me to tell them where I'd gone or why. I said nothing about my night alone. By this time, the sadness and anger had lifted. I felt cleansed by my aimless walk through the forest, those hours spent in darkness and the sweet perfume of cinnamon still lingering on my fingertips.

⌒

A good many writers are walkers too. Edward Hoagland, in his collection of essays, *Walking the Dead Diamond River*, tallies up some of the pedestrian achievements of English poets: "Samuel Taylor Coleridge is said to have walked as far as forty miles in a day, and Carlyle once logged fifty-four in twenty-four hours on a walking tour. Wordsworth, the champion in this league, was calculated (by De Quincey) to have toted up 175,000 to 180,000 miles in a lifetime of peregrinations afoot. 'I have two doctors,' said Sir George Trevelyan of English-style walking, 'my left leg and my right.'"

Though he doesn't quote Thoreau, Hoagland refers to his legacy. "The American brand of walking of course has a different mystique, almost forgotten lately, which dates back to the frontier and has little to do with the daily 'constitutional' and therefore should be exercised in a setting so brawny and raw that the mileage can't even be guessed."

In search of this experience, and disillusioned by the war in Vietnam, Hoagland uprooted himself from New York City in the 1970s and purchased a farm in upstate Vermont, with a hundred acres of woodland. Here he could walk freely in the forests surrounding Mount Hor, one of the least developed regions of New England. Yet even in this isolated Eden, he writes about an awareness of limits: "Against the sense of exuberant release I felt on long walks in the woods was the knowledge that this in fact was just a hermetic patch of wilderness with highways on all sides, scarcely larger than a park: it was a ship in a bottle, and I was only hiding out."

This problem afflicts us all, both as writers and as walkers, the shrinking margins beyond which our natural surroundings no longer extend. In the Himalayas, as much as any other place on earth, there is a growing sense of containment, even in the wildest forests and remote valleys. Except on the highest peaks, we are never more than a day's walk from some kind of settlement. As the network of roads expands along rivers and over ridgetops, the world of concrete, polythene, and human ordure proliferates. India's ballooning population, well over a billion now, includes growing numbers of Himalayan residents, as well as seasonal migrants. On one level, it seems selfish, perhaps unethical, to complain about a walk in the woods being disturbed by the encroaching needs of those who struggle for a meal each day. But conservation is a good and righteous thing, just as important as the alleviation of poverty. Some activists have shown that the two objectives complement each other. In the race for survival, however, human beings have a distinct edge over other species, and the natural world is becoming more and more constricted and polluted by the day.

It will be a sad moment when every trail in the mountains leads to a dung heap, and one cannot walk for a couple of miles, up or down, without crossing a motor road where the exhaust fumes of vehicles foul the air. I think of Megathenes's mythical race of Himalayan inhabitants who sustained themselves through smell alone, living off the perfume of apples. They would not survive today as "too strong an odor would readily kill them." Neither would those other "fabulous" creatures with their feet turned the wrong way round. Where would their footsteps lead them, except backwards into the future, where extinction awaits us all?

KAILASH

A Pilgrim's Crossing

*We had found the peace which is the reward of those
who seek to know high mountain places.*

Eric Shipton

Entering the Mandala

Driving across western Tibet, somewhere between Lhasa and Mount Kailash we approach the crest of an unmarked pass, roughly 15,000 feet above sea level. All at once, a low canopy of cloud dissolves into rain, a rare moment of precipitation in this arid landscape. The windshield on our vehicle is speckled with drops. Dust turns to mud and streaks the glass. We open our windows, admitting the welcome fragrance of moist earth.

At the beginning of our journey, the rolling steppes seemed almost colorless, like monochromatic tints in a sepia photograph. But as we travel over the Tibetan Plateau, mountain light reveals a range of mineral hues in the soil, from rust to ochre, amber, and gold, as well as the whiteness of salt. Wherever there is a hint of water, living shrouds of muted green unfold within the valleys. Sand dunes glow like burnished copper. Bruised and dented, the surrounding ridges are varying shades of purple or indigo, their pigments changing with the shafts of sunbeams that slant in across the high Himalayas.

Stepping out of our vehicle at the top of the pass, I let the rain fall on my face, sprinkling my hair and clothes. After the suffocating heat of the drive, the breeze is cool, and clouds obscure the sun with shadows of moisture.

A few minutes later, descending from the pass, we cross a shallow draw, where two gazelle race off into a canyon. Suddenly, several hundred yards head, I see a rainbow. It marks the edge of the storm, a perfect arch of primary colors like strings of prayer flags erected by luminous vapors in the atmosphere. Appearing as if out of nowhere, the rainbow could be a window to another world. Our road passes directly beneath this ethereal gateway, as if built to celebrate our passage. The driver, Sonam, guns the engine on his Land Cruiser, accelerating toward the rainbow. I expect it will disappear before we get there, vanishing because of the angle of the sun or a gust of wind. But there it is in front of us. The bow remains taut, an invisible arrow pointing our way to a hidden land. . . . Shambala? Sunlight gilds the slopes beyond.

Our vehicle leaps and plunges over the rutted road. Sonam will not slow down. Seconds later, we drive through the arch, cheering as we cross this gaudy frontier of light. All of us laugh with excitement, shaking hands, congratulating ourselves. Sonam grins and blows his horn. After hours and days of tedious driving, this is a brief moment of exhilaration and delight that makes us feel as if we have finally reached our destination, though we are only halfway there.

When I look behind us, the bright bands of color are gone.

⁊

Tibetan mythology and folklore explain that the land itself has many guises. Rainbows represent the auras of saints and teachers who have passed away, or numinous markers leading to promised lands. What we see around us is only the surface, beneath which lie hidden realities—lost cities, subterranean lakes, and buried treasure. In one account, the undulating highlands of the trans-Himalaya are actually the body of a female demon (some would call her a goddess) who lies asleep beneath our feet. Another myth describes the mountains as tent pegs that hold the sky in place. Countless stories of Shambala promise the discovery of a secret, peaceable kingdom, closer at hand than we think, just beneath the taut dry membrane of these barren steppes. Only those who are blessed with sacred access can find the invisible gateways and forbidden caves that lead us into this idyllic country. Our ignorance makes us blind to sheltered valleys and neighboring worlds.

The myth of Shambala, or Shangri-La, echoes the narratives of a pastoral people for whom plentiful meadows lie just beyond their reach. Legends of Tibet recall journeys of migration and exile, a time before cities and towns, when families moved with the seasons, following flocks of sheep and goats. Their faith, their superstitions, and their instincts are formed out of a nomadic existence that interprets the landscape on different levels, from the harsh realities of sand and snow to underlying hopes of flowing streams, wildflowers, and verdant pastures. Wandering priests and shamans who minister to these herdsmen identify landmarks that others cannot perceive: sacred texts or *terma* secreted beneath huge boulders or tucked into the crevices of cliffs; bones of saints and warriors; the foundations of ruined fortresses or monasteries; lumps of gold and precious relics locked within the earth.

For pilgrims like us, who travel in search of a sacred mountain, the routes we follow take us beyond the contours of this world into a mysterious realm of magical secrets, terrifying obstacles, and questions for which there are no answers. Ultimately, the hardship and doubts of our journey lead us back into ourselves, for the true pilgrimage is not about distances covered or altitudes gained but follows only pathways of the mind.

∽

Before setting off for Kailash, if I had been told that I would be travelling for two weeks with a group of forty Hindu pilgrims from Gujarat and Maharashtra, driving ten to twelve hours a day over unpaved, dust-smothered roads, and sharing accommodation, sometimes as many as ten of us in a room together, beds crammed end to end and side by side with no privacy or ventilation, and no baths for the duration of the journey, I might have reconsidered my options. However, the decision to travel to Mount Kailash and Lake Manasarovar was impulsive. Making arrangements at the last minute, I had no choice but to let a travel agent in Kathmandu squeeze me into a group that was already organized and approved by Chinese authorities.

For someone who prefers to travel alone, without a fixed itinerary, finding my own transport and lodging, this would be a new experience. But after all that had taken place over the past two years, I was urgently in need of something different. Ameeta understood that I needed to get away and she did not stop me, though it seemed a foolish, unplanned journey without any particular purpose. She knew that this was part of the process of healing, and did not question my reasons for going, though she had no interest in coming with me.

Kathmandu itself was unknown territory. Though I have lived most of my life in the Indian Himalayas, I had never visited Nepal before this trip. Just as my fellow pilgrims began their spiritual quest at Hindu sites in the city, I made my rounds of Kathmandu's major shrines, starting with Pashupatinath Temple, where Shiva is worshipped behind silver doors that are closed to foreigners. On the banks of the Bagmati River, I watched a line of funeral pyres that burn all day and night. After circumambulating Boudhanath stupa in the Tibetan quarter of the city, I took darshan of the Maitreya Buddha at another shrine. And in the old city of Kathmandu, I wandered about the sanctuary of the living goddess, a prepubescent Newari virgin who is worshipped until her first menstruation, after which her place is taken by another, younger girl. I also paid my respects to the ferocious Kal Bhairav idol in Durbar Square, a wild-eyed deity carved out of black stone. All of this seemed the appropriate thing to do before setting off for Kailash, though I felt more like a tourist than a pilgrim, pursuing the exotic instead of the divine.

In the winding streets of Thamel, foreign backpackers and latter-day hippies hung out at coffee shops. Every kind of souvenir was available, from brass thunderbolts and *khukuris* to prayer wheels. As I walked through the bazaar, touts offered to buy dollars or sell hashish. At the Pilgrim Bookstore, which has a large collection of Himalayan literature, I bought a pirated edition of George Schaller's *Stones of Silence* and a map of the region surrounding Kailash, with all of the distances and altitudes marked. In addition to motor roads, the map portrayed the Kailash Kora, our route of circumambulation. At a scale of 1 inch to 175,000 feet, the journey ahead looked straightforward and simple, carefully surveyed and accurately rendered.

Back on the streets of Thamel, I was lured into a shop selling thangka paintings, both on cloth and paper. Dozens of images exhibited differing degrees of artistry, from abstract mandalas with geometric lines to wild-eyed Jambhala figures, guardians of the sacred realm.

But the thangka that caught my eye was a painting of Shambala. I paid more than I should have, but it was not expensive—a contemporary artwork produced in one of the monasteries or sweatshops of Kathmandu. And yet, this painting had been conceived with care and detail, depicting a wonderful, magical world. I could not resist its spell.

Unlike the trekking map that I had purchased a few minutes earlier, the thangka was not to scale and its perspective was skewed, so that I felt as if I were hovering directly above this secret world. Two rings of mountains, each of them a stylized image of Kailash, formed the primary outlines of the mandala. Surrounding these were Bodhisattvas and other celestial figures floating on wisps of cloud. Inside Shambala, like the petals of a lotus, were various scenes of human figures and buildings, travelers on horseback, streams and gardens, monasteries and mansions. It seemed an enchanted garden, the promised land, a country of eternal happiness.

The Russian émigré artist, Nicholas Roerich, whose paintings are some of the most evocative modern images inspired by the Himalayas, wrote a book called *Heart of Asia* in which he explores the myth of Shambala. Roerich quotes a Tibetan lama that he interviewed:

> "Only in the time of Shambhala shall all languages be understood without previous study. Because we hear and understand not the outward sound; and we see not through the physical eye, but through the third eye, which you see symbolized on the forehead of our images—this is the eye of Brahma, the eye of all-seeing knowledge. In the time of Shambhala, we will not need to rely only on our physical sight. We shall be able to evoke our great inner forces ... By passages through wonderful ice-caves under the earth, a few deserving ones, even in this life have reached the holy place, where all wisdom, all glory, all splendor are gathered."

Despite my instincts toward disbelief, there is a part of me that seeks out those mysteries that lie beyond the natural, sentient world, if only to probe and question their authenticity. This doesn't mean I carry my skepticism with me like a compass or altimeter, constantly measuring and refuting the beliefs of others. In Hindi, the word *yatra* means both pilgrimage and journey, as if the only purpose of travel is to seek the truth. Whether a *yatri* boards an airplane, bus, or train in pursuit of business, pleasure, or salvation, it fulfills that person's dharma and leads them on a quest, both secular and spiritual.

More than anything, the purpose of my journey was to try to understand the significance of Kailash, the most sacred mountain in the world, the protruding navel of the cosmos, a celestial snow peak that represents the ultimate destination for those who seek to release themselves from the grinding wheels of suffering and rebirth. This pure white summit and the pristine lake in the foreground are the two most powerful icons of the Himalayas.

Kailash and Manasarovar are surrounded by myths, mantras, and mandalas, a mystical geography that has fixed coordinates in every Hindu or Buddhist imagination, as well as in the minds and souls of other believers. This is the axis mundi of several faiths. For Hindus, Kailash is the "abode" of Lord Shiva, the supreme creator and destroyer, who takes the form of an immortal ascetic and lives on the mountain with his female consort in a state of elevated abnegation.

For Buddhists, Kailash represents Mount Meru, the sacred summit of the gods where the world originated. Kang Rinpoche, precious jewel of the snow, is the name given by Tibetan Buddhists who worship Kailash as a Tantric emblem of mystery and power. Followers of the Jain faith know this mountain by two names—Ashtapada and Padma Harada—where the founder of their religion achieved enlightenment. And for the Bon, followers of an ancient shamanistic tradition that predates Buddhism in Tibet, the peak is named Mount Tise or Yungdrung Gutse, the nine-story swastika mountain.

Geographically, Kailash and Manasarovar have immense significance, for they lie at the center of the high tablelands of western Tibet and mark the watershed of South Asia's greatest rivers. From the slopes of this mountain and the glaciers that feed this lake, the Indus and Sutlej flow westward through the Himalayas, before crossing into Punjab and Sindh, on their way to the Indian Ocean. The Karnali River also originates near Kailash, carving its way southward through the mountains of Nepal to become a major tributary of the Ganga. And draining to the east is the Tsangpo, or Brahmaputra, which flows in a huge arc across Tibet before entering northeastern India and setting its course for the Bay of Bengal.

Tibet! Here too was a name that called out to me because of romantic and exotic associations. Nineteenth-century explorers risked their lives to survey this unknown corner of the world. Even on contemporary maps, Tibet has the look of terra incognita, with few roads and towns scattered across a vast expanse of seemingly empty space, a vacant landscape where travelers could easily get lost for days . . . perhaps forever.

For me, Tibet has always represented a forbidden country. My hometown of Mussoorie is one of the places in India where Tibetan refugees have settled. Accompanying the Dalai Lama into exile in 1959, they established a displaced community and culture outside their homeland. In 1962, when I was an impressionable six-year-old, India and China fought a war over disputed Himalayan boundaries, and these regions became inaccessible to most civilians, especially foreigners. I had always imagined that entering Tibet would be like crossing a closely guarded frontier, traversing a dangerous, unyielding border that might close behind me without warning, like mountain passes buried in a sudden avalanche of snow.

In fact, there is nothing impossible or heroic about this journey, which is undertaken by thousands of pilgrims every year. I simply paid my fare and took my seat in a Toyota Land Cruiser. Our driver, Sonam Tsiring, with his Stetson, cigarette, and laconic manner, could have been a Tibetan incarnation of Clint Eastwood from *The Good, the Bad and the Ugly*. Frontier culture permeates these Himalayan highlands and several times on the journey, I felt as if I was driving through Colorado or Wyoming, though at twice the altitude. The air contains only half the oxygen there is at sea level but, except for the trek around Kailash, I barely exerted myself. In many ways, this was an easy trip compared to most I've undertaken, though the extremes of heat in the day and cold at night tested my endurance. Boredom too became a challenge. As with most journeys, there was a lot of hanging around, waiting for checkpoints to open and barriers to be lifted, slowing our progress and making destinations seem farther away than they really were.

Why was I doing this? What made me travel to Kailash?

I do not know the answer. It was a decision that came upon me suddenly, through a combination of impulse and desperation. For two years following our attack, I had been tied down by a full-time administrative job that made me restless, with responsibilities I would have preferred to avoid. My contract ended on June 30, 2010. The very next day, on the first of July, I boarded a flight from Delhi to Kathmandu. Except for my immediate family, I didn't tell anyone where I was headed or try to explain my motives. Going to Kailash seemed the only way to leave behind the tensions, anxieties, and frustrations of the past twenty-four months.

On another level, buried deeper in my psyche, was a need to come to terms with those violent memories and raw veins of fear. Though my wounds had healed, the scars continued to erode my physical and mental confidence, like ravines in the mountains scoured by corrosive storms. Perhaps that was why I was going on this yatra, to escape my own immediate cycle of suffering and rebirth, to find solace and redemption in the sacred aura of Kailash.

Then again, maybe it was something much less complicated and more instinctual, like the genetic compass and homing reflex that guides a migratory bird, winging its way across the Himalayas.

Frontiers of Faith

4:15 a.m. My wakeup call comes earlier than expected. I have forgotten to adjust my watch to Nepal time, a quarter of an hour ahead of India. Throughout this journey there will be continuous uncertainty about time, as if clocks are meaningless. All of China operates on Beijing time, two hours and fifteen minutes ahead of Kathmandu, though our Nepali guides and Sherpas refuse to advance their watches. Adding to the ambiguity, after crossing the border we will be traveling four hundred miles westward. According to Chinese clocks, sunrise at Mount Kailash can be as late as 10:00 a.m.

Before departure, a group of pilgrims gathers in front of our buses and perform a brief *pooja*. They sing an off-key hymn and recite a Sanskrit incantation, led by one of the elderly women. At the end, they cry out in praise of Shiva: "Jai Gaura Shambhu! Bam Bam Bholey!" The ritual is improvised and awkward but satisfies a need to invoke blessings for our journey.

Yesterday, we were given a briefing by ABC Travels, the company that has organized our yatra. The pilgrims from Gujarat and Maharashtra were herded into a conference room at our hotel and spoken to in Hindi. Meanwhile, in the coffee shop, I am introduced to four NRIs (Non-Resident Indians) from the US and England, who are part of the pilgrimage. One of the travel agents briefs us in English and gives us a lecture on the rigors of the journey and the importance of maintaining a "positive attitude." He tells us that yatris come in three varieties: those who see the trip to Kailash as a spiritual journey; those who are interested in nature; and those who feel they are buying a chance to boast about having been to Mount Kailash. The third category, he explains, are the ones who cause the most problems. We are instructed to travel light and leave behind unnecessary items. Our clothes and other belongings must fit into a small duffel bag provided by the agency. The rest of our luggage will be left at the hotel in Kathmandu. Our duffel bags are numbered for easy identification, since they are transported by truck. My number is 51. I am permitted to carry a day pack with me. The tour operator then recites a litany of rules. We will not be allowed to bathe for the duration of the trip and shaving is discouraged. The guesthouses where we will stay have no running water. Toilets will be a hole in the floor. Nausea and headaches are to be expected. Our tour leader will dose us with Diamox, the standard prophylactic for altitude sickness. The agent ends by commenting that the Tibetans aren't particularly hospitable. "The yaks and horses are more cooperative," he says.

Kathmandu is already stirring as we drive through the outskirts of the city into terraced hills. Bhim, our tour leader, reminds us that we won't see greenery for the next two weeks and urges us to appreciate the monsoon foliage of Nepal. Playing several roles on this journey, Bhim has a look of perpetual anxiety on his face, softened by an occasional smile. His favorite word is "compulsory," which he inserts into all of his instructions. Bhim handles logistics—room assignments, requests for drinking water, negotiations with drivers and horsemen. But he also interprets the sacred stages of our yatra, explaining the significance of certain myths and spiritual landmarks, directing our attention to necessary rituals at various sites. As we leave the Kathmandu Valley, he points out "the tallest statue of Shiva in the world," a recent construction that looks like a gigantic comic book superhero made of reinforced concrete. All of Bhim's speeches begin with "Om Namah Shivaya" (in the name of Shiva), our mantra for the journey.

For the next three hours we drive through constricted gorges and over bridges above the swollen waters of the Bhote Kosi River, which flows from Tibet. Passing through a village of six houses, our bus stops as ducks waddle down the middle of the road, refusing to give way. Eventually, we reach Khodari, a gloomy border town choked with trucks, many of them stuck in the mud. Through a gray drizzle, our group is led to a riverside hotel, where money changers swoop in to exchange rupees for yuan. Two men, one Chinese and the other

Nepali, work together. They have a briefcase full of yuan and a pocket calculator, moving from table to table in the restaurant. No receipts or exchange certificates are issued. A few of the pilgrims try to haggle over the rate, before surrendering wads of Indian currency. Because of counterfeiting, large notes are not accepted, only denominations of Rs 100 or less. By the end of these transactions, the money changers have a garbage bag full of Indian rupees, which rips open as they carry it out of the restaurant.

Setting off across the Friendship Bridge, we are besieged by children clamoring to carry our day packs. A few trucks are crossing but mostly porters hauling heavy loads. Beneath us, the Bhote Kosi crashes through the rocks, as monsoon waters flood a deep cataract. Between Kathmandu and Khodari we have been stopped at half a dozen checkpoints, but here at the border nobody seems bothered by our departure. Nepali policemen in blue camouflage are taking shelter from the rain under a tin awning and wave us through. In contrast, the Chinese put on a stern display of martial discipline. Halfway across the bridge, two guards in lime green camouflage inspect our passports and scowl at us with rehearsed suspicion. Farther on, a pair of sentries wearing dress uniforms stand at attention inside glass booths. Their jaws twitch and eyes flicker, but otherwise they could be made of wax.

The immigration and customs hall on the Chinese side of the river has X-ray machines, a duty-free shop, and uniformed officials wearing white gloves. Signs are written in Chinese characters and in English. Yet, the whole effect of regimentation and formality is defeated by the procession of Nepali porters ferrying baggage back and forth. Each of them has a blue transit pass, which they wave at the Chinese officials as they shuffle by, bent double under bales of fabric and boxes of other merchandise. Both women and men carry huge loads on their backs, most of the weight supported by straps across their foreheads. This route has always been an important trade link between Nepal and Tibet, traversed by Newari merchants for generations. Today, instead of butter, tea, and salt, the consignments are cartons of mango juice in tetra packs, cheap rubber sandals, and denim clothes. On both sides of the border, glaciers of packing materials have been discarded down the hillsides into the river.

Gradually, I am getting a sense of my fellow travelers. Our party is made up of three pilgrimage groups clubbed together for the convenience of the travel agency and Chinese authorities. While I am eyeing my companions to assess their stories, they too are watching me. A few of the pilgrims have made small talk and word has gone around that I speak Hindi, but everyone is cautious, not wanting to seem too inquisitive.

Our official Chinese guide meets us in the immigration hall. He is a Tibetan from Lhasa, working for the China India Pilgrim Service Center, an agency that handles Hindu pilgrims visiting Kailash. A thin, agitated man with a nervous grin, he speaks some English. When he learns that I am from Mussoorie, he tells me that his wife studied there at the school for Tibetan refugee children. We follow his instructions, joining one queue and then another, until we emerge on the other side. After an hour's wait, our luggage and supplies are carried across and loaded onto a truck. Though customs notices forbid importing fresh vegetables and fruit, our group is vegetarian and huge baskets of cauliflowers, okra, bitter gourd, cucumbers, and tomatoes are being carried with us from Nepal. While we stand and wait, money changers ruffle wads of yuan in our faces, taunting us for having exchanged our rupees at a lower rate on the other side.

Procedures and rituals of crossing a border make these political boundaries apparent, though the physical features of the mountains are no different on either side of the valley. As we complete the process of exiting one country and entering the next, it seems as if we are transiting a much greater divide. An illusory chasm exists between nations, far deeper and broader than the Bhote Kosi River. Ceremonies of departure and arrival convince travelers like us that we are entering a different land, one as difficult to reach as Shambala.

After everyone has cleared immigration and customs, Bhim hands out slips of paper on which are written the license numbers of the Land Cruisers. Each vehicle carries four passengers, along with the driver and a Sherpa, who rides in the back. I have requested a front seat but must assert myself. Knowing this will be where I sit for the next two weeks, I rush to the front door and squeeze inside with my day pack. The last member of our group to reach the vehicle is put in the middle of the backseat, a dour looking man with a fatalistic frown.

Our caravan consists of eleven Land Cruisers and a truck carrying luggage and kitchen supplies. Sonam, the driver, eyes us cautiously, lighting a cigarette as he gets behind the wheel. We begin to climb out of the gorge, up a steady zigzag of switchbacks. After three or four miles we pass through the border town of Zhangmu, built accordion-like on the near-vertical slopes. The narrow streets are lined with restaurants and provision shops, as well as a Sexy Cat boutique, selling slinky lingerie.

Beyond the town, we ascend through moist green shadows, trees overhanging the road. Near the river grow elms, alders, and rhodo-dendrons, after which we move up into conifer forests of cedar and hemlock. One variety of spruce has purple cones as big as mangoes. At places the road has washed away. Laborers are rebuilding walls as bulldozers remove debris. Across the valley, we see precipices extending thousands of feet up and down, like scroll paintings: brushstrokes of bamboo, a cragged profile, clouds of negative space, and water-falls that drop as silver threads down moss-covered slopes. The humid warmth of the valleys gives way to a damp chill. When we stop at a checkpoint, the armed guards are wearing quilted uniforms. In the gorge below, the Bhote Kosi writhes and roars like a chained dragon.

౿

Nyalam is situated 12,000 feet above sea level. Since we will be spending the next twelve days at higher altitudes, our group breaks journey here for two nights, acclimatizing. Most of the pilgrims are already taking Diamox to prevent altitude sickness. Several are suffer-ing from headaches and nausea. Though Bhim insists it is compulsory, I avoid taking any pills. Unlike the other yatris who have come from sea level, in Gujarat and Maharashtra, my home in Mussoorie lies at an altitude of 7,000 feet.

We have crossed the main thrust of the Himalayas but have yet to reach the Tibetan Plateau. Though Nylam sits above the tree line, there is plenty of moisture and greenery. The next morning, I climb a nearby hill covered with juniper and wildflowers—edelweiss, geraniums, thistles, musk roses, and yellow primulas. But the most spectacular flower of all is a blue poppy growing halfway up the ridge. It is a deep cerulean hue, like the sky immediately after monsoon clouds have parted. In our garden at Oakville, Ameeta has been trying to grow this species for several years, but the seeds refuse to germinate, while here it blooms with hardy impunity amid the rocks.

The market in Nyalam extends for a quarter mile, with shops and shabby restaurants on either side of a concrete avenue, where sleeping dogs don't seem to have moved since we arrived last evening. Most of the stores are general merchants selling bottled drinks and household goods. At a trekking shop there is no equipment, only cheap canvas sneakers and knitted caps. I pass a public bathhouse, its windows opaque with steam and soap scum.

Entering a restaurant near our lodge, I discover a bar serving Chinese beer and liquor. When I order a cup of black tea without sugar, the sullen waitress nods as if she understands. Instead, I get a mug of over-sweetened brew made with yak milk, which has a barnyard aroma. For half an hour I nurse my tea in disappointment. Blaring in one corner is a television. Tibetan and Chinese pop stars perform a medley of songs. The music has a country-western twang and the singers are dressed in fur-lined costumes. Five or six customers are seated at a corner table, chain-smoking and drinking bottles of Lhasa beer. Later in the afternoon, I see two men in suits come staggering out of this bar, arguing. One of them is weeping. Shoving his companion aside, he tries to flag down a truck headed for the border. Three women who have followed them out of the bar try to restrain the drunks, but they keep breaking down in fits of giggles. Getting plastered on a Saturday afternoon in Nyalam seems the only way to pass the time.

Boredom and stagnancy drives me back into my room at the guesthouse, while loneliness and eddies of depression make me wonder if this journey is a mistake. I study my map obsessively to see what progress we have made, tracing our route to Mount Kailash. The tangkha painting of Shambala has been left behind in Kathmandu, along with my excess luggage.

I know that I must be patient, though I can't wait to get moving again. Here in Nyalam the excuse for our immobility is acclimatization, as if my body has to catch up with itself, having traveled faster in a short period of time than the bronchioles and alveoli in my lungs will allow. My organs must recalibrate themselves to handle reduced levels of oxygen in the air. Reading Bruce Chatwin's *The Songlines*, one of the books I carry with me, I come to a passage in which he describes a group of porters who insist that they stop for a day after several forced marches, so "their souls can catch up."

Reading and writing are the only two distractions. Going back and forth between *The Songlines* and Vikram Seth's *From Heaven Lake*, I read a few chapters of one before switching authors. Knowing I have two weeks to go before I find another bookstore, I force myself to read slowly. I am also carrying Schaller's *Stones of Silence* and Shekhar Pathak's new biography of Pandit Nain Singh Rawat, *Asia ki Peeth Par* (On the Shoulders of Asia). Rawat was an Indian cartographer and spy who first mapped Tibet for the British in 1865. He traveled from Kathmandu to Kailash, as well as Lhasa, crossing the Himalayas west of here at a place called Kirong.

The story of Nain Singh Rawat and his fellow "pandits" is one of the great adventures of Himalayan exploration. Being secret agents of the British Raj, Rawat and other men from the border villages of Uttarakhand were recruited by officials of the Survey of India. They were trained in techniques of cartography and equipped with sextants hidden in boxes with false bottoms. Disguising themselves as Ladakhi merchants, they worried strings of prayer beads specially adapted to count their strides—100 beads instead of the usual 108. The maps they produced are remarkably accurate, though their equipment was unsophisticated. To gauge the level of the horizon, they carried bowls of liquid mercury. Altitude was calculated by measuring the temperature of boiling water, a procedure that required precision and patience, as well as plenty of yak dung for fuel. The pandits mapped the course of the Tsangpo and discovered that it became the Brahmaputra beyond the impenetrable gorges of the eastern Himalayas. Captured and jailed on several occasions, they returned to India with valuable intelligence. Their reports were published by the Royal Geographic Society in London, but their names were erased from the records, anonymous explorers in ambiguous lands.

As I write in my journal, my left hand keeps brushing flies off the page. I wonder if they are attracted to the odor or taste of ink. I also wonder whether the first surveyors were aware of hidden lands that lay beneath their maps, those secret passageways and border crossings from this world into the next. Did the pandits understand that their crude instruments were actually measuring the body of a goddess (or was she a demon)? According to Tibetan mystics, her supine limbs and torso stretch from one skyline to the next in an attitude of divine repose. As they counted their strides and read the stars, were they conscious of ancient mysteries that British geographers would never comprehend? I wonder if they kept those secrets to themselves.

Meanwhile, it is growing dark and the pilgrims from Maharashtra have whipped themselves into a frenzy of singing and clapping. They belt out *bhajans* with tuneless chauvinism, celebrating Shiva's predominance. A conch shell moans like a disgruntled yak. I am glad for a room of my own tonight, keeping my distance from these spiritual sing-alongs. At moments like this, the Bon vision of Kailash makes more sense to me, an animistic tradition that celebrates the natural history of these mountains. Just before dusk, I step outside and watch a flock of yellow-billed choughs riding the wind on deft black wings. The sky has changed from poppy blue to the color of wet ash. Rain has turned to sleet.

Trans-Himalaya

As we depart from Nyalam at dawn, a herd of yaks is leaving town to graze on the nearby hills. With downcast eyes and shaggy, lumbering forms, the yaks appear to be half-asleep. Nobody is tending them as they walk unguided down the street. These animals have only been domesticated for a few generations. Herds of wild yak used to roam the Tibetan Plateau, but most were killed off by hunters or captured by herdsmen. Now, with sanctuaries in Changtang and other parts of Tibet, the wild herds are making a comeback, much like the American buffalo.

Sonam has turned on his music, a recorded collection of Tibetan and Chinese pop songs that accompany us for the rest of the journey. The music is saved on a small flash drive plugged into the dashboard, and this medley is repeated constantly on a two-hour loop. From time to time, Sonam sings along with the lyrics. One of his favorites is a song with a refrain that sounds like "Bye Bye Molokai." The only English song is "Take Me to Your Heart," which I later learn was written by Jascha Richter and Jacky Zhang. By the end of our journey, after hearing it again and again, "Take me to your heart, take me to your soul/Give me your hand before I'm old . . . Standing on a mountain high/Looking at the moon through a clear blue sky . . . ," the inane lyrics are embedded in my mind.

Though Sonam speaks no English and I don't know Tibetan, we communicate through fluent gestures. Among the drivers, he is clearly the "dude," with his leather jacket and cowboy swagger, a silver stud in his ear. On his dashboard is a small shrine with a stylized "Om Mani Padme Hum." Most of the time he wears his hat, though he removes it occasionally to brush back his ponytail. His key chain is adorned with a white strip of rabbit pelt that has been dyed with snow leopard spots.

We climb steadily for half an hour toward the Thong La pass, 16,896 feet above sea level. The Land Cruisers slow down with the altitude, losing acceleration. Finally, one of the vehicles ahead of us stops completely, less than a mile from the crest of the ridge. We pull over to help. Sonam and the rest of the drivers huddle around the open hood, tinkering with the fuel pump and carburetor. The sun has come out, but the wind slices across the slopes, shearing through my fleece. Noticing a movement on the ridge below, I take out my binoculars and spot two gazelle. They are grazing about half a mile away. Fawn-colored, with pale rumps and delicate horns that curve up like raised eyebrows, the gazelle blend into the dry landscape. I can see their ears flicking. When they turn toward the sunlight, it is easy to trace their profiles, though seconds later they disappear into sand and rocks. On the hill above, a flock of choughs keep up a plaintive chorus and take to the air in unison, like punctuation marks flying off a page. Just below the road, I can see burrows in the ground. Out of one comes a gray pika, or mouse hare. He studies me for a moment then darts across to another den. A small brown bird alights close by and begins to harass the pika every time he emerges from his hole. I assume the bird is some kind of lark but later learn it is a Tibetan ground-tit. Mouse hares were once considered pests and blamed for the destruction of sparse pastures in Tibet. After an unsuccessful campaign to eradicate them with poison, scientists discovered that pika are crucial to the survival of this harsh but delicate environment. Rather than destroying the pastures on which the nomads of Tibet depend, these small rodents contribute to the regeneration of grasslands by dispersing seeds and aerating the soil. Even the ground-tits depend on pikas, for they often build nests in abandoned burrows.

The Land Cruiser's engine roars back to life and we hurry to reclaim our seats. Three minutes later, we reach the Thong La pass and stop again. Here the wind is much stronger, buffeting the parked vehicles and flapping the massed streamers strung from a flagpole. A man in monk's robes is selling prayer flags and tiny packets of printed prayers.

From the direction of Nyalam, a motorcycle arrives, the rider wearing a heavy woolen cloak, his hair braided with red ribbons. Buying a packet of paper prayers, he tosses these into the air like confetti and shouts into the wind as the multicolored scraps scatter across the road and down the hill. Nearby is a line of wooden prayer wheels with cupped propellers that catch the wind. The wheels turn constantly on greased axles, driven by a steady gale at the top of the pass. Our drivers have trouble lighting their cigarettes. They hunker down and shelter their lighters between the upturned collars of their coats. While we are stopped, two Japanese cyclists on mountain bikes arrive at the pass. They look exhausted, having pedaled all the way from Lhasa, but I can see the relief in their eyes as they survey the downhill route ahead.

Eight miles farther on, we turn off the main highway and begin heading west toward Saga, our destination for today. Almost immediately, our progress is interrupted. The Land Cruiser that was having engine trouble earlier has broken down again. We stop at the side of the road to wait. By now the sun is unrelenting, and we are stranded on an exposed patch of dust and grass, next to a marshy meadow. Yaks and goats are grazing nearby. A cluster of shepherd's tents is arranged in the distance. Soon a crowd of women and children gather, begging for food and money. One of the women has a bracelet made out of a conch shell, which looks like a white gauntlet on her wrist. A few of the yatris give the younger children cookies, and one of the Gujarati women sticks *bindis* on the foreheads of the girls. The herdsmen's clothes are tattered. None of them seem to have washed their faces for days, though there is plenty of water nearby.

Our halt allows me to get acquainted with my fellow travelers. Sharing the Land Cruiser with me are three men. One is a Gujarati named Satish, who runs a transport company in Kutch. He is close to sixty, a grizzled, pensive man who quickly joins the other Gujaratis every time we stop. Stuck in the middle of the back seat is Gopal, a bank manager from Aurangabad in Maharashtra. When I mention that I have visited the famous Kailash temple at Ellora, near his home, he smiles for the first time, and tells me enthusiastically about other monuments in Aurangabad. "You must see the Bibi ka Maqbara. It's

155

just like the Taj Mahal!" Both Satish and Gopal speak little English, and even their Hindi is weak. Conversations are halting, and my questions often go unanswered.

The third person in our vehicle is Dineshbhai. He seems to be harbouring a grudge against me for having claimed the front seat, but now that we are on our way, I am forgiven. Dineshbhai is a cloth merchant in Mumbai, though originally from Porbandar in Gujarat. He can speak Gujarati with Satish and Marathi with Gopal. With me, he insists on using English. Dinesh tells me that he is sixty-two years old and weighs 110 kilograms. In his younger days, he was a semi-professional actor in Gujarati theater, and he enjoys telling stories of his thespian adventures. Some years ago he toured America with a drama troupe. In New Jersey, the Gujarati community welcomed them like Bollywood stars. Dineshbhai went on to visit Las Vegas and enjoyed the casinos and dancing fountains. "But I'm not a gambler," he tells me. "I'm a spendthrift. Mostly, I spend my money on travel, like this journey. Someone says to me, 'Chalo, let's go,' and I'm ready!" He rubs his hands together. "Next year, I think I'll go to South Africa."

Dineshbhai has a theatrical manner. He entertains Satish and Gopal with lines of dialogue from Gujarati plays. Occasionally, he breaks into song—mostly old favorites from Hindi films. He claims to have little interest in his family company, which he shares with two brothers, but recounts in detail how they specialize in selling *bandini*, a kind of tie-dyed fabric.

After a while, our conversations cease. Stuck at the side of the road, we begin to get frustrated, as the sun grows hotter. An hour passes. Two hours. Finally, after three hours of waiting, the other vehicles arrive and we set off again. By this time, I have a splitting headache. The rough road makes it worse, with deep ruts and detours where bridges have washed out. The pain moves from my forehead to the base of my neck and back again, as if my brain is being booted around like a football. I assume it must be the altitude. When we stop for lunch at a desolate resthouse with a courtyard full of yak bones, I decide to take a Diamox tablet. Hardly have I swallowed the pill, when I break out in a cold sweat. I cannot finish my lunch, and stagger outside to get some air. Beyond the courtyard wall is a stream banked with green grass and snow peaks to the south, but I can't appreciate the view. After taking the Diamox, I feel drunk and disoriented. I keep thinking I've lost my hat, then realize it's on my head. Just as we are about to start off again, I take a pair of sunglasses from my pack, which ease the glare. It isn't the altitude that caused my headache but the harsh sunlight.

As we drive on, snow peaks continue to appear to the south, along the border with Nepal. Seeing them I feel even more disoriented, for I am used to having the Himalayas rising up in the north. Everything seems to be turned around and my sense of direction is confused. At times I cannot tell if these are clouds or mountains. Some of the peaks have enormous hanging glaciers and others are broken spires. I feel as if I am hallucinating, seeing an endless panorama of snowfields and summits that may or may not be there. As the landscape grows drier and more desolate, sand dunes begin to appear—waves of gold with rippled patterns. On ahead, a mirage warps the horizon. Conscious of a watery blue surface, I tell myself it is an illusion, my vision distorted by pain. Then, all at once, we come to a large lake, fed by glaciers to the south. The blue expanse of water looks like a patch of sky that has fallen on to the plateau. For a moment, I think we have arrived at Manasarovar, though it is still more than three days drive from here. Later on, checking my map, I discover the name of this lake is Paigu Tso. I have lost track of time, delirious, drifting in and out of consciousness, despite the jostling and shaking of the vehicle. When I open my eyes again, there is another lake. This one is completely white. At first, I think it must be frozen, covered with snow, then realize it is salt. Far off on the perimeter, I can see men digging and remember a section of Nain Singh's journals in which he describes two alkaline lakes where caravans load up to carry this mineral cargo across the Himalayas.

~

Soon after arriving in Saga, we discover that the next leg of our journey, a stretch of 150 miles to a town called Paryang, is undergoing roadwork. The police are closing the highway during the day, from 9:00 a.m. to 6:00 p.m. This means that we will be forced to travel at night. Bhim and the Sherpas consult with the drivers and decide to set out at 2:00 a.m., though the exact time of our departure remains unclear. While our Nepali guides continue to operate on Kathmandu time, the drivers and Chinese officials are functioning on Beijing time, and it is impossible to know exactly what to expect.

A dose of Ibuprofen has helped ease the pain between my temples. Just after dark, I force myself to stagger down the steps of our guesthouse and across the street to a grocery store, where I buy a bottle of water. Our drinking water is being boiled by the Sherpas, but knowing how difficult it is to heat water at this altitude, I don't want to take any chances.

Saga has a couple of moderately upscale hotels, but ours is a cheap flophouse, the most poorly designed building I have ever stayed in. Recently built, it consists of three floors of rooms, most of which can sleep eight or ten people. But the architect has forgotten to include any plumbing. Washrooms and latrines are situated outside, at the edge of a parking lot. Here too there is no running water. The signage is deceptive: GENTLEMEN, LADIES. Inside, the unlit toilets are nothing but shit-encrusted cavities in the floor through which the desert wind funnels up the sickening odors of a dung heap below.

Despite the extended misery of today's journey, I am eager to leave Saga as soon as possible. When I go out to buy my bottled water, a woman with a baby strapped to her back begins begging for money. She is a young Tibetan in her twenties, haggard and dressed in tatters. It seems odd that anyone would need to be begging on the street under Communist rule, with all the promises of a paternalistic state. But almost everywhere we stop, women and children greet us with open hands.

This time, the woman is unusually persistent. She follows me to the entrance of our guesthouse, the year-old child still slung across her back. As we enter the empty lobby, she makes a gesture that I think I have misunderstood. Waving her off, I tell her in Hindi—which is unintelligible to her—that I'm sorry but she won't get anything from me. She pursues me up the stairs, her voice a plaintive cooing, almost a whimper. When I reach the door of my room, which I am sharing with four other yatris, she is still at my elbow. As I turn to shoo her off, she repeats the gesture with her right hand. This time it is unmistakable. Her fingers curl into an open fist and her wrist jerks up and down in a pantomime of masturbation. Her baby eyes me drowsily. Confused and unsettled, I hand her a ten-yuan note before escaping into my room and latching the door behind me. My roommates notice the look of dismay on my face. When they ask me what has happened, I shake my head.

The pathetic obscenity of this encounter leaves me with a sense of remorse and disgust, particularly the image of the child on the woman's back, and the futile desperation that must drive her to offer hurried sex to strangers in this wayside town.

❧

Just after midnight, I am awakened by a banging on our door. The Sherpas bring us tea—lukewarm and over-sweetened. After a couple hours' sleep, my headache is gone. Only a mild itch of pain lingers around the rims of my eyes, which reassures me that it was caused by the sun, not altitude. Though we set out in the dark, I make sure my Raybans are easily accessible.

Sonam and the other drivers don't look as if they've slept at all. As we drive out of Saga, many of the shops are still open, including a Sichuan Barbeque with marinated birds in the window impaled on skewers. Our headlights pick up the shapes of dogs roaming the streets. A young couple, fashionably dressed and totally drunk, staggers out of an apartment building, waving goodnight to their hosts, and awkwardly try to climb onto a motorcycle. At 1:00 a.m., Kathmandu time, we pass through a checkpoint at the edge of town.

Six miles beyond Saga, one of the vehicles breaks down again. Sonam swings irritably over to the side of the road and takes charge of the situation, siphoning petrol from a jerry can in the back of our vehicle and trickling it into the fuel pump. The engine roars and everyone climbs back into their seats. We drive another half mile before the Land Cruiser stops again. This time we are stalled on a steep incline, halfway up a series of switchbacks, where a section of the road has been recently excavated. Huge pieces of earth-moving equipment are parked close by, amid mounds of earth. Every few minutes a truck labors past, sending up a cloud of dust and diesel exhaust. Whatever we might have gained from our early start is lost as we remain stranded at the side of the road, while the drivers disassemble the fuel pump and carburetor. They work in complete darkness, with only a couple of headlamps.

During this delay, most of the pilgrims doze in their seats, but I find myself pacing back and forth to stay warm, staring up at the stars. The night sky is a pointillist fantasy, every bead of light shimmering amid infinite patterns of the universe. I can imagine Nain Singh Rawat on a night like this, trying to get his bearings. Having taken his sextant from its secret compartment, he must have hesitated before fixing his coordinates, with so many stars from which to choose. I try to connect the dots of constellations, but the sky is so crowded that all I can recognize is the Big Dipper, and Orion with his belt of stars. Beside him is Canis Major, his hunting companion.

The temperature is close to freezing. All of the drivers smoke incessantly, despite the fact that they are working with petrol, which could easily ignite and send the Land Cruiser up in flames. At one point, Sonam alternately puffs on his cigarette and blows through the fuel jets. In the end, he puts his mouth to the hose on the fuel pump and sucks in a mouthful of petrol, then spits it out with a grimace, saying, "Mai Tai!" Everyone laughs, though the situation seems hopeless. I worry that we will have to return to Saga. Finally, around 4:00 a.m., as the sky is beginning to brighten above the ridges to our east, the Land Cruiser miraculously comes back to life, and the engine settles into a ragged growl.

Now that we are finally moving again, the road is even rougher than yesterday, with hundreds of detours across the rolling steppes. As Robert Fleming explains in his book *Across the Tibetan Plateau*, western Tibet is really a series of high valleys and ridges, rather than an open plain. Crumpled by the collision of continents, the horizon is corrugated with hills.

The drivers are exhausted, having been awake all night. Soon after sunrise, they stop for breakfast at a shack by the side of the road. Sonam and the others ignore the pleading of our guides to continue so that we can cross a police checkpoint before it closes at 9:00 a.m. Setting off again, at last, we find the barrier only a few hundred yards ahead. Here, we are told that we can't proceed until nightfall. The barrier closed five minutes before our arrival. After a long discussion with the sentry, Sonam comes back shaking his head. "Police say no chalo!" he reports. Then he grins and steers his Land Cruiser off the side of the road, across open ground, while the sentry watches with helpless disapproval. On ahead, a yak herder flags us down. He insists that we are crossing his pasture and demands ten yuan, which we gladly pay, circling over a marsh before rejoining the highway, still within sight of the police barrier.

Surprisingly, there isn't much construction along the next fifty miles of road, and the two police patrols we pass ignore us. At a crossroads is a petrol pump and two hundred yards of asphalt, wonderfully smooth. After filling their tanks, the drivers decide to have a picnic in the middle of this paved section of the road. Dineshbhai begins to protest, but the Tibetans are in no hurry to make up for lost time. Stripping down to their undershirts, they sunbathe, smoke, drink tea from thermos flasks, and tease the baby-faced driver whose vehicle keeps breaking down.

A woman named Sarita strikes up a conversation. She is a Sanskrit scholar from Mumbai, and her business card has a saffron "Om" embossed above her name. She says that she has noticed me taking notes and asks if I am a writer. She too is planning to write a book on Kailash and is also working on her PhD in German philosophy. "I've read all of Kant and Nietzsche," she tells me. "Now the only one I have left is Schopenhauer. The Germans were influenced by the Upanishads, you know, and Hindu philosophy." She asks if I have read the Upanishads. I nod but confess that I am not a scholar. Sarita seems disappointed that I am unable to have an academic conversation with her about epistemology and Übermensch. She has a friendly but strident manner and begins to lecture me about the etymology of

Kailash, rattling off a series of Sanskrit words and syllables: a cryptic code I cannot understand.

"This pilgrimage will give me the strength to finish my thesis," she tells me.

Three hours later, we finally reach Paryang, another dusty, low-roofed town. In the distance, I can see the northern profile of the Himalayas framed by clouds. We are following the Tsangpo River, though our route crosses into parallel valleys and over broad passes that lead us north, then west, in circuitous detours. Each time we return to the river, it seems to have grown smaller, now a shallow stream. I find it hard to believe that this is the same river I crossed several years ago in Assam, where I could hardly see from one bank to the other. It took hours to navigate the vast, muddy current of the Brahmaputra by riverboat. Here, I roll up my jeans and wade across.

The guesthouse at Paryang is laid out in a square courtyard. All of the rooms face inward. It is just past noon, and we have to wait for our supply truck to arrive before we have lunch. Leaving my bags in my room, I decide to set off for a walk around town. Fifty yards from the guesthouse, a pack of roaming dogs comes out of a side lane and confronts me. They are Tibetan mastiffs, as shaggy as yaks. Two of them begin to bark when I stop to gauge their intentions. I realize that the main road through the center of Paryang is littered with dogs, some asleep and others rising to their feet with menacing growls. Nobody else seems to be venturing out, and the path I was going to take no longer holds any interest. Quickly, I retreat into the safety of the guesthouse.

The dogs remind me of our three Tibetan mastiffs in Mussoorie. As a breed, they have a reputation for being ferocious guardians, protective of their territory and their masters. Though our mastiffs can put on an intimidating performance when strangers arrive, they have been badly spoiled and would never bite anyone unless they sensed a serious threat. Still, their presence is reassuring, and I know that they are the most reliable form of security that we could install, totally loyal to Ameeta and me. With thick manes and dense under-coats, these dogs are well adapted to the Himalayas, able to withstand the cold, snow, and harsh winds. Many of the mastiffs I saw in Tibet looked as if they were feral animals with long hair hanging in matted clumps like dreadlocks. Packs of these dogs scavenge along the margins of most settlements we pass.

Though pedigrees are hard to come by, the largest and most imposing Tibetan mastiffs are bought and sold for hundreds of thousands of dollars in China. When Marco Polo traveled across this region, he marveled at the size of these dogs, exaggerating when he claimed they stood as tall as donkeys. By some accounts, in earlier centuries many of the monasteries in Tibet kept mastiffs for protection against bandits and also to consume corpses. As a funeral rite, it was believed that feeding human flesh and bones to dogs, just as vultures are fed during sky burials, was an act of compassion. This gruesome yet humane ritual symbolizes the impermanence of our bodies and the continuous cycle of life through which our own mortality contributes to the survival of another species.

Brahma's Dream

Crossing Tibet, I am constantly aware that this is a country under occupation. Though sparsely populated, much of the region has been dominated by Chinese military and recent immigrants. Because of Beijing's resettlement policies, ethnic Tibetans have become a minority in their own homeland. Though officially referred to as the Tibet Autonomous Region, there are few signs of independence, and any form of protest is ruthlessly suppressed.

As transient pilgrims, we had few opportunities to observe the social and political dynamics of Tibet. But along the highways there was evidence of dramatic changes underway: concrete colonies and army installations appearing out of nowhere, walled enclaves blaring martial music. The road gangs working on the highway were mostly Tibetans, supervised by Chinese engineers and foremen. At several points during our journey, I saw evidence of intrusive power and an authoritarian regime that governed with arrogance and insensitivity.

All along the route to Kailash, we were stopped and made to wait, ostensibly because of roadwork but often for no reason at all. On one occasion, during our return journey, we were stranded for twelve hours without any explanation. Two policemen had set up plastic stools in the middle of the road and blocked our way. A line of trucks and other vehicles stretched for a quarter mile. Hours dragged on while the policemen seemed content to sit in the middle of the road forever, accepting cigarettes from drivers but refusing to budge. Their jungle camouflage seemed out of place in the arid steppes.

After four hours of waiting, two jeeps came roaring toward us from the opposite direction. Everyone sat up hopefully, thinking the road might open. Seeing six policemen emerging from one of the jeeps, I felt sure they had come to inform us that the highway was clear. Instead, they went around to the back of the jeep and took out a watermelon. The size of a basketball, its color matched the variegated green hues of their uniforms. As all of us watched, the melon was placed in the middle of the road, like some sort of fetish object. Meanwhile, a Chinese woman dressed in tight black leather stepped out from behind the driver's seat of the second jeep. She wore dark glasses and high-heeled boots, as if she were a dominatrix hanging out with men in uniform. The only thing missing was her whip. A senior police officer also emerged from this jeep, adjusting the red and gold epaulets on his shoulders. He and the woman stared past the line of waiting vehicles, as if we were not there, though everyone's eyes were on them. At a signal from the officer, one of the policemen took out his knife and butchered the watermelon with ceremonial precision. It was cut into slices and handed around among the policemen. The woman laughed as she took a bite. While the stranded drivers and passengers watched in silence, the policemen devoured the bright red flesh and spit out the seeds, leaning forward to avoid dripping juice on their clothes. When they finished, each of them hurled the watermelon rinds into the desert like boomerangs that would never return. Then, without once acknowledging the long line of vehicles still waiting to move, the policemen and the woman in black got back in their jeeps and drove off in the direction from which they had come.

We remained there another two hours, until finally, one of the guards punched a number into his mobile phone and spoke for a while. He consulted with his colleague and then, all at once, they removed their stools and waved us forward. Everyone dashed to their vehicles and engines roared to life, as the stranded convoy set off along the road with a screeching of tires.

Five miles ahead, however, a police vehicle with its blue light oscillating wildly, came driving past us waving everyone to one side. Pulling over, Sonam shrugged impatiently and got down to see what was going on.

The senior officer in command of this stretch of highway arrived in his jeep. He was a caricature of a tiny dictator, hardly four and a half feet tall, wearing a uniform two sizes too large, a peaked hat, and a pair of aviator shades. A cigarette holder clenched between his teeth, he marched about with a belligerent swagger and started barking orders. With him was a junior officer, carrying a construction helmet turned upside down.

As all of us watched, the officer ordered each of the drivers to put their keys and registration papers into the helmet. It was hard to know exactly what was going on, but later we learned that he was accusing the drivers of having jumped the checkpoint. He was furious because he hadn't given an order to open the road. When the drivers protested that the guards had released them, the officer called back to the checkpoint, where the policemen must have denied letting us through. All this we pieced together later, but at that moment the only thing I could see was the officer gesturing and shouting, as if we had broken every law in the country. Going up to one of the Land Cruisers, he demanded to know whose vehicle it was. When nobody came forward to surrender his keys, the officer picked up a rock and began hammering on the hood.

Immediately, a driver jumped forward, complaining loudly and waving his arms. Once again, the rock came down on the hood, denting the metal and scratching the paint. Rallying together, the crowd of drivers converged on the police party. In addition to our group, twenty other vehicles had been stopped. The drivers surrounded the policemen in an angry mob, and I noticed Sonam picking up a rock in each hand. The policemen were Chinese, the drivers Tibetan. For several minutes, it looked as if we are going to witness a riot, with the officer screaming and the owner of the damaged vehicle bellowing back at him.

Amid the tension, I could see one of the junior constables frantically calling for backup. Just as the situation was about to escalate into serious violence, we heard a siren and saw two police vehicles coming in our direction, trailing plumes of dust. The drivers retreated as a group, marching away defiantly across the open plain, abandoning their vehicles and passengers. Again, we didn't know what was going on, but it turned out that they were headed to a military outpost a mile away to register a complaint. Meanwhile, the officer strutted about, triumphantly puffing on his cigarette holder. Our Sherpas and some of the pilgrims tried to reason with him, but he cut them short with an angry, "No!" Being in charge of this stretch of road, he wasn't about to have his authority questioned. The whole episode was like watching a cartoon in which the bellicose villain rants and raves, while everyone else looks on helplessly. The Indian pilgrims muttered to each other, wishing they were back in their own country, "where we could pay off the cops with a hundred rupees."

By now the sun was going down, and there was nothing but empty highway stretching in both directions. After dark, the policemen departed and our driverless vehicles stood in a lonely queue by the side of the road. For supper, the Sherpas handed out apples, which was all they could muster. As the temperature dropped, each of us put on as many layers as we could and tried to sleep in the vehicles, heads lolling from side to side, windshields fogging over with our breath. The seemingly limitless landscape shrank into darkness.

A few minutes past midnight, I was jolted out of a fitful sleep as the driver side door was yanked open. Sonam pushed himself behind the wheel with an angry grunt and started the engine. Offering no explanation, he set off along the detour, circling the police barrier that was now deserted. Fifteen minutes later, we reached a guesthouse. In an airless room with beds jammed together, we scrambled for the nearest horizontal surface and finally fell asleep.

⌒

A cloudy dawn paints the snow peaks to the south with gold and violet pigments as we leave Paryang. Seeing the mountains to the south, my sense of direction remains disoriented. All my life the Himalayas have been situated to the north, and it confuses me to face them from this perspective, with the sunrise to my left.

If all goes well, Bhim assures us that today we will finally see Lake Manasarovar and Mount Kailash. The road beyond Paryang is marginally better than the one we traveled yesterday, though the dust is thicker. Whenever we pass a vehicle or follow close behind one of the other Land Cruisers in our convoy, the clouds of dust are so thick that visibility drops to inches and the drivers are blinded. At one point, we pass a recent collision between a motorcycle and a jeep on a perfectly straight and open stretch of road. It seems absurd that the two vehicles would run into each other head-on in a place like this. The only explanation is the dust.

Though none of the Land Cruisers breaks down today, our drivers keep stopping and progress is slow. Just before 10:00 a.m., they decide it is time for lunch. We park near some tea stalls close to a police checkpoint. Outside one of the huts is the mummified head of a yak. A few yards away, I see an argali skull with broad curving horns forming a double spiral. These wild sheep were described by Marco Polo when he wrote about crossing Central Asia. The largest of the subspecies bears his name. In a tent at the edge of the settlement, a man is butchering the carcass of a goat. Sitting cross-legged on the floor, he has the skin spread out in front of him, the wool side down. Neat piles of offal—lungs, liver, heart, kidneys, stomach, and intestines—are arranged on the skin. The internal organs are still steaming, and the goat must have been killed not more than half an hour earlier. For a moment, I think he's a Bon shaman who can read the future in the entrails of a sacrificial goat. But this man's motives are commercial, not psychic. The meat is for sale, and no part of the animal is going to be wasted.

I wonder who slaughtered the goat. Most Tibetans eat flesh but observe Buddhist injunctions against killing living creatures. All of the Hindu pilgrims in our group are vegetarians, and we do not eat at any of the roadside canteens or restaurants where the drivers order noodles with yak meat or mutton. The Sherpas too eat meat, though our cook prepares only rice, lentils, and curried vegetables, a monotonous but healthy diet. I am more than content to be vegetarian for the duration of this pilgrimage.

While waiting to be on our way again, I get a chance to talk with the NRIs. One of them, Niranjan, is a plastic surgeon in the UK. He tells me that he owns a Lexus SUV and has recently taken a course in off-road driving, learning to negotiate a 70-degree slope and how to maneuver through snow, sand, mud, and water. I ask him how his Lexus would have handled the roads in Tibet. "Just fine," he says, glancing across at the Land Cruisers, which have none of the standard luxuries, not even air conditioning or seat belts. These are stripped-down models, made for the Chinese market. On Sonam's vehicle, the manufacturer has painted a slogan: "I love to have fun. I love my family and friends. I love this beautiful planet earth. The reason why I chose this car is because it will totally satisfy my requirements for outdoor living. Well . . . tomorrow, where shall we go?"

As Niranjan and I are talking, one of the Gujarati women comes up to us and remarks: "You are American but living in India. . . . He is Indian but living in UK." Her eyebrows twitch inquisitively. Niranjan responds by quoting Socrates: "I am a citizen of the world." Our group is is an eclectic mix of cultures. At least six languages are operating at once—Gujarati, Marathi, Hindi, English, Nepali, and Tibetan. My Hindi and English allow me to speak to almost everyone, except the drivers. I remember reading an anthropologist's theory that pilgrimages like this are as much about cultural integration and breaking down social barriers as they are about sustaining religious beliefs.

Niranjan introduces me to his friend Shivram, an accountant with IBM, based in Binghamton, New York. He and Niranjan have often traveled together. A few years ago they hiked up Machu Picchu, and, more recently, they sailed to Antarctica on an educational cruise. They admit this yatra isn't quite the style of travel to which they are accustomed. Shivram visits India once in a while, though most of his family now live in the US. I ask if his wife considered coming to Kailash. "No way!" he says, with a laugh, "She couldn't handle this. Even the hotel in Kathmandu would have been difficult for her. When I come to India, she goes to Florida and plays golf. That's what she enjoys most. She's not an atheist, she just prefers golf to visiting temples." Shivram's son, Suraj, is a doctor in Philadelphia. He has just finished his residency, specializing in emergency medicine. The complete lack of sanitation in Tibet is a challenge for him, but he has brought a generous supply of antiseptic hand lotion and sterile wet wipes. The fourth member of their group is Lalit. Like Shivram, he too is an accountant. His family were originally from Gujarat but settled in Kenya several generations back, then emigrated to England in the 1980s. This group of four men, all of them Hindus, represent the Indian diaspora. Yet, the pull of the Himalayas draws them back to South Asia. A mountain like Kailash has a magnetic force, a spiritual and geographical lodestone that attracts us all to its ancient source.

While talking with Lalit, I notice one of the Gujarati women eating a mango. She has carried it all the way from India and is sucking on the seed. When our eyes meet, she gives me a guilty smile. Niranjan has discovered that the Gujarati pilgrims have smuggled two extra duffel bags containing dry fruit and nuts, savory mixtures, and other snacks.

ॐ

After another four hours of driving, we finally come within sight of Manasarovar. Ascending out of a shallow streambed, our vehicles crest a saddle with a chorten and flagpole at the top. Prayer flags radiate in all directions, like a sagging circus tent. The drivers complete a clockwise circuit of the chorten and park the Land Cruisers on a level patch of ground overlooking the sacred lake.

After four days of anticipation, we are suddenly here, and our abrupt arrival takes me by surprise. Manasarovar is larger than I imagined, though I can see the opposite shore. The circumference of the lake is 55 miles. Ordinarily, we would be able to see Kailash from this spot, but the sky is overcast and Bhim points in the direction where it stands, promising us that it is "compulsory" for the clouds to eventually clear. The lake has a dark blue tint that turns to turquoise when the sun comes out from behind the drifting clouds. Partially visible to the south are the mountains and glaciers that feed Manasarovar. Gurla Mandhata (25,243 feet) is the main peak, a massive whale-backed summit fully clad in snow. In 1905, Tom Longstaff and the Brocherel brothers attempted to climb this peak and were swept three thousand feet down its slopes by an avalanche, which they survived. The treeless landscape conveys stillness, despite the wind that riffles the prayer flags. Nothing else moves except for the clouds and their shadows that cross the water like phantom shoals. One moment the tawny ridges have hardly any color—then, as the sun emerges, it brings out hidden pigments in the rocks and soil, a subtle alchemy of light.

Manasarovar is known as Mapam Tso in Tibetan, a name that means "undefeated," commemorating Milarepa's victory over a Bon shaman. The Buddha's mother, Maya, is said to have bathed in this lake before Gautama was conceived. In Sanskrit, "manas" means mind and "sarovar" is a lake. Hindus believe that Manasarovar was first created within Brahma's imagination—a divine illusion that became a geographical reality. It is the highest freshwater lake of its size in the world, and the clarity of its waters reflects the purity accorded in mythologies of different faiths. Those who bathe in Manasarovar are cleansed of sin and guilt, not only from this life but from all previous and future incarnations. Even the gods descend from heaven to baptize themselves in its waters. The most devout pilgrims complete a *kora*, or circumambulation of the lake on foot, which takes three days, though trance walkers who practice lung-gom are said to circle it in a day.

Early nineteenth-century explorers William Moorcroft and Hyder Hearsey went fishing in Manasarovar, more interested in sport than spirituality. Swami Pranavananda, who made his first pilgrimage to Kailash in 1928 and subsequently visited the region on nine different occasions, wrote a guidebook, *Pilgrim's Companion to the Holy Kailas and Manasarovar*. Though a spiritual traveler, Pranavananda was scientifically inclined and kept records of the temperature and water level of the lake. On one of his visits, he had a motorboat hauled up to Manasarovar and puttered about on its surface, taking soundings of its depth at various places. In 1948, a portion of Mahatma Gandhi's ashes were also immersed in the lake.

Historically, this region yielded gold and turquoise, though most of the mines in the surrounding hills are now abandoned. One of the popular legends is the story of a huge nugget of gold, the size and shape of a dog, that was unearthed by chance near Manasarovar. When it was found, nobody dared keep it, believing this was sacred treasure. The miners took it to Lhasa and offered it to the Dalai Lama. Instead of accepting the lump of gold, he instructed them to carry it back to the shores of Manasarovar, where it was reburied exactly as it was found. A stupa was built on the spot and named Serkyi (or Kyiro Serpo), which means "golden dog."

Our route takes us around the eastern rim of the lake, circling Manasarovar in a clockwise direction. After eight miles we stop at a pebbled beach, where Bhim announces that anyone who wants to take a ritual bath is welcome to do so. "It's not compulsory," he says, "but please, no shampoo or soap." Inside the Land Cruisers it is hot and stuffy, but outside the wind has a sharp edge and the temperature drops every time a cloud passes overhead.

The glacier-fed waters of Manasarovar are not as cold as I expect, being shallow and warmed by the sun. Some say that hot springs heat the lake, though it remains frozen for nine months of the year. The deepest point at the center is more than 250 feet but near the shore its depth is less than a foot. We spread out along the beach, and most of the men strip down to shorts. A few of the women enter the lake in their saris. Others scoop a little of the water into their hands and splash it onto their faces. The pebbles underfoot make it awkward to walk, but I wade out about twenty yards from shore, where the water reaches my knees.

Lowering myself backwards, I go under completely and dunk myself three times. Surfacing, I can feel the dust and grime of four days' travel rinse away, along with the adhering filth of the places where we have stayed. My skin is pale, except where the sun has burned my arms and face. The scars on my body are a dull red color, particularly the gash on my left calf and the stab wound on my thigh. Though fully healed, my injuries are still sensitive, and there is a numbness from damaged nerves. As I scrub myself in the clear waters of Manasarovar, I try to imagine the scars washing away, releasing me from the violent memories of our attack. Opening my eyes underwater, I can see the colorful patterns of pebbles and the glint of sunlight on the rippling surface above. I want to swim out farther from shore, but after a few strokes, I let myself sink below the surface again, content to float in the shallows. I feel a sense of buoyancy and calm, immersed in Brahma's dream. Though I submerge myself in the lake, none of my sins slough off; at least none that I am aware of. Yet I feel cleansed by these sacred waters.

The Gujarati and Maharashtrian pilgrims have broken into separate groups and huddle together, performing poojas along the shoreline. The cloying smell of incense taints the breeze with synthetic odors of sandalwood and jasmine. A flock of terns is squabbling above a sandbar. Manasarovar contains several varieties of fish on which these migratory birds feed. In 1945, Dr. Salim Ali, India's eminent ornithologist, took an expedition to Manasarovar to study different species that summer here in these waters, particularly greylag and bar-headed geese. The mythological equivalent of these birds is Shiva's swan, which is said to nest on the shores of Manasarovar. There are no shrines nearby, not even a pile of *mani* stones, but it is a quiet, meditative place, a natural sanctuary imbued with an atmosphere of peace.

I collect a handful of pebbles from Manasarovar to take home with me as mementoes. Most of the other pilgrims are doing the same. Satish, the Gujarati in our vehicle, rushes over holding a strangely shaped stone. "Can you see Ganesh?" he says with excitement, pointing to the raised contours on the surface of the stone. I nod, though it is impossible for me to make out the elephant's head that his mind's eye has discovered.

After an hour, everyone has completed their rituals. Returning to our vehicle, Dineshbhai distributes *prasad*, a gram-flour candy that has been blessed during the pooja. Only Sonam refuses to eat this sacrament, though he has accepted other food and candy along the way. The drivers and Sherpas perform subtle acts of veneration, fingering prayer beads, but none of them goes near the water. They watch the Hindus with a mixture of amusement and some derision. Occasionally, they imitate the pilgrim's cries of, "Bam Bam Bholey!" laughing among themselves.

We continue circling the lake, passing a couple of small monasteries and pilgrim shelters that look deserted. Crossing a stream swollen with snowmelt, one of the Land Cruisers gets stuck, water swirling halfway up the doors. Fortunately, the driver is able to reverse out of the current and makes it across on his second attempt. From the southern shore of the lake, the road loops up a broad bluff, and we are able to see Rakshastal, a second lake almost as big as Manasarovar, but irregular in shape and about fifty feet lower in altitude. *Rakshas* means "demon," and this lake, which is salty and undrinkable, is associated with the darker forces of Hindu mythology. The two lakes lie side by side, like a misshapen ying and yang. It may be the gray canopy of clouds or the angle of the sun as it descends toward the horizon, but Rakshastal has a menacing demeanor, its surface rough with waves.

Minutes later, as we descend the other side of the ridge, a miracle occurs!

Our route, which has been unpaved for more than 350 miles, suddenly merges with a perfectly tarred road coming in from the south. Asphalt never looked so beautiful, and the yellow line down this two-lane highway is a ribbon of gold. We have joined the road that comes up from Taklakot, a historic trading post near the border with India and Nepal. For centuries this has been one of main centers of commerce, where tea and butter are still bartered for pashmina wool and yak tails. The short section of highway, hardly twenty miles from the border to the roadhead at Darchen, has been paved by the Chinese to create the illusion of development. On the Indian and Nepal side of the border there is no motorable approach, only rough footpaths winding up precipitous gorges. In 1866, Nain Singh Rawat escaped from Tibet along this route and returned to India. Despite ongoing border disputes, a bilateral agreement between India and China permits a limited number of pilgrims to cross into Tibet on foot. From Taklakot they are taken by bus to Darchen. Originally, I had hoped to make the journey to Kailash by this route, which starts in Uttarakhand and avoids the long detour to Kathmandu. But permits are issued by lottery, and the Indian government does not allow foreigners to cross the "inner line" and pass through border regions.

The paved road feels as smooth as polished granite, and the Land Cruiser hums over its perfect surface with effortless ease. All of us are in awe of the road, opening our windows to enjoy the air unladen with dust.

⌇

I would be happy to drive for another hour like this, but after twenty minutes we reach Chiu Gompa, where we spend the night at a guesthouse that is decorated with brightly painted yak skulls. Nearby is a dry channel that connects Manasarovar with Rakshastal, though water only flows between the two lakes during years of heavy rainfall, when the level of Manasarovar rises. This is interpreted as an auspicious omen. The shore of the lake at Chiu is surrounded by mud, and it is impossible to reach the water. One of the pilgrims goes too close and sinks up to his thighs in gray ooze. I walk out as far as I dare and find thousands of tiny snail shells, bleached white by the sun.

The clouds disperse at nightfall, and we are treated to a spectacular display of stars. Unlike night skies in other parts of the world, where an electric glow allows only a few constellations to shine through, here the firmament above us flickers with millions of lights. The Milky Way spreads like a celestial glacier above the eastern horizon, its reflection faintly visible on the still, dark surface of the lake. Sirius, the Dog Star, gleams like a nugget of gold. A satellite passes overhead, a blinking firefly weaving its way through a net of lights. I keep expecting it to collide with one of the stars. Though the sky appears crowded, it is actually an empty sieve through which years of ancient light have drained to illuminate this moment. There is no moon, but to our south the faint profile of the Himalayas rise above Manasarovar like horns of ice. Alone in the starlight, I feel as if I am standing on the skull of the world.

Upon This Threshold

Hoping to see the sunrise over Manasarovar, I get up early the next morning and stumble past my sleeping roommates. Once outside, I am disappointed to find the sky is overcast. A murky dawn seeps through the clouds. After a few minutes, however, shafts of sunlight penetrate the gray curtains and shoot across the surface of the lake, giving it a metallic sheen. A little later I meet three of the Gujarati pilgrims, who tell me that they have been awake all night and claim to have seen lights descending from the sky into the water. One of the myths of Manasarovar is that these lights are deities who descend to bathe in Brahma's lake. I ask what kind of lights they were, and they describe something between a shooting star and an emergency flare, phosphorescent streaks that drop out of the darkness before disappearing into the water. Others have described this phenomenon before, which is sometimes explained as St. Elmo's Fire, atmospheric bursts of static electricity. Whatever it may be, the pilgrims are delighted, and they tell their story to everyone in the group.

Later in the morning, I notice one of the women who saw the falling lights sketching a horoscope for another member of her group. On a wrinkled scrap of paper, she draws squares and triangles, calculating the date of birth and charting out a diagram of her companion's future. She also claims to read palms, tracing the intersecting lines and squeezing the woman's fingers together to make the creases more visible and easier to decipher.

After breakfast, Niranjan and the other NRIs invite me to join them on a short trek up the ridge above the guesthouse. Today we are scheduled for a late start, leaving Chiu Gompa after lunch and driving only as far as Darchen, which is fifteen miles away. Part of the reason for our walk is to test ourselves for the circumambulation of Kailash, which begins tomorrow. Manasarovar lies 15,000 feet above sea level. Oxygen is scarce, and we keep stopping to catch our breath. Kailash is still obscured by clouds, and I begin to wonder if we will ever have a clear view of the mountain. The landscape around Manasarovar is like a dented bowl that rises up on every side. Windswept and dry, the folded ridges are covered with patches of Tibetan gorse, a hardy plant with dark green leaves. Though it provides forage for wild and domesticated animals, its thorns protect it from overgrazing.

From the ridge above Chiu Gompa, we can clearly see the dry streambed between Manasarovar and Rakshastal. Sections of the channel appear marshy, and at places it has a rime of salt caused by evaporation and minerals leeched out of the soil. Known as Ganga Chu, this occasional stream carries the pure waters of Mapam Tso into the demon's lake, rendering it sacred as well. One myth describes the creation of the stream by two golden fish that swam in Manasarovar many years ago. As one fish chased the other, they plunged out of the water and plowed a channel between the lakes, linking them together. This year, Ganga Chu is inauspiciously dry. Summer rains have been scarce, and the snowmelt off Gurla Mandhata is not enough to make Manasarovar overflow its banks.

A large black dog has followed us with expectant eyes. He lags behind for a ways, then races off after a scent, ranging two or three hundred yards before returning to join us again. Lalit mentions the story in the Mahabharata in which a dog leads the Pandava brothers into the Himalayas to Swargarohini, where they are carried off to heaven. In this myth, Lord Indra comes to fetch the heroic brothers but refuses to let the dog climb aboard his chariot because the animal is unclean. Yudhisthira declines to go with him, insisting the dog has been a faithful companion and deserves to ascend with them. Eventually, Lord Indra relents, and the dog is revealed to be Yudhisthira's father in disguise.

Our morning trek is hardly mythical and certainly doesn't lead to heaven. Clouds still hide Kailash from view. Atop the highest ridge we climb is a cairn of rocks, where we have a dramatic view of the lake. From this angle, Manasarovar looks much larger, almost a perfect oval. Moved by the sight, I pick up a disc-shaped stone and place it on the cairn to mark our visit. Almost immediately, the dog trots up and debunks whatever sanctity I might attach to this experience, raising his hind leg and urinating on the cairn.

୶

Following a heavy lunch in which the last of our fresh vegetables are consumed, we pack up and prepare to drive to Darchen. From here on in, our meals will consist of dehydrated soya protein and lentils, as well as packaged curries. Before we set off, Sonam switches on the music system in his Land Cruiser. Four of the younger Gujaratis begin dancing to the beat of Tibetan pop songs, filming each other with a camcorder. In their heavy down jackets and knitted caps, they wiggle about self-consciously, as if trying to stay warm. At the same time I notice one of the elderly couples, a government servant and his wife from Pune, facing northward with folded hands, praying fervently. Mount Kailash has suddenly emerged from hiding and stands out above the ridge with unexpected brilliance. The sun gleams off its snowclad features. While several of us grab for our cameras, one of the women throws herself on the ground and lies face down in the dust. For a moment, I think she has fainted, and then I see her extended fingers steepled together, trembling with devotion.

Darchen lies at the foot of the ridges below Kailash, though the mountain itself cannot be seen from the town. A dusty, unkempt settlement with two main streets that cross in the middle and rows of identical buildings, it is not a hospitable place. A line of shops sells trinkets and souvenirs to pilgrims, as well as dried herbs collected from the nearby hills. At the center of town is the Good Luck To The Supermarket and an Abundance Wholesale Store. Our accommodation is a government guesthouse that looks more like a jail than a hotel. Several yatra groups are staying here, and we are allotted C-Block, a desolate yellow barrack. The usual jigsaw puzzle of beds is squeezed into each room, with barely enough space for anyone to enter.

After unloading our bags, we set off again to visit the starting point of the Inner Kora. Sonam drives us up a series of switchbacks, along a steep, rough road. Less than three miles above Darchen, the valley opens out into a broad meadow with a stream flowing through the middle. From here, the south face of Mount Kailash rises directly above us, no clouds obscuring its brilliance. Bhim described this as a "Kailash darshan," providing us with our first close view of the mountain. When we stop, even the drivers take out prayer rugs or spread their jackets on the grass and prostrate themselves in front of the mountain. Conversations cease, and each of us drifts off to separate areas of the meadow to contemplate Kailash, alone with our thoughts.

A short distance away, on the slope of a ridge, lies a *gompa* associated with the Jain religion, though it looks very much like any other Buddhist shrine, with red mud walls and prayer flags. In front is a chorten with a gilded spire. But at this moment, I have little interest in visiting man-made structures. Instead, I follow a small footpath leading up a dry, windswept ridge at the head of the valley. Several pilgrims, part of another group, are ascending this path, and I decide to follow them. It is a steep climb, much more strenuous than our hike this morning, and I walk slowly upward, eyes fixed on the mountain.

The poet-saint Milarepa described Kailash as it appeared in his dream, the verses translated by Lobsang P. Lhalungpa:

> I dreamed that in the vast North of the world
> A majestic snow-clad mountain arose.
> Its white peak touching the sky.
> Around it turned the sun and moon.
> Its light filled the whole of space,
> And its base covered the entire Earth.
> Rivers descended in the four cardinal directions,
> Quenching the thirst of all sentient beings,
> And all these waters rushed into the sea.

Kailash grows larger the closer I get, its south face ribbed with snow. Down the center of the mountain is a deep gash, which Bon mythology tells us is the path by which Tonpa Shenrab, the great magus, descended from heaven. In a contrary Buddhist myth, the gash was caused by a Bon sorcerer falling from the summit after he was defeated by Milarepa. While the peak remains clad in snow all year, during summer, the black striations become more visible. Similar markings appear on the surrounding hills, and I can see where bands of softer rock have eroded, leaving intervening layers of harder stone intact. The Bon identify a sacred Swastika in the patterns of these rocks. If one stares at the mountain long enough, the shape appears like a giant petroglyph. In India and Tibet, the swastika represents good luck and fertility. Many Hindus interpret it as a stylized image of Natraja, the dancing form of Shiva.

While the peak itself is considered the austere throne of Shiva, who sits here in eternal meditation, a broad hill in the foreground is known as Nandi Parbat, representing the bull of Shiva, who lies attentively at his feet. As I look at the shapes in this tableau, they remind me of the Great Pyramid of Cheops with the Sphinx crouched in the foreground. One of the nearby ridges is known as Kuber Parbat, where the god of wealth resides. Another ridge is revered as the abode of Vishnu. But at this moment, all of these myths and legends become superfluous. As Nicholas Roerich has written: "One experiences a special emotion in these remote mountains, on discovering the living words of that which he has read in the pages of distant books."

Climbing the winding path, I feel no religious narratives guiding my feet, no songlines carrying me aloft, no divine coordinates centering my soul. At the same time, irrepressible emotions well up inside of me at several points along the trail. My vision blurs with tears, and my throat constricts, not from altitude but from a sense of having arrived. Several pilgrims, coming down the path, greet me with repeated cries of "Om Namah Shivaya!" but I am speechless, unable to respond. It could be awe or reverence that evokes these emotions, or a sense of release at having accomplished the simple goal of being in the presence of Kailash.

When I reach the top of the ridge, I find a seat away from the path, next to a rock the size of a yak. Its rough texture is daubed with orange and yellow lichens. Focusing on Kailash, I let my eyes and mind explore its surface. At 21,778 feet above sea level, the summit has never been climbed. To ascend this peak would be a form of sacrilege. Some years ago, Chinese authorities issued a climbing permit to a group of Spanish mountaineers, but this was withdrawn after angry protests. Staring up at the mountain, I try to imagine how anyone could scale its vertical face, which looks impossibly steep.

For all its sanctity, I approach Kailash with a reverent sense of disbelief. While the myths and metaphors of different faiths provide vivid interpretations and intriguing riddles, the physical presence of the mountain dispels religious lore and dogma. In and of itself, Kailash is nothing but an enormous mass of rock covered in snow and ice. There are no hidden worlds hovering beneath its vast façade, no Shambhala, no *terma* waiting to be revealed, no deities enthroned upon its summit. The only mandalas are those projected in the minds of devotees. While I have come here as a pilgrim, my convictions as an atheist are reaffirmed by the material reality of Kailash. There is no Shiva, Brahma, Buddha, or Tonpa Shenrab. No goddesses. No *dakinis* dancing through the clouds. Whatever mysteries confront us are not mysteries at all, but simply enigmas of our own making that confuse the beauty and omnipotence of nature for something beyond this world. Sitting here in front of the mountain, leaning against this rock, I realize that nothing exists outside of this experience. Neither is there any merit gained, no consequences, no salvation at the end of this pilgrimage. All myths are fiction or distortions of historical facts. That is the only secret this mountain reveals. Its summit is neither sacred nor celestial. Kailash is a mountain, nothing more or less. Accepting this simple realization, I transcend the illusions of belief. Sometimes, negation can be a form of affirmation, when we reconcile ourselves to what is here and now, rather than chasing after future lives and other worlds. Yet, none of this makes the experience any less profound.

Here in front of me is a huge slab of the Gangdise uplift, part of the primal continent of Pangea that broke apart and drifted thousands of miles around the globe, only to join together again with other fragments in a series of tectonic collisions that forced the mountain upward. Here is a truth much older than any religious doctrine, its text inscribed and embedded in stone. Understanding a geological phenomenon of such magnitude takes me beyond the tentative limits of doubt and faith to a rational form of enlightenment. Despite the awe and reverence I might feel, there is no need for me to demonstrate piety or devotion. For an hour, I simply sit alone beside the lichen-covered rock, emptying my mind of rational and irrational thoughts, experiencing only the transcendent vision of Kailash.

Circling the Summit

Hindus and Buddhists circumambulate sacred sites and shrines in a clockwise direction, while those who follow the Bon faith insist on walking counterclockwise. My instincts are to follow the latter route, but I must stick with my party of Hindu pilgrims and we will follow the conventional circuit of Kailash. Three of our group have decided to stay behind in Darchen and will not attempt the *parikrama*. They are suffering from altitude sickness and other ailments. Early this morning, when I went outside to the toilets, I passed a woman retching near our block of guestrooms. When I tried to offer help, I saw it was Sarita, the Mumbai Sanskritist and philosopher. She looked at me and shook her head, asking with desperate eyes to be left alone in the privacy of her nausea. For all of us, much of the journey has been like this, a combination of the squalid and sublime.

Last evening, the Sherpas were testing a portable compression chamber that is used for treating extreme cases of altitude sickness. The chamber is the size and shape of an inflatable kayak, with a clear plastic window on top. Just the sight of it gave me a feeling of claustrophobia. The victim is zipped inside. When air is pumped into the chamber it fills up and approximates the pressure at lower altitudes. From what I've heard, it is a terrifying solution to a fatal condition. Pulmonary edema causes the patient to froth at the mouth inside this plastic cocoon. When I ask Bhim whether he has used it before, he shakes his head but tells me, "Every year, ten or twelve Indian pilgrims die on the kora. It is compulsory!" The only effective treatment for altitude sickness is to quickly take a person down several thousand feet. But the problem in Tibet is that there is no place to escape, for the entire country lies at high altitudes. The closest airports where a person could be evacuated are either Lhasa or Kathmandu, five days' journey from Darchen, by which time it is too late.

After breakfast, the Land Cruisers drop us at Tarboche, three miles west of Darchen, where the kora route begins. During the Saga Dawa festival in late spring, Tarboche is inundated with thousands of pilgrims. Each year, a huge flagstaff is erected, from which strings of prayer flags radiate like the fluttering spokes on a giant wheel. Tarboche is located at the mouth of a broad gorge that wraps around Kailash on its western side. Nearby is a sky burial site, where the mortal remains of eighty-four Buddhist saints were fed to vultures and eagles. According to traditional Tibetan funeral rites, their bodies were cut up into small morsels of flesh, and their bones emptied of marrow, then mashed up with barley flour and presented as offerings to birds of prey.

When we arrive at Tarboche, the trailhead is deserted. Yak and bharal skulls are stacked on piles of mani stones, giving this place a gloomy atmosphere. A ring of dark clouds hides the summit of Kailash, but we can see the mountain's lower slopes encrusted with bands of snow and ice. At Tarboche stands a small chorten with a passage through the middle. Hindu pilgrims call this Hemdwar, which means "gateway to the snows." The shape of the chorten reflects the shape of Kailash, with a tiered base and pure white dome. While the yatris debate whether they must circle this shrine thirteen times or just once, I complete a quick circuit of the chorten and pass through Hemdwar, stooping to avoid colliding with the doorframe. Sticking out of the ceiling above my head is the hoof and foreleg of a mummified goat, which has been plastered into the ceiling, an alarming relic for vegetarian pilgrims.

From this point onward, until we complete the kora, most of our party will be riding horses, with yaks and porters carrying tents and supplies. Only two of us have chosen to complete the kora on foot, myself and a man named Chandrashekhar from Mumbai. Bhim and the Chinese tour guide must organize the caravan of men and animals that will travel up the valley. We have been told that nobody is allowed to share a horse, and you cannot carry your pack while riding. This requires a porter to shoulder the extra load for an additional fee. Happily leaving behind the bickering and chaos of pairing horses with riders and yaks with loads, I set off up the valley. Chandrashekhar and I walk together for a ways, then agree to each continue at our own pace, glad for the solitude of the Lha Chu valley, known as the gorge of the river gods.

A good-sized stream, thirty feet wide and milky with snowmelt, flows through a broad expanse of valley, almost half a mile across at its mouth. On either side spectacular cliffs of red rock ascend above me, framing the sky with weird formations. It reminds me of the settings for western movies like *Mackenna's Gold*. I can almost imagine Gregory Peck riding out of one of the box canyons or Julie Newmar bathing in the river. Two horsemen are coming down the valley toward me. Both are wearing broad-brimmed hats that make them look like cowboys. Reining in their horses, they ask if I want a ride. I shake my head, and they carry on, the embroidered saddle cloths and strings of brass bells around the horses' necks reminding me that I am in Tibet, not Colorado. A few minutes later, two motorcyclists overtake me, heading up the valley. Their bikes are loaded with supplies. The trail is nothing but a rough footpath. They maneuver between the rocks until one of them takes a corner too sharply and topples over. By the time I catch up to him, he has righted his bike and kicked the engine back to life. Within minutes, the roar of the motorcycles is consumed by the silence of the valley.

Waterfalls cascade down the cliffs, their fluid strands bending in the wind like frayed ropes dangling from the rocks. Between the jagged spires and layered towers of stone, I catch glimpses of snowfields and glaciers. The sun is straight above me, and I am sweating as I walk. After seven days of sedentary travel, it feels good to be carrying my pack. Though the air is thin, our ascent is gradual and my breathing is not strained. I feel the exhilaration of being alone, moving of my own accord. Nobody is responsible for my progress except me. Clouds keep passing overhead, their shadows sweeping across the canyon walls, casting transient pools of shade that disappear as quickly as they form.

At almost every turn of the path stand cairns of stones, reminding me that millions of pilgrims have gone before us. Some of the cairns are not man-made but natural mounds of conglomerate rock with stones of different sizes, from tiny pebbles to massive boulders that have been fused together. The variety of rocks seem infinite, every shade from crystal clarity to creamy white, burnt umber, and tawny gold, salmon with streaks of yellow, orange, pink, and rose. Each of them looks like hardened fragments of light. From a distance the ridges around us appear a uniform color of reddish brown. Kailash itself is stark black granite, but the stones in the valley are variegated hues of every shade and texture.

The colors in the landscape, the myriad shapes of rocks around me, and the trail of footprints in the dust make me think of a giant sand mandala, with the sacred mountain at its axis. Created through eons of erosion, it could easily be a natural diagram of the cosmos. Compared to Kailash, each of the boulders is a granule, and the mineral pigments create mysterious patterns, like a maze that leads beyond perception.

Constructed over days and weeks, sand mandalas are a schematic vision of a spiritual landscape, a labyrinthine map that guides the seeker to its mystical core. Buddhist monks painstakingly put the mandala together, one grain at a time, its creation a form of meditation. After the mandala has been completed, it is worshipped briefly and then swept away at the end of the ritual, a metaphor of the illusory existence of the material world. Buddhists believe that everything we perceive is artifice, even this mountain at the center of the universe. Viewing the mandala, we experience the mysterious symmetry but also understand that the cosmos is not limited to Kailash. It lies nowhere and everywhere. Each of us can discover it within ourselves.

The valleys and mountains around Kailash are believed to be full of terma, buried texts and treasure that will be found when the time is right. Many Buddhist teachers seek out these messages and artifacts secreted in the earth by ancient masters centuries ago. Hidden scriptures and sanctified objects are intended to be discovered at auspicious moments by protectors of the Dharma, tertons and oracles who reveal the truth contained in terma, thereby renewing and reaffirming the faith. Many of the terma are said to have been buried by

Guru Rinpoche, Padmasambhava, the sixth-century Indian saint and teacher who was a great reformer of Buddhism and set the faithful on the true path of righteousness. The concept of terma also takes on a special significance in more recent history, when many relics and texts were hidden to protect them during the Cultural Revolution, which destroyed and desecrated most of the monasteries and religious sites in Tibet.

Padmasambhava is said to have rescued Buddhism from occult and profane influences, including the so-called sorcery and shamanism of Bon tradition that permitted animal sacrifices. He preached nonviolence and compassion as the key tenets of Buddhist doctrine, though the religion continued to promote Tantric rituals, which are rooted in the older shamanistic practices. This inherent paradox between the multifaceted and orgiastic Buddhism illustrated in sexually explicit thangka paintings and the stark asceticism of monastic life is one of the perplexing contradictions in Tibetan culture. For Buddhists from other traditions, the Tantric practices in Tibet are often disturbing. Ekai Kawaguchi, a Japanese visitor to Kailash, described with dismay the erotic and sometimes violent manner in which Padmasambhava was venerated. Kawaguchi complained that the great teacher was depicted during lama dances as "a devil in disguise of a priest as if he had been born for the very purpose of corrupting and perverting the spread of the holy doctrines of the Buddha."

Pilgrims who journey to Kailash are confronted by the never-ending vistas of the steppes as well as microscopic visions of a sand mandala. The dimensions of the cosmos are so infinite as to be unknowable, while at the same time infinitesimal and unseen. The only thing that is not hidden from view is the mountain itself, a stacked pyramid of rock and snow. As I walk around Kailash, following timeless paths that wheel about its axis, I become conscious of the hidden taproot of this mountain. Even as it rises more than 21,000 feet above sea level, Kailash extends deep into the earth. What lies above the surface is huge and magnificent, but even more compelling must be the molten currents beneath the earth's crust, where the mountain floats upon a raft of magma. The geological forces that thrust Kailash into the sky hundreds of millennia ago also formed its subterranean structure, the buried weight of rock that provides its hidden foundation. Just as Hindu artisans imagined, while carving the great Kailash temple in Ellora, this is the fiery realm of the demon Ravana who shakes the earth with his fury, only to be subdued by Shiva's toe. Myths like these translate the magnitude of natural phenomena, sculpting the buried terma into symbols of faith, even as science explains their geological origins, revealing the continental keel that steadies the earth beneath our feet.

The landscape in this treeless valley has a hypnotic quality. Rocks and boulders take on weird and magical shapes like an optical illusion. Lama Govinda, the Bolivian-German mystic who helped introduce Tibet to the West, writes about lung-gom. While on an extended pilgrimage to Kailash and the abandoned kingdom of Guge in far western Tibet, Govinda claims to have experienced trance walking himself, after getting lost in the mountains.

> [T]o my amazement I jumped from boulder to boulder without ever slipping or missing a foothold, in spite of wearing only a pair of flimsy sandals on my bare feet. And then, I realized that a strange force had taken over, a consciousness that was no more guided by my eyes or my brain. My limbs moved as in a trance, with an uncanny knowledge of their own, though their movement seemed almost mechanical. I noticed things only like in a dream, somewhat detached. Even my own body had become distant, quasi-detached from my will-power. I was like an arrow that unfailingly pursued its course by the force of its initial impetus, and the only thing I knew was that on no condition must I break the spell that had seized me.

On my pilgrimage, I do not experience this levitating trance that Lama Govinda compares to sleepwalking, but several times I find myself staring at a fixed object in the distance while everything else around me blurs into insignificance. Rather than entering an elevated state of consciousness, my mind and body simply move in rhythmic harmony with the land.

༃

By noon, I reach a cluster of teashops, where Bhim has instructed us to wait for lunch. The western face of Kailash is clearly visible now, another facet of the pyramid with the same horizontal bands of rock and snow. But from this angle, the mountain seems to have a different character, somber and almost menacing. The base is guarded by gargoyles of red rock, fearsome sentinels chiseled by the wind. As I gaze up at the mountain, the sun is in my eyes. While Kailash itself remains imposing and serene, here in this valley there seems to be a surrounding chaos of eroded precipices that suggest wild and threatening forces, as if fierce storms and mountain demons have petrified into solid shapes.

The teashops are large tents, their outer fabric a sturdy green canvas but the inner fly is made of printed cotton, a floral pattern of blues and pinks. In the center of the tent stands a cast-iron stove, where two cauldrons of tea are brewing slowly over smoldering yak dung. These tea shops are set up during the pilgrimage season, from the end of May through October, and will be dismantled during winter when the kora route is closed. Tables and benches are arranged along one side with displays of Coke and Red Bull cans out front, as well as bottled beer. Entering a tent, I ask the proprietor for tea. She serves it to me in a thimble-sized glass, a murky pink infusion with a mildly salty flavor. After all of the over-sweetened chai made with powdered milk, it tastes wonderful. She refills my glass from a thermos flask corked with a knob of wood. Her daughter, a toddler, wears a whimsical plastic hat with propellers and spring-loaded baubles that nod as she walks, proud as a princess modeling her first crown.

An hour later, our group begins to arrive. The yaks carry on toward our campsite, two hours farther up the valley, while the pilgrims straggle in on horseback. Some have decided to walk because the trail is almost level and the saddles uncomfortable. We are served a simple lunch of rice and lentils. I quickly eat and hurry on, not wanting to be caught in a slow procession of horses and porters.

It would be impossible to get lost in this valley, though there are dozens of trails that separate and reconverge along the eastern bank of the Lha Chu River. These paths seem to have been laid out over centuries by the wandering footsteps of pilgrims, each taking their own circuit around Kailash. Coming from the opposite direction, I pass a group of Bon pilgrims who shout "Tashi Delek!" I respond with equal enthusiasm, glad for a change from "Om Namah Shivaya!" After an hour's walk, I come to a bridge that leads to Drira Phuk Gompa, on the opposite side of the valley. Though tempted to explore, I don't know where our camp is pitched and whether I can cross the river farther up.

When I reach the campsite, another mile on ahead, the yaks are being unloaded near a level patch of ground beside a cluster of resthouses, which look even less inviting than those we've stayed in so far. Fortunately, we will sleep in tents tonight. The only part of the settlement that intrigues me is a well-worn billiard table that stands outside, directly under the north face of Kailash. Its green baize surface is badly scratched and torn. One leg is broken and nailed together. The mesh pockets at each corner are full of empty tins and other trash. The table stands there as if it were a decrepit relic of arcane rituals—cue sticks and balls of different colors. Like almost everything else on this journey, it is symbolic of something that I can't quite comprehend.

As the Sherpas set up our tents, I find a rock to lean my back against and watch the pilgrims arrive. The horsemen are a colorful group. Many of them are women, wearing ankle-length dresses with brightly striped aprons. Most of the women have covered their faces with surgical masks because of the dust. Though it looks as if it might be a sign of modesty, none of them seem shy and they bully the pilgrims, communicating in exaggerated sign language. A young couple lounge on the grass beside their horses, having delivered riders and loads to the campsite. The woman leans close to the man, as they peer down at the small handheld screen of a battery-operated video game.

Exploring above our camp, I reach a pile of mani stones. Ahead of me is a gorge that leads to the foot of Kailash, which looks deceptively close. I decide not to go any further, for the wind has picked up and I have left my jacket behind. Far below me, I watch one of the pilgrims preparing to conduct a pooja near our tents. He looks like a gnome in his puffy jacket and woolen cap, stooping over an unruly square of plastic weighted down with stones. The corners are flapping in the wind as he tries to set out each ritual object, a conch shell, incense, a framed picture of Shiva.

Returning to camp, I put on my down jacket and find a place to wait for the sunset. I want to get a photograph of Kailash with the last rays of light tinting the snow. Right now, in full daylight, the stark whiteness of the peak makes it seem almost two dimensional. Mahesh, the tour leader for the group from Maharashtra, joins me. We sit together on the ground, facing the sacred peak.

Hesitantly, Mahesh asks if I am a believer. Without giving me a chance to reply, he then quickly inquires how much I know of Hindu mythology. I tell him that I am a skeptic, but mythology is a subject that interests me very much. Mahesh is an earnest young man whose faith has none of the strident overtones of others in his group. This is his second trip to Kailash. He admits he doesn't have any patience for the ecstatic singing and clapping of the pilgrims he leads. One man in his group gets possessed during rituals, though Mahesh believes he is acting.

As we sit together, he tells me a couple of stories about Kailash, recounting them slowly, with liberal digressions. "First," he says, pointing at the cornice of snow on the summit, "that overhanging snowfield never melts. It has always been there on the northern side of the mountain. You can look at photographs taken years ago. It is the hood of the Shesh Nag, the great cobra who resides with Lord Shiva." In many Hindu images, the cobra is coiled around Shiva's neck. Its extended hood rises protectively above his head, sheltering him in meditation. The shape that Mahesh describes is easily recognizable. When he tells me this, I can picture the summit of the mountain transformed into a cobra's hood.

The second story is about Ravana, the demon king of the *Ramayana*. "From the earliest times," Mahesh explains, "Ravana was a devotee of Shiva and worshipped him for centuries at Kailash, performing all kinds of *tapasaya* and acts of extreme austerity. One day, he approached Shiva for a boon. Ravana wanted to carry Kailash to his home in Lanka. Because the demon was his most faithful devotee, Shiva could not refuse this request, but he insisted on one condition. Once Ravana lifted Kailash onto his back, he could not put it down until he reached his destination. If he lowered the mountain to the ground, it would remain at that spot. Being a powerful giant, as huge as the mountain itself, Ravana accepted this condition and braced himself to lift Kailash."

Though the temperature has dropped below freezing, Mahesh is warming to his story. "Those lines you see on the surface," he continues, "are where he tied the ropes, each one cutting into the rock. On the south face of the mountain, you must have seen a vertical line down the center. That's where Ravana's spine dug into the cliffs as he lifted Kailash onto his back." Hearing this myth, the image that comes to mind is a Nepali porter, shouldering a mountainous load to carry across the border.

Mahesh blows into his cupped hands to thaw his fingers and carries on with the story: "As soon as Ravana uprooted the mountain, Lord Vishnu and the other gods became worried, not wanting this sacred summit to leave the Himalayas. Vishnu used his divine powers to stop the demon by filling his bladder to overflowing. Before Ravana could take a giant stride toward Lanka, the demon felt a sudden urge to urinate. As a result, he put the mountain down on this spot and shrugged off the ropes. Then he stood and relieved himself in this valley. The demon king's urine flowed down to Rakshastal, and even today its water is unfit to drink."

Both of us laugh at the punch line, but Mahesh tells the myth with quiet sincerity. His story brings the mountain to life. Never again will I be able to look at the lines on those cliffs without thinking of the ropes straining against the weight of Mount Kailash and Ravana's superhuman strength.

By now, the clouds have deceived us several times, making it seem as if the sun has already set. More than a century ago, in 1907, Sven Hedin, the Swedish explorer whose expedition was bankrolled by Alfred Nobel's dynamite fortune, experienced the same vigil:

The sun sets and we sit still and wait, confused by the rush of the spirits of the air and water. This time they have played a pretty trick, and we have been caught. To the north rises Kang-rinpoche, lofty and bright as a royal crown. Its summit is like a chorten on the grave of a Grand Lama. Snow and ice with vertical and slightly inclined fissures and ledges form a network like the white web of a gigantic spider on the black cliffs.

I am just about to give up on the sunset and retreat to my tent when I notice a faint amber glow on one of the lower snowfields. To the west, banks of clouds begin to part, as the sun slips behind the western crags of the La Chu valley. "Each of those peaks are the *rishis* and *munis* who sit in meditation. . . ." Mahesh begins another story, but I am no longer listening. He too falls silent, as a golden light ascends the mountain. Within a few seconds, Kailash is completely gilded, and the cobra's hood shines like a cornice of gold. The black striations stand out in contrast to the burnished snow, and it feels as if the mountain has changed from two dimensions into three and then, perhaps a fourth—each crevice and cliff line standing out in bold relief. Holding my breath, I take a few pictures, then lower my camera, wanting only to experience this spectacle with my eyes, rather than viewing it through a lens. Already, the light is fading. Within three minutes the sunset is over and shadows enfold us in a frigid embrace.

Cave of Mysteries

We are awake at 3:00 a.m. An early breakfast of vegetarian soup and bread is served in the dark. Bhim keeps announcing to everyone, "Soup is compulsory!" Though I am not suffering from altitude sickness, I can't stomach the thought of tepid broth at this hour of the morning and drink an extra cup of tea instead. To cross the 18,500 foot Dolma La pass today and reach our next campsite, we have been told that we must start by 4:00 a.m. The stars are brilliant, and Kailash glows like a pale slab of marble leaning against a sequined sky. The yaks arrive in silence, matted shadows lumbering in the dark. The only sounds are the shrill whistles of their handlers. Just as we are about to leave, a new moon comes up over the ridge. For a couple of minutes, the entire circumference is visible as it rises, then the moon fades quickly into a thin crescent.

Setting off, there is just enough light for me to see where the path angles across the valley. Though the wind has ceased, it is still bitterly cold. Stars begin to disappear as the sky brightens before dawn. A number of Tibetan pilgrims are already on their way, and I pass a couple of groups loaded down with tents. Soon enough, we cross a bridge over one branch of the river, its rocky banks encrusted with dirty snow. Yesterday, some of the pilgrims scrambled up the ravine above our camp and brought back chunks of ice and snowballs to show the others. For most of them, it was the first time they had touched snow.

Hiking up the trail, I feel stronger than I expected, walking slowly but feeling no need to stop and rest. The climb takes me diagonally up a rocky slope, with a few switchbacks at the steepest points. An hour from camp, I find myself at the top of a rise, where a Tibetan family has stopped to drink tea from a thermos flask—a father and mother with their teenage daughter and son. Unlike most of the other Tibetans, they are wearing Western clothes and look like a prosperous, middle-class family. The boy is about eighteen and carries a prayer wheel in one hand, which he keeps spinning even when they stop. The barrel of the wheel is covered in a crocheted bonnet of lime green yarn. Two other groups of Tibetan pilgrims have halted here and greet me with cries of "Tashi Delek!" Most of them are carrying prayer beads, which slip silently between their fingers.

While these groups have spent the night in Drira Phuk, other pilgrims circle Kailash in a single day, walking more than thirty miles. Some prostrate themselves at every step, lying flat on their stomachs and progressing by lengths of their body. One man has wooden blocks in each hand and pads on his knees, but instead of flattening himself completely, he moves forward in a tight squat, like a frog. Two companions are walking with him, and I wonder if he will make it over the pass today. Several of the older Tibetans are chanting, and their low voices sound like the guttural roar of the river we've left behind.

Across the valley from us, Kailash is visible again after being hidden for most of the route from camp. While we remain in shadow, the peak is lit by the first rays of sunlight. Though not as dramatic as the evening glow, the morning light has a startling brilliance, its intensity increasing until I cannot look at the mountain without dark glasses. From this angle, the main profile of the peak is identical to what I saw last evening, but the eastern ridge is now in view. Below this lies the main glacier that skirts the north face.

The advantage of climbing at this hour of the morning is that we have no direct sun and the air is calm. The pass is still not visible, and I'm not sure which of the valleys we will ascend, but it isn't difficult to recognize our route. Most of the large rocks we pass have been turned into shrines, wrapped with scarves and smeared with grease and ochre. My maps and guidebooks indicate specific sites, a rock where Milarepa's footprint can be seen and the famous "sin-testing stone," but there is no signage and it is difficult to know which landmarks are which amid hundreds of boulders that pilgrims have marked as totem sites. At various points, the Tibetans stop to pray, pressing their heads against stones in silent obeisance.

One of these natural shrines is a place where pilgrims shed an article of clothing as they pass. It looks like a laundromat hit by a hurricane. For almost two hundred yards, the rocks are covered with mounds of old shirts and trousers, socks and gloves. Several hats are perched on top of cairns. A pink woolen ski cap, with a knitted pattern of skull and crossbones, has been placed over a stone the size of a child's head.

All along the way, a trail of litter and garbage is strewn, everything from sardine and Pepsi cans to candy wrappers, even pharmaceutical sachets and broken vials from glucose injections, where ailing pilgrims must have been given an intravenous boost to get them over the pass. Strangest of all are aerosol cans that look like air freshener. For a long time, I can't figure them out because the writing is in Chinese. Finally, I realize that these are empty oxygen containers. The trail of garbage has accumulated over many years. For much of the route it feels as if I am walking through a junkyard.

While the discarded clothes represent an act of faith, the rest of the rubbish is nothing but a sign of careless indifference. For those pilgrims who throw garbage along this sacred route—and many of our group contributed to the pollution—there seems to be no connection between their pious prayers and the trash they leave behind. Stepping over plastic bags and empty juice packets, I find myself getting angry and frustrated. Like everything else on this journey, it seems symbolic of something greater, a paradox that defines the contradictions of human nature. Whatever we worship, we also defile and desecrate. There seems to be an equation between faith and filth. Contained inside superficial layers of dogma resides whatever elemental mystery there might be. What we often confront is only the superficial packaging and gaudy wrappers. Sometimes I feel that religion is nothing more than the detritus and debris of spirituality discarded on the refuse heaps of credulity.

By now the barren ridges on either side have been touched with light. Each of the summits has a name—Chenresi Ri, the peak of Avalokiteshvara, or Jampelyang Ri, the pinnacle of Manjushree. Though the trail at my feet is littered with trash, these summits rise up in pristine grandeur, inaccessible to man.

One of the landmarks I have been searching for is a small pond called the Mirror of Yama, the looking glass of death. There is only one pool of water on this side of the pass, hardly fifty feet in circumference and a short distance from the trail. A large rock overlooking the pond is draped with hundreds of strips of cloth and bits of yarn, most of them red and saffron. It is here that people leave shreds of fabric recovered from garments of the dead, remembering those who have left this life behind. Unlike the discarded heaps of clothing lower down, this memorial has an eerie beauty that makes me stop and gaze across at the reflective surface of the lake. Each thread is a life that has unraveled and will ultimately be woven back into the fabric of existence. The valley around it lies in shadow, but the water captures the bright blue of the sky. To the southwest, Kailash stands out. This will be the last clear view I have of the mountain during my kora. Though I will see its eastern face after descending the pass, only sections of the mountain are visible beyond this point.

7:00 a.m. Three hours have passed since I left camp, and now the horses are beginning to catch up. I can hear the sound of their hooves on the rocks and the clucking of the horsemen urging them on. As I step aside to let a group go by, some of the pilgrims greet me, while others sit slumped in their saddles with expressions of misery. Their heads must throb under woolen hats, and nausea makes every turn on the trail a stomach-churning ordeal. Last night, one of the yatris from Maharashtra became violently ill and was taken back to Darchen. Nobody knows if he has survived, and his companions are anxious. The sure-footed ponies pick their way through patches of snow, which are covered with dung and dirt. Heading directly east, into the sunrise, it is impossible to see the crest of the pass because of the glare. A hundred yards from the top we cross from shadow into sunlight, the harsh rays blinding as they light up thousands of colored prayer flags that cover Dolma La like a patchwork quilt.

Arriving at the pass, the pilgrims dismount. Aside from a few cairns and flagpoles, the high point of our journey is a broad expanse of windswept rock, surrounded by saw-toothed ridges, edged with ice and snow. Dolma is one of several names for the goddess. As with

Hindu deities like Nanda Devi, she has many aspects and attributes, from fierce eroticism to motherly calm. At times, the goddess can be dark and forbidding, lashing pilgrims with her unrelenting storms, but on days like this, when the breeze is gentle and the morning sunlight warms the rocks on which we rest, she is benign and welcoming.

Near the top of the pass, covered with layers of prayer flags, is a huge, angular boulder. Tibetan pilgrims leave locks of their hair and decayed teeth that have fallen out squeezed into the crevices of this rugged monolith. Others take away bits of rock or some of these human relics as a talisman. Having promised friends and family that I will bring them souvenirs from my journey, I collect a dozen pebbles from the pass, tiny fragments of the mountain, each of which is a miniature version of Kailash.

Though I feel a sense of elation on reaching the pass, there isn't the same experience of awe and reverence that I felt when we approached Kailash on the first day, or last evening when I saw the sunset lighting up its northern face. Dolma La is as dramatic a landscape as any we've crossed, but, emotionally, it does not move me beyond a feeling of relief and appreciation for the eroded features of the mountains. Kailash itself is hidden from view. A group of Gujaratis are seated on the rocks just below the pass. They hail me and insist on touching my feet because I have walked the route. The pilgrims also touch each other's feet in a gesture that acknowledges our having completed the most arduous stage of the sacred journey. By simply being in the presence of Kailash, we have acquired enough merit to receive deference from one another. The yatris insist that I share a bottle of Pepsi with them, as if it were some form of sacrament. At 18,500 feet above sea level, the carbonation fills me up faster than at lower altitudes. Even though I drink very little, I feel bloated.

Just below Dolma La is another pond, slightly larger than the Mirror of Yama but no more than thirty feet across. Hindus call this Gauri Kund, and Buddhists refer to it as the Lake of Compassion. For much of the year it remains frozen, but in summer the water melts to a chalky green color. The snow-capped ridge above is reflected in the surface. Being several hundred feet below the pass and surrounded by steep cliffs and rocky slopes, the lake is seldom visited by pilgrims, who follow a trail that circles above Gauri Kund. Some yatris brave the difficult descent to bathe in the water, but most take darshan from a distance, allowing their prayers to reflect upon the jade-like surface of the pool.

According to Hindu mythology, this pond is associated with Parvati, the mountain goddess and consort of Shiva. By most accounts, Parvati bathed in Gauri Kund, and this is where Ganesh was born. An immaculate conception, his birth reflects the earthy qualities of Hindu lore. According to some accounts, Parvati created her son out of sweat and skin exfoliated from her body. When he was fully formed, his mother asked him to guard her bathing place. Ganesh made sure that nobody intruded on Parvati's privacy until Shiva himself arrived. Neither son nor father recognized each other, and when Ganesh attempted to stop Shiva from approaching, the lord of destruction lost his temper and opened his third eye, vaporizing the young man's head. Learning what had happened, Parvati was distraught, and the only way that Shiva could console her was to resurrect Ganesh. At that moment an elephant appeared and Shiva transplanted its head onto the decapitated boy. This myth is a familiar episode in Hindu mythology, and I have visited more than one place that is said to be the setting for this story. Here in Tibet, well above the range of any elephants, I wonder: if the myth were played out in front of us today, would Ganesh have the head of a yak, or perhaps an argali sheep, with twisting horns instead of a coiled trunk?

From the crest of the pass, we can see our trail cutting down a steep slope, traversing a field of rocks and boulders. Farther on, the Lham Chu valley opens up and leads us back toward Manasarovar. Many of the pilgrims are taken by surprise when they realize that they must descend on foot. The path is too steep for horses to carry riders to the valley floor, and the horsemen quickly vanish. As I start down, I see them hurrying ahead of me, abandoning their riders. While the trail is treacherous at points, not all of it is impassable on horseback, and this seems more of an excuse for the horsemen to rush ahead and have tea at the foot of the hill.

Descending beyond the pass, I come across a Tibetan woman and her four-year-old son walking hand in hand. She is part of our group of horsemen and yak drivers but is not carrying a load. The boy has wind-blushed cheeks, and he is bundled against the cold. When I offer him some chocolate, he hides behind the folds of his mother's *chuba* but she accepts it for her son. A number of Tibetan pilgrims are coming up the path, undertaking the Bonpo Kora, following our route in reverse. For them, the climb to the pass is much steeper, a straight ascent from the valley, up a zigzag trail. Descending slowly, I stop at several points to sit in the shadow of a boulder and write in my journal. The sun grows brighter and hotter as it rises above us.

It is clear that our group will take several hours to descend from the pass. The horsemen have unsaddled their animals to let them graze on a sparse meadow near the river. Not knowing exactly how far on ahead we will go before camping, I decide to find some shade and take a nap. As I walk down the path, there doesn't seem to be any place where I can escape the sun. Finally, I find a small cave, three feet deep and two feet high, into which I can squeeze my head and shoulders. It is a relief to lie in the cool semi-darkness, though I keep wondering if the cave is the den of some creature that might resent my presence. The only wild animals nearby are marmots, which shriek at anyone who walks by, before disappearing into their holes. But in my burrow I am alone and doze for a couple of hours until the rest of the yatris begin to wander past.

As it turns out, we still have seven miles to walk, though most of this is level ground and easy trekking. Kailash remains hidden from view, except for brief glimpses of its eastern face. Unlike the other three sides of the mountain, there are no telltale bands of rock and snow. Instead, this side of the peak is a pure white cone wedged between clefts in the ridges.

Early in the afternoon, I come in sight of Zutrul Phuk, a monastery and settlement where the poet-saint Milarepa took shelter in a cave and meditated for many years. The gompa, with its red walls, stands next to a whitewashed boulder shaped like a natural chorten. There are several guesthouses and shelters, but we camp in an open field close to the river. By the time our tents are set up, the wind has gained force, a relentless torrent of air that tugs at the fabric, straining the guy ropes. The broad valley offers no protection from this fierce gale, which seems intent on blowing us back toward Dolma La.

✑

Next morning, as the rest of the pilgrims set off after breakfast, I head up to the gompa at Zutrul Phuk. None of the Hindus seem interested in visiting Buddhist shrines. I have read about the Cave of Mysteries, where Milarepa achieved enlightenment and composed many of his poems. Of all the Tibetan religious figures, both historical and mythological, Milarepa is one of the more accessible and intriguing. His life story is characterized by moral preaching, yet he has human qualities and failings that distinguish him from other saints, who seem to have more virtues than character or personality.

In his youth and early adulthood, Milarepa was brash and violent, ignoring the precepts of Buddhist teaching. But after a transformation brought on by the death of his mother, he retreated into the mountains and committed himself to austerity and contemplation. Most images of Milarepa depict him as a pale, ascetic figure, almost as gaunt as the fasting Buddha. He is said to have survived for years by eating only nettles, which gave his complexion a greenish pallor. In his wanderings, he circled Kang Rinpoche many times and finally chose this eastern valley as his hermitage. Like Padmasambhava, Milarepa is often presented as a savior of Buddhism, reasserting the divine principle of compassion and self-denial over superstition and shamanism. One of his most popular stories involves a contest with Naro Bon-chung, a Bon shaman who challenged Milarepa to a race to the summit of Kang Rinpoche. On the morning of the contest, the shaman got up early, well before daybreak, and set off for the top of the mountain, carrying his *damru*, a small two-sided drum that is used to invoke an occult trance. Meanwhile, Milarepa completed his morning prayers and rituals. When his disciples urged him to depart before it was too late, he showed no haste or anxiety. As the sky brightened, the shaman was beginning his final ascent, racing up through the snow. But Milarepa remained in his cave at Zutrul Phuk, absorbed in meditation. When the first rays of sunlight breached the cragged peaks along the eastern horizon, the saint was instantly transported to the sacred summit astride these golden sunbeams. Defeated and cowed by the powers of Milarepa, the shaman dropped his damru, which tumbled down the southern face of the mountain, making a loud banging sound and leaving a vertical gash in the cliffs.

Arriving at the gompa, I can hear a steady drumming. The monastery is built over the rock chamber in which Milarepa meditated. I enter a rectangular courtyard that seems deserted, though the sound of the drum is coming from somewhere inside. Opening off the courtyard are dormitories where monks and visitors stay, but right now there is nobody around. I can smell incense and notice an enamel basin in which clods of yak dung are burning, with fragrant juniper twigs and needles sprinkled on top as incense. Last night my tent was filled with smoke from the horsemen's fires, and the acrid stench almost asphyxiated me, but this morning the resinous juniper tempers the smoke and has a pleasant, peaty odor.

The main sanctuary lies in front of me, but the doors are locked. Two large frescoes dominate the walls, with fierce guardians keeping watch. To the right, a staircase leads me into a second sanctuary, where a single monk is chanting verses while beating slowly on a large drum suspended from the ceiling. He acknowledges me as I enter but does not stop, turning the pages of scripture that lie in front of him. At one end of the room are three brass idols, a demonic figure and two images of the goddess, one riding a horse and the other a snow lion. These are draped with gauze scarves and stoles. In the foreground are butter lamps flickering in the breeze that enters through an open window. The walls are covered with thangka paintings, most of which depict divine coition, the goddess seated on her lover's lap. The couple's faces are contorted in a grimace of passion, a sexual union that appears more grotesque than erotic, more painful than pleasurable. After a few minutes, the monk concludes his chanting and closes his book by arranging the loose pages in a neat pile and folding these up in layers of silk brocade.

He is a stout, slow-moving man, about forty, wearing a yellow down vest over ochre robes. The monk does not seem disturbed by my early arrival and gestures for me to follow him into the main sanctuary. On either side of the door are two large prayer wheels the size of oil barrels, painted bright colors. Inside the main temple are two Buddhas, one of them larger than life. These are seated against the back wall of the sanctuary, alongside images of the goddess and Milarepa. One of the Buddhas looks as if it could be plated in gold, though it is hard to tell in the shadows. The chapel lies mostly in darkness. A small skylight and two butter lamps are the only illumination.

The room is square, with supporting columns in the middle. An altar is arranged in front of the images and there is a ceremonial throne, draped with scarves. Most of the walls are covered with thangkas. Along the right wall is the library, a lacquered bookcase that rises from floor to ceiling. Each text has its own pigeonhole, like sacred postboxes, and all of the books are wrapped in silk.

Milarepa's cave lies in one corner of the sanctuary, at ground level, tucked between the idols and library shelves. I have to stoop down to see inside for it is barely three feet high, about the size of the cave in which I took refuge yesterday. An impression of Milarepa's hand appears underneath the stone slab that forms the ceiling—though I can barely make out an indentation of what might have been his palm and fingers. Inside the cave are a dozen or more images, including a silver idol of the saint in a meditative posture. A few photographs of aged monks are on display but no pictures of the Dalai Lama, whose image is forbidden in Tibet.

While I sit in front of the cave, trying to imagine what it must have looked like before the gompa was built, the lama busies himself opening packets of butter. These will be melted to fill the votive lamps. When the butter hardens, it is like candle wax and burns with a sooty yellow flame. Whatever solitude and stoic simplicity the saint encountered here is now encased in an elaborate shrine. The religious images and paraphernalia seem to contradict whatever meaning the place must have had in the past. Yet, the gompa has a peaceful feeling of antiquity despite the clutter of images and fetish objects. Seated on the floor, I light a lamp and stare into the flame—a pure, unadulterated vision of brightness and energy. It could have been the same flame that illuminated this cave hundreds of years ago, a mute tongue of fire.

☙

Leaving the gompa, I notice a few clumps of nettles growing amid the rocks. These are the plants that sustained Milarepa, and Tibetans still cook them as a vegetable. When boiled, the spines lose their sting and the stewed leaves taste like spinach. A short ways down the valley, I see an enormous cave above me, large enough to contain an entire monastery. It seems deserted, though the canyon above it is decorated with prayer flags suspended from one ridge to the other. Unlike the stark red rocks in the western valley, this corridor is lined with elaborate formations of granite, shale and other stones. There is more vegetation too, low plants like gorse and juniper, even a few flowers—blue asters and yellow buttercups.

Soon after departing Zutrul Phuk, I see a moving shape silhouetted against the sky between the yawning jaws of a canyon. For a moment it is there, then it vanishes. A few seconds later, it reappears, like the fleeting shadow of a crescent moon. Though far away, I recognize the outstretched wings of a large bird circling on the air currents. As it flies above me, I try to identify what it is, but only when it turns can I see the distinctly wedge-shaped tail of a lammergeir or bearded vulture. These magnificent raptors have the largest wingspan in the Himalayas, nearly nine feet from tip to tip. According to Hindu and Buddhist mythology, they are associated with Garuda, the vehicle of Vishnu. Bon tradition also celebrates these birds with stories of horned eagles that carry shamans across the sky. To see a lammergeir circling the slopes of Kailash seems an auspicious sign and confirms for me the significance of this place—a sanctuary open to the sky, a place where mountains rise above us like natural cathedrals cloaked in snow and brushed by the wings of raptors.

Elated by this vision, I carry on. An easy two-hour walk from Zutrul Phuk brings me to a small settlement called Tangsar, where the Lham Chu valley narrows into a horseshoe gorge. By the time I reach the end of our circuit, the drivers and Land Cruisers are waiting for us. My fellow pilgrims are overjoyed to have undertaken the parikrama. They embrace their companions and touch one another's feet in acknowledgement of having completed the most sacred pilgrimage of all. It is moving to see how happy they are despite the struggles and deprivation of the last ten days. The loudest and most abrasive of the Gujarati pilgrims puts his arms around me and bursts into tears of joy. We hold each other as brothers, though we have hardly spoken until now and, after this journey, will never meet again.

BANDARPUNCH

Returning Home

Whence this creation has arisen—perhaps it formed itself, or perhaps it did not—the one who looks down on it, in the highest heaven, only he knows—or perhaps he does not know.

Rig Veda (translated by Wendy Doniger)

Healing Light

Artists know that light in the mountains is different. Altitude makes everything clearer, defining shapes and contours more sharply. Colors take on a bolder hue, particularly during morning and evening, when the day ripens at sunrise and then rots at sunset. Instead of encompassing broad sightlines that stretch toward a flat horizon, mountains have a way of compressing and compacting light, breaking it up into messy, disorderly exaggerations, enfolding it with shadows and stretching it in all directions.

Photographer Sankar Sridhar has spent several winters in Ladakh, where temperatures drop twenty degrees below freezing at altitudes above 14,000 feet and fingers lose all feeling in the few seconds it takes to remove a lens cap. He has captured psychedelic images of dawn breaking over frozen lakes, which have an otherworldly quality, as if the pictures were taken on a distant planet orbiting somewhere farther out in space.

Himalayan landscapes reflect a luminosity that doesn't exist on the plains. Partly, it is the clarity of the air but also the angle of the sun, slanting above the earth's curvature to meet the sudden upheaval of these high ranges. Refraction in the atmosphere at extreme elevations contributes to a greater brightness, as well as subtle adumbrations that tease our perception, as if the light were emanating from the mountain itself.

Mountain sunlight seems omnipresent. As all-sustaining as air, it feels as if you can breathe in lungfuls like a glassblower, exhaling weightless orbs of color. At other times, light in the mountains is like water—so deep that we could drown in it. Our eyes focus on dramatic displays of radiance, the pyrotechnics of daybreak and dusk.

Everything in us responds to light, a kind of human photosynthesis that sends streams of life rushing through our veins, nourishing the cells in our skin and tissues, even our bones.

Clouds form the negative space in a mountain landscape, the unpainted margins of the sky obscuring and filtering light. An art teacher in college once taught me how to draw with an eraser, sketching nude shapes out of a graphite blur, penumbral outlines of human flesh and form where the pencil's shadow has been removed. Another professor, Paul Horgan, with whom I served an apprenticeship as a writer, used to tell me how he carried a blank notebook with him during his travels, which he filled with small watercolor sketches so that he could recall the light he encountered on his journeys. Paul's two-volume history of the Rio Grande translates into words the magnificent panoramas of high deserts in Colorado and New Mexico, prose descriptions rendered from the fluid pigments off his brush.

When a peak serves as a sundial, light becomes time, the dark profile of a mountain moving across a canyon wall with the measured inevitability of a clock. Light changes with the hours. Light travels in waves, as constant as vibrations in the quartz crystals at the heart of my wristwatch. Light washes over the mountains, adjusting each day to the turning of the seasons. I have raced shadows up a ridge, trying to keep pace with the sunlight as it advances. Mornings, I have waited as the brilliance creeps up a meadow before consuming me in its blinding warmth.

There is a popular Himalayan myth about a magical herb called jwala booti, which emits an ethereal light. It grows in high pastures near the snow line and can be found only after the sun goes down. The leaves glow in the darkness, and the stems burn like filaments in an electric bulb, as delicate as fireflies. By other accounts, the upper portion of jwala booti does not give off light; instead the roots do, which makes it even harder to find. Digging these out of the soil, we find the glimmering tendrils aglow, like a fuse ignited by fires deep inside the earth.

Lights upon a mountain carry supernatural connotations. Late at night, they glitter near a summit or a pass, moving across the dark face of the mountain. Some say they are the votive lamps of saints who wander over these heights, offering prayers to Himalayan deities. Others believe they are the eyes of unknown creatures that stalk us in our dreams or stars fallen to earth, meteors that gradually cool in the snow and finally disappear.

Mystics use the metaphor of light to explain divine revelation, those moments of epiphany that defy reason and rhetoric. Mountain light, in particular, conveys an intense radiance associated with transcendental experiences. Auras are pathways of illumination. The poet-saint Milarepa traveled on sunbeams to the summit of Mount Kailash. Yet, light can also create deceptive illusions. Inspired by eastern lore and myths, William Butler Yeats composed a sonnet titled "Meru," with these concluding lines:

> Hermits upon Mount Meru or Everest,
> Caverned in night under the drifted snow,
> Or where that snow and winter's dreadful blast
> Beat down upon their naked bodies, know
> That day brings round the night, that before dawn
> His glory and his monuments are gone.

Ocular perception is a product of neural consciousness, processing myriad messages of light that travel from cornea to retina and through the nerves that enter our brains, generating synaptic impulses to form patterns of memory and imagination. We create these convincing illusions for ourselves, a subjective interpretation of what exists within our field of vision. Looking at a mountain, we believe it's there and accept its presence, appreciate its beauty, but all we really see is the distant fire of the sun reflecting off its surfaces, a cosmic form of artifice as abstract as these words upon a page. For all its grandeur in our minds, the mountain remains unseen, an optical echo of itself.

Sometimes, however, a revelation occurs when separate forms dissolve and we can observe a mountain with an acute perception that draws back the veil of projected reality. The camera obscura falls apart, and we see and don't see all at once. Not only do we perceive the mountain in a different light, but we comprehend its presence within ourselves. At last the lost horizon comes in view. But is it real or is it a hallucination, a phantom image that haunts our vision? Georgia O'Keeffe, whose iconic paintings of New Mexico convey the numinous intensity of mountain light, often saw crosses in her landscapes, ethereal visions that she tried to frame upon a canvas.

Philosophers like Edmund Burke and Immanuel Kant have attempted to describe human responses to nature's most dramatic phenomena, through the aesthetic dichotomy of the sublime, in which a mountain landscape evokes both horror and awe. The extreme contrasts of darkness and light that we observe high up in the Alps or in the Himalayas, particularly at dawn or dusk, elicit simultaneous feelings of fear and elation. Essentially, the sublime defines a kind of emotional vertigo that leaves us both unsettled and inspired. This experience places us at the edge of a metaphorical precipice that is even more disturbing and uplifting than the cliffs that drop away beneath our boots. It is, perhaps, the primal reflex that provokes in some their search for a divine creator and destroyer.

Mountain worship is far older than any of the major faiths today, but it is often dismissed as "fuzzy new-age logic," naive devotion to inanimate objects that science has fully explained. Investigated and interpreted by the high priests of geology, biology, and physics, nothing more remains to be discovered. Yet, somehow, we cannot break away from the embrace of mountains, their healing depths and resonant stories. We believe in them because they symbolize so much that we fail to understand, another dimension that lies beyond those paths where our feet cannot take us. At the same time, mountains seem so obvious and omnipresent, immensely real and constantly there.

Despite our doubts and disbelief, the spiritual radiance of a mountain flows off its glaciers and shines like a beacon of eternity. The sublime magnitude of the Himalayas leaves us with profound feelings of reverence as well as trepidation. We reconcile ourselves to this greater power only when we surrender to the mountains with humility and compassion, accepting our place among them. As we climb those staircases of ice and rock, our burdens fall away. Our bodies and souls vanish into a bottomless crevasse, even as we continue to seek the summit.

Certain light, found only in the mountains, travels with us as we ascend.

Ascent and Retreat

A goat path follows the blade of the ridge, less than eight inches wide, with a drop of several hundred feet on either hand. We are climbing the crumbling remnants of an extinct glacier that carved this valley into a scalloped bowl centuries ago. A steep rib of moraine rises out of a boulder field and leads to the peaks above. Its surface is loose scree with sparse ground cover, dwarf rhododendrons and juniper that grow close to the soil. From a distance it looks as if the ridge were bare. Yesterday, I watched a herd of bharal cross these slopes, moving with the agility of mountain creatures for whom the cliffs and fissured rocks offer countless hoofholds. Commonly known as blue sheep, the bharal's natural habitat lies above the tree line. These are one of the highest-ranging mammals in the world.

I wish I had a bharal's sense of balance instead of my two clumsy feet, which stumble and trudge up the narrow trail. Keeping my eyes fixed on the ground, I take short, careful steps. My breathing is labored because of the altitude: 13,000 feet above sea level. The load I carry is not heavy—thirty pounds—but my pack is bulky, filled with mountaineering boots and crampons as well as other gear, which makes me top heavy and less secure on the climb.

Looking back, below us I can see our tents pitched on a rocky meadow beside a stream that flows from the ice. The synthetic domes look like orange blisters, out of place amid the dour gray rocks. A pair of choughs glides above me, sleek black birds with yellow beaks that whistle plaintively as the wind tosses them about. To the east, amid the clouds, I can see the summits of Srikantha and a dozen other mountains above Gangotri, the flared crest of the Garhwal Himalayas rising to almost twice our elevation.

Each time I think we've come to the end of the ridge, there is a further ascent, until we reach a point where the trail disappears under a wedge of dirty snow that funnels into the valley. We sit and rest after an hour's climb, and my breathing slows. Looking up, I cannot make out any route, only sheer slopes of grass and rocky ledges that lean outward from the mountain. My companions seem untroubled by the vertical expanse above. When I ask which way we go from here, they wave casually upward, as if we are going to catch a thermal like the birds and sail effortlessly to the top.

Crossing the snow, I kick at the frozen surface with my toes to gain purchase on the crust of ice and use my trekking pole to keep from sliding. On reaching the other side, we begin to climb again without bothering to search for a path. At first, dry tussocks of grass provide uneven steps that allow us to negotiate the slope with relative ease. The open flank of the mountain is steeper than the spine of the ridge below, roughly 60 degrees but quickly straightening to an angle that feels almost perpendicular. I am grateful for patches of rhododendron, which give me something to hold onto, spreading roots clutching the earth as desperately as I cling to their matted stems.

After every five steps, I stop and gasp for breath, as much from fear as exertion. I do not have the courage to look down anymore. If I slip, there is nothing to stop me except an intervening rock or two and then the boulders far below. Whenever I glance upward, the back of my head knocks against my pack. Ordinarily, I do not have a fear of heights, but memories from boyhood, of climbing slopes like this, still terrify me. Several times, while scrambling about the mountains near Mussoorie, I found myself stranded on a grassy cliff that seemed to drop away in all directions. I have fallen more than once, tumbling down hillsides in a frantic plunge, grabbing for anything to stop myself. But more than the fear of falling, it is a paralyzing sense of immobility that terrifies me, being unable to go up or down.

Thankfully, the clouds come in and obscure the valley. Peering down between my knees, I can see the wall of grass vanishing into the mist. There is no choice but to keep on going. Those who are with me take their own routes, each of us searching for paths of least resistance, though gravity weighs us down and our loads drag us away from the face of the hill. I am using both hands now, having abandoned any pretense of walking up the mountain. My ascent has become a precipitous crawl. The useless pole in my hand makes it even more awkward as I reach for tufts of grass. A nugget of rock breaks free in my fingers. A juniper root bends but does not snap.

I am sweating, and my glasses repeatedly fog up. Finally, I take these off and stuff them into a pocket. There is no exultation in this climb, only a constant clutch of danger. At places, I feel as if the mountain is leaning outward, a weird sensation of vertigo in which I can't tell if I am climbing up or down, my body hugging the earth that seems to have been upended. *It's not so bad,* I tell myself. *If it weren't for the drop, I could easily scramble up this slope. I've climbed worse heights than this. Just think of it as ten feet . . . then another ten feet, that's all. One step at a time.* But there is no consolation in these thoughts, and I can feel my arms trembling, not from fatigue but from having reached a psychological limit, an abyss of the mind. My lungs are pumping oxygen into my blood, but there is also a steady stream of adrenalin entering my veins. I feel my knees begin to lock, refusing to take another step. I want to cry out for help though my throat has gone dry. The brittle grass between my clenched fingers begins to unfasten from the soil. If the wind were stronger, it would blow me off the mountain like the dry husk of a leaf. Time has stopped, though my pulse is racing over a hundred beats a minute. We haven't even reached the mountain I hope to climb, yet already I want to turn back, even if the descent from here is as treacherous as the way up.

The Monkey's Tale

In the *Himalayan Gazetteer*, published in 1886, E. T. Atkinson quotes William Fraser, one of the first Europeans to explore Garhwal in the 1820s. Fraser's description of Bandarpunch is probably the first account in English of this mountain, which he observed on his way to Yamunotri. Both the mountain itself and the sacred lore of this peak caught Fraser's imagination:

As seen from the south-west two lofty and massive peaks rise high above the rest, deep in snow, from which all the other inferior ridges seem to have their origin. These peaks are connected by a sharp neck, considerably lower than themselves. The south and south-east exposure is the least steep and bears a great depth of pure unbroken snow. Little or no rock is seen, except a few points at the ridge of the connecting neck, where it is too sharp and steep for snow to lie; and there it appears of a red colour. Here and there lofty precipices are seen in the snow itself, where the lower parts have melted, and masses have given way and slidden down to the ravines below, leaving a face several hundred feet high, that shows the depth of snow which has accumulated for ages. The name of Bandarpunchh properly applies only to the highest peaks of this mountain: all the subordinate peaks and ridges have their own peculiar names. Jamnotri has reference only to the sacred spot, where worship is paid to the goddess and ablution is performed. According to native accounts there are said to be four peaks which form the top of Bandarpunchh, only two of which are seen from the south-west and in the cavity or hollow contained between them tradition places a lake or tank of very peculiar sanctity. No one has ever seen this pool, for no one has ever even attempted to ascend any of these peaks. Besides the physical difficulties, the goddess has especially prohibited any mortal from passing that spot appointed for her worship.

The landholders aver that every year, in the month of Phagun, a single monkey comes from the plains by way of Hardwar, and ascends the highest peak of this mountain, where he remains twelve months and returns to give room to another; but his entertainment must be very indifferent and inhospitable, as may be inferred from the nature of the place; for he returns in a very sad plight, being not only reduced almost to a skeleton, but having lost his hair and a great part of his skin.

☙

Two years after my first attempt on Bandarpunch, I return to the mountain a second time, determined to reach the top. Several friends had planned to join me, but, for one reason or another, they dropped out. In order to facilitate permissions and clearances from the Indian Mountaineering Foundation and the Uttarakhand Forest Department, I engaged a private outfitter, Rimo Expeditions, which handles treks and climbs throughout the Himalayas. The high peaks of Garhwal and Kumaon are some of the most regulated ranges in the world, with all kinds of restrictions, especially for foreigners like me. The Person of Indian Origin (PIO) card, which allows me to stay in India without a visa, states clearly that it isn't valid for "missionary activities, mountaineering and research." Somehow, I feel as if they've singled me out, but after making inquires, Rimo tells me that Bandarpunch is an "open peak," for which special permission can be granted on payment of exorbitant climbing fees.

Being a novice when it comes to mountaineering, I have asked that an experienced Sherpa accompany me. The only person in the group with whom I've trekked before is Titu, who climbed Bandarpunch in 2011 and will serve as guide. We begin to make plans six months ahead and complete all of the paperwork and other formalities. But then, on the first of June, just as I am about to leave Mussoorie, word comes in that one signature is still required. The chief wildlife warden of Uttarakhand has yet to approve our permit, and he is away from his desk and "out of station."

Eventually, losing patience after three days' wait, Titu and I head off for Sukhi, the roadhead from where our trek begins. Driving from Mussoorie to Uttarkashi, then further up the Ganga, I feel a sense of déjà vu, for I have traveled this route more than a dozen times. Twelve years ago, I walked these roads while writing a book about the sacred sources of the Ganga. Being the pilgrimage season, tour groups of yatris crowd the guesthouses and restaurants along the way. The roads are as bad as ever, with washouts and landslides. Though the monsoon is still to come, it has already rained, and unpaved stretches are awash in mud. As our vehicle grinds its way through potholes and over rutted sections of the highway, I feel a depressing awareness of erosion caused by human beings—bulldozers clearing rubble, road crews breaking rocks by hand. Equally discouraging are signs of religious vehemence, which has increased in recent years. Billboards advertising spiritual discourses by self-proclaimed gurus line the roads. In every wayside village, posters of politicians offer felicitations on the journey to "Holy Ganga," though they have done little to plan or prepare for this spiritual invasion.

The Bhagirathi tributary, full of silt washed down from the mountains, is the same color as the strong, thick tea brewed at roadside stalls. Just above Uttarkashi, we pass Gangori, where the traditional route to Bandarpunch cuts off and climbs to Dodital. A year ago, flash floods on the Assi Ganga washed away the bridge and a dozen buildings. The military Border Roads Organization has replaced the bridge, but Gangori still looks like a disaster zone. Hundreds of people died in last year's floods, many of them undocumented laborers working on a hydroelectric project along the Assi Ganga, trying to harness the power of the river, which turns lethal in the monsoon. Five weeks ago, training for my climb to Bandarpunch, I trekked up this route to Dodital and the Darwa Pass.

Everywhere along the road lies the pious squalor of religious tourism: guesthouses with sanctimonious names and quilts that are laundered every two or three years. Many of the newer buildings stand well below the high-water mark of earlier floods, inviting disaster. The Ganga View hotel on the outskirts of Uttarkashi has its foundation in the riverbed. The town of Bhatwari is sliding into the Bhagirathi and may disappear within a couple of years. At Gangaria, hot mineral baths and lines of tea shacks have turned a cluster of thermal springs into a fetid slum. And as we approach Sukhi, winding our way up switchbacks, we get stuck in traffic jams. Enormous pilgrim buses, almost too wide for the road, come face to face on narrow corners, inching past one another and blowing horns impatiently. Zipping around the vehicles like a swarm of venomous wasps are gangs of motorcycle yatris, young men with saffron headscarves and fluttering pennants emblazoned with Oms and swastikas. They race up to Gangotri to bathe in the seminal waters of the Ganga, absolving themselves of every sin except religious chauvinism.

The Himalayas are often depicted as the pristine seat of spiritual enlightenment, the fountainhead of Hindu tradition, the reclusive retreat of sages and sadhus. But along these valleys, where increasing numbers of pilgrims travel in a continuous caravan of zealous fundamentalism, the politicized face of Hinduism has evolved into a grotesque visage spouting dogma, prejudice, and venal theologies. The mountains themselves rise above the Ganga, which flows resolutely on, washing away the filth of millions who pollute its waters, even as they chant her praises and call her "Mother." Natural phenomena are turned into religious metaphors and then debased by the tawdry embellishments of faith. Even ancient myths lose resonance here.

When we finally arrive at Sukhi late in the afternoon, I find the team from Rimo Expeditions camped in a village house at the side of the road. Kunzang, the trip leader, whom I have met before in Delhi, introduces me to the others, including our liaison officer. He is Nandan Jaiswal, a young mountaineer in his late twenties, from West Bengal. The others in the group are Phurbu and Tenzing, both Sherpas from Darjeeling. Our cook, Gokul, is Nepali, and our three high-altitude porters are from Kumaon—Soop Singh, Kamal Singh, and Dhan Singh. Kunzang explains that another fifteen porters are arriving tomorrow to help ferry loads up to base camp.

Suddenly, my fantasy of a small, compact team has expanded into the equivalent of a minor military campaign. It seems absurd that so many people have to be marshaled together to accompany me up the mountain. Documents from the IMF identify me as "team leader," but I feel immediately self-conscious and ambivalent about being the instigator of this elaborate operation. I'm not sure what I had imagined, but certainly not marching out of Sukhi at the head of a band of twenty-five men. Of course, mountaineering is very different from trekking, and my outfitters are experts in this field, so I quietly retreat to a room at the Sunshine Hotel, Sukhi's finest, awaiting word that the chief wildlife warden has signed our papers. His approval is essential, since our party will be passing through reserve forests, the protected habitat of rare species like musk deer, panthers, and bear. Obviously, he is a busy man, attending a Railway Board meeting in

Delhi to discuss recent collisions between wild elephants and express trains, and then rushing on to Ramnagar, where a tigress has been found dead in Corbett National Park. Compared to these crises, our expedition to Bandarpunch is hardly worthy of the ink in his pen. So, we wait at Sukhi another twenty-four hours until we are finally told that permission has been given and we can move forward.

Setting Off

Walking comes as a relief after sitting around and marking time. The porters' loads have been divided and they start off ahead of us, strung out along the winding trail that climbs 2,000 feet to the pass above Sukhi. In my haste to get moving, I take a wrong turn and find myself tangled up in barricades of thorn bushes along the terraced margins of potato fields. But, eventually, we are on our way, and the trail leads up toward a notch in the ridge, from where we will descend into the Son Gad gorge. Two years ago, I returned this way and finally got a signal on a borrowed mobile phone and spoke to Ameeta, who told me that my father had lost consciousness. The musk roses and spirea are blooming, but it is two weeks earlier in the year and none of the other flowers have appeared. The ache of memory eases as my muscles stretch. We stop for lunch along the way, having started at half past noon. By two thirty, we are at the pass. I remember finding a snake on this trail last time, a pit viper that someone had killed with a rock, its tail still coiling and uncoiling sluggishly with the dying reflexes of its nerves. The viper's brown and gray scales matched the mottled rocks on the path.

At the pass, Nandan and I sit together, waiting for the others to catch up. When I ask him how he got into mountaineering in Asansol, a mining and industrial city in the lowlands of West Bengal, he says he started rock climbing when he was a boy. "We have pure granite hills," he tells me. Nandan is a member of the Vivekananda Mountaineering Club. Last year he climbed Kamet, the third highest peak in India at 25,446 feet. But he complains that it was a "boring mountain" because they had to slog their way across miles of moraine to reach base camp. Only one section, a rock face above Camp 4, offered a serious technical challenge.

Nandan is built to be a rock climber, slight and compact, with an economy of movement in his limbs. His restless but attentive eyes look as if they could decipher the most cryptic rocks. This year, he applied to the Indian Mountaineering Foundation to be a liaison officer, as the post would give him a chance to climb more peaks. He plans to add Bandarpunch to his resume, though it is much lower than Kamet. Next year he hopes to tackle Everest, if his club can raise the funds. Their motto quotes Vivekananda: "Take a handful of soil from your home and carry it to the top of a mountain." In 1900, Vivekananda attended the world conference on religion in Chicago, one of the first interpreters of his faith to export Hindu teaching to the West. He founded the Ramakrishna Mission, which promotes Vedanta theology, perceived by many to be a "pure" strain of Hindu philosophy distilled from Sanskrit texts like the Bhagavad Gita.

From the pass, we drop into the valley on the other side, so today there is no net gain in altitude. I remember the steepness of this descent and the blood blisters that formed under my toenails, clambering down these slopes, glissading on pine needles and braking with my boots. After a while, the trail disappears altogether, and we find our way as best we can, eventually crossing a shepherds' bridge made of twigs. At the foot of the gorge we choose a campsite under a stand of fir trees. Last time, we camped farther up the valley, but this seems a better place to stop, with a spring nearby.

Gokul has spotted edible ferns sprouting near the spring, and he quickly sets about gathering them for dinner. The Garhwali name for these fiddleheads is *lingra*, which means "phallus." Most ferns appear after the monsoon begins, but here is an early crop. Gokul tells me that he grew up in the forests of western Nepal, where he learned to identify all kinds of wild vegetables and herbs. He claims he can even make a dish with dock weed, picking only the smallest leaves and cooking them with potatoes. He plucks another plant near our tents and tastes it, then spits it out, saying he mistook it for something else. Gokul has a boyish, infectious laugh. Though we speak in Hindi most of the time, his English is good, and occasionally he interjects comments that take me by surprise, saying, "Life is a struggle," or, nodding seriously, "I understand the situation." For dinner, he cooks a robust pasta with tomato sauce and lingra stewed in garlic. Watching him in the kitchen tent, I can see that he is a master chef of the outdoors, juggling pots and pressure cookers over kerosene stoves.

By any standards, this is a luxurious trek. The team pitches a Mountain Hardwear expedition tent for me, which I have all to myself, on a level patch of ground cushioned with fir needles and goat dung, where herdsmen have camped before us. On my earlier expedition to Bandarpunch I shared a tent with six other men, a claustrophobic intimacy that tested my solitary nature.

Dawn in the Valley

Next morning, I wake up early. Everyone is still asleep, and in the half-light I see three figures weaving their way down the hill through the trees. They are Gujjar herdsmen carrying twenty-liter jerry cans of milk on their backs. Every summer, these Muslim nomads migrate with their buffalos from the plains and foothills to high pastures in the Himalayas. Moving silently, they pass by our tents without stopping. Dressed in loose cotton *lungis* and black vests with plastic shoes on their feet, each of them has a neatly trimmed beard. As they race by me without a word, I see a drop of perspiration fall from one man's nose. They deliver milk every day to a roadhead three hours down the valley.

Before our team starts stirring, I have an hour to myself, sitting alone on a boulder below the tents. Here, amid the tall conifers and maples, looking up at a chevron of snow peaks, I listen to the wild rush of melt water in the river below. Each of the trees above me represents more than a human lifespan, but they have been here for only a fraction of a second in comparison to the soil that nourishes their roots and the rocks that give them purchase on the slope. Yet, even these mountains are not eternal. In the extended timeline of geological history, the Himalayas are relatively "young," though a thousand years of their existence is equal to a minute of my life.

This gorge is a fulcrum of tectonic change, where massive plates of rock converge and buckle upward, enormous slabs cantilevered one upon the next, where ancient continents are fused together. The Himalayas are accordions of stone, stacked by the slow pulse of time.

Drinking tea a short while later, I watch the porters huddle around a fire, baking chapatis on an iron skillet. In 2008, after our attack, police suspicion was directed to migrant laborers from Nepal. "Did they look Nepali? Did they sound Muslim?" we were asked. Yet these men, who have hauled our gear this far seem utterly innocent. They greet me cheerfully when I ask if they were warm enough last night. One of them grins and points to a cave in the rocks above us where they slept—true mountain hardwear. I see no trace of hostility in their faces, only the rootless poverty that drives them far from home to shoulder heavy loads for a daily wage.

We break camp after breakfast and set off up the right bank of the valley, through fir forest, pine, and yew, then into stands of birches. A species of white lilac is blooming, and I can smell its fragrance as my pack brushes the blossoms, scattering them on the ground. Farther on, Nandan discovers his first wild strawberries in an open glen. Though bright red, they have a dry texture and little flavor.

After traversing an old landslide, we stop to rest. Two Gujjar girls come down the trail carrying containers of buttermilk. Their camp lies across the river, over which they have built a seasonal bridge. Instead of crossing here, we keep to the right bank and continue climbing through groves of birches, where wild irises and rhubarb are blooming. At the head of the valley, we descend along a steep escarpment to a snow bridge. Above us is a waterfall that crashes down the cliffs before disappearing under a sheath of ice. This snow bridge is all that remains of a massive glacier that must have dominated this valley years ago. Atop the cliffs we can see the maw of the upper glacier, hanging there like fractured battlements of a frozen fortress.

Clouds have gathered as we cross the snow bridge, which creaks underfoot. As I clamber up the opposite slope, rain begins to fall. Gokul and I take shelter in a narrow cave under a giant boulder. Below us, we can see the porters crossing the snow, like a line of beetles moving over bauchy ice. When Kamal Singh joins us, he shows me a shard of mica he has found, peeling it apart and passing me a slice. Through its crystal lens, I can just make out the shapes of the mountains. And when I cup my hand around it, I stare into the reflective surface and see a faint mirage of myself. The mica reminds me of old glass negatives, scratched and faded but preserving fossilized images inside translucent leaves, tectonic chapters overwritten from the Carboniferous or Eocene age, a palimpsest of geological history.

Half an hour later, when the rain stops, we arrive at base camp—a sloping field of grass and rubble next to a stream—from where we can look back down the valley. Porters straggle in. One of them had to be sent back because he was suffering from altitude sickness. The rest shrug off their loads and quickly leave as soon as they've been paid, almost running down the trail.

Explorers and Forebearers

Bandarpunch was originally climbed in 1950 by Tenzing Norgay, who went on to higher summits, including the first ascent of Everest in 1953. John Martyn, headmaster of the Doon School, and Jack Gibson, his colleague and successor, led several expeditions to Bandarpunch before they succeeded. Both men had developed a fascination for this mountain. One of the youngest members of the first Doon School expeditions was Gurdial Singh, a history teacher, who went on to make his name among the first generation of modern Indian mountaineers.

A few months before setting off on our expedition, I met Gurdial in Dehradun, at the home of Nalni Jayal, an alumnus of the Doon School and former environment secretary of the government of India. Both men have climbed together on several expeditions, and Nalni now runs the Himalayan Trust, advocating ecological awareness. Gurdial, whose friends and students call him "Guru," tells me that he will turn ninety on January 1, 2014. Despite his years, he is a tall, imposing man, with a camouflage cap on his head. His memory remains sharp as an ice axe, recalling early attempts on Bandarpunch.

Their team approached the mountain from the southeast, walking from Mussoorie to Dodi Tal, then climbing onto the high bugyal meadows and working their way up through the watershed of the Hanuman Ganga. Through his connections in the Himalayan Club, Martyn recruited three Sherpas from Darjeeling for their expedition, one of whom was Tenzing. Gurdial shows me a photograph of the summit ridge taken by another Doon School master, R. L. Holdsworth. His Leica captured the stark dawn shadows, outlining snow and rocks against a sky that is almost black, the kind of image that digital photography cannot replicate. Gurdial's finger traces the route. "Martyn and the rest of our party got up this far and then turned back because it was too difficult, but Tenzing carried on to the summit."

He shakes his head in disbelief. "We had very little equipment. When I think of what we wore . . ."

Gurdial was inspired by mountaineering books in Martyn's and Gibson's libraries, classic accounts of Himalayan exploration by Shipton, Tilman, and Smythe. I ask if he had any training as a mountaineer, and he laughs. "We learned as we went along. After all, climbing is little more than putting on crampons and tying a few knots. In those days we didn't know what pulmonary edema was. We didn't know anything about acclimatization. We just kept going."

Though Gurdial didn't make it to the top in 1950, he returned to Bandarpunch twenty-five years later, in 1975. With an expedition from the Nehru Institute of Mountaineering, he successfully climbed the mountain by the route we are attempting.

"May I ask how old you are?" He fixes his eyes on me. When I tell him fifty-six, he nods. "Still young," he says. "You must tell me about the climb when you get back."

Several writers have identified Gurdial Singh, Roy Greenwood, and Dawa Thondup's climb of Trisul in 1951 as the advent of Indian Mountaineering. Nalni Jayal was also a member of this expedition, though he did not reach the summit. Gurdial, Greenwood, and Thondup were the second team to reach the top of Trisul, which was first climbed by Tom Longstaff in 1907. They approached the mountain through a section of the Rishi Ganga gorge, now part of the Nanda Devi sanctuary.

"It was perfectly still and clear on the summit," Gurdial tells me, "with a layer of clouds below us at 20,000 feet. I remember kneeling in the snow and changing a reel of film. I had an Agfa camera."

A famous photograph published in the *Himalayan Journal* shows him doing a headstand on the summit of Trisul. When I ask if he had planned it ahead of time, Gurdial shakes his head and smiles. "No, it was a spontaneous decision. Roy Greenwood had done a handstand, so I decided to do a headstand." The picture, taken by Greenwood, shows a carefree exuberance for the adventure of climbing and reminds us of an innocent age of mountaineering. Instead of planting flags or posing triumphantly on vanquished summits, Gurdial and Greenwood literally turned the heroics of the climb on its head.

Gurdial recalls: "A few years later when I went to teach for a year at Gordonstoun, the British Council asked me if there was anyone I would like to meet. Immediately, I mentioned Tom Longstaff. They arranged for a visit, and I went up to his home in Scotland by train and stayed the weekend. Longstaff told me how much he liked *gur* (raw cane sugar), though he couldn't pronounce it." Presumably, he had the same trouble pronouncing Gurdial's name. They compared notes on their climb of Trisul—two men of different generations and cultures, brought together by a mountain.

Willi Unsoeld was also a friend of Gurdial's. They met when the young American first came to India in 1949 and attempted Nilkanth. The two of them spent almost a month together, including a week in the Bhyundar Valley, climbing nearby ridges and photographing wildflowers. When Unsoeld returned to India in 1976 to climb Nanda Devi with his daughter, they had planned to get together in Dehradun. But after Devi died on the mountain, Unsoeld went straight back to America, and they didn't have a chance to meet.

Nalni Jayal recalls the Trisul expedition with Gurdial and a later expedition to Kamet. He is a gentle, self-effacing man, though responsible for tough administrative reforms that led to the protection of Himalayan environments, including the creation of the Nanda Devi biosphere reserve, which he has described as "a unique garden of the Gods." As we sit on his veranda, drinking tea and eating a mandarin orange cake that Gurdial has brought from his home in Chandigarh, stories of climbs and conquests give way to an ongoing appreciation for the natural history of the Himalayas. Nalni and Gurdial, along with Nalni's cousin, Nandu Jayal, the first director of the Himalayan Mountaineering Institute in Darjeeling, were all together on the Kamet expedition in 1952. The memory of that climb is marked not so much by daring adventures or life-threatening storms, but rather by the discovery of a rare flower, *Christolea himalayensis*, growing at an altitude of 20,000 feet, one of the highest signs of life in the world.

Blue Sheep

The day after we reach base camp, Phurbu, Titu, and several of the others set off on a load ferry to advance base camp. This will give them a chance to reconnoiter the route and assess what lies ahead. Though feeling strong and experiencing no ill effects of altitude, I decide to stay behind and acclimatize. Base camp lies at 12,000 feet. While impatient to keep moving, I reconcile myself to resting here and exploring the valley in which we are camped.

It is still early in the year for wildflowers, but we find plenty of herbs, including thyme and a species of allium with white, star-like blossoms. Known as wild garlic, its leaves have a pungent, oniony smell and taste. Yesterday, Gokul collected enough to make a vegetable dish mixed with potatoes. Armed with my camera, I wander about the rocks and meadows, crossing snowfields above our camp to reach the outer margins of the valley. Pikas, or mouse hares, populate the glacial debris, darting from one rock to the next. They are skittish animals, and I've never been able to get good pictures. But this time, with some patience, I am able to sit still, until their curiosity gets the better of them.

Three of these tailless rodents, which look like hamsters, come out to investigate. At first, they scurry back and forth, whiskers twitching irritably and sharp eyes fixed on me. Gradually, they grow bolder and do not seem to mind the camera. Their fur matches the colors in the rocks, a combination of rust and gray that makes them disappear the minute they stop. One of the pikas has a nick in his ear, where I imagine a predator has snapped at him. Mouse hares provide a steady diet for foxes and birds of prey, like the pair of black eagles that sweep overhead, wings dueling with the wind as they circle the cliffs, casting swift shadows on the grass.

The enforced idleness of acclimatization makes me restless. Though Bandarpunch itself is not visible, some of the lesser peaks crown the ridge above us. They look dangerously sharp and steep, even where the snow softens their rugged contours. Clouds scroll and unscroll off the ridges. Weather is our main concern. Though meteorologists in Delhi have predicted another two weeks before the monsoon arrives, the Himalayas often attract early storms, and clouds chase each other across the sky. Every time they close off the valley, I feel a discouraging sense of having arrived too late. The four days we lost waiting for permission seem crucial now, though we plan to stay on the mountain until June 21, which gives us a window of two weeks.

Wandering about, I keep an eye out for keeda ghaas, especially along the edges of the snow, where it is usually found. One of the strangest natural phenomena in these mountains, keeda ghaas (which means "insect grass") is actually a fungus that grows out of dead caterpillars. The insect, which matures into a species of ghost moth, has many unusual traits. In its caterpillar stage it is a voracious feeder, but as a moth it has no mouth. Some of these caterpillars become infected with fungal spores, which kill them before they are able to pupate. The following spring, as the snow melts, a thin, thread-like mushroom emerges out of the dead caterpillar's head and casts its spores in a parasitic cycle of rebirth. These caterpillar mushrooms contain a potent steroid and are used in Chinese medicine. According to some accounts, it is an undetectable ingredient in performance-enhancing drugs for Olympic athletes. A single piece of keeda ghaas can fetch four hundred rupees (eight dollars) and a kilo makes a man rich. Kamal Singh told me that he had recently been up at the Kuari Pass, and whole families were camped out there, searching for the desiccated remains. Though the conditions in the Son Gad valley were ideal for finding keeda ghaas, our searches went unrewarded.

A light drizzle begins to fall as I reach a cluster of boulders near the center of the valley. These huge blocks of granite are as big as pilgrim buses parked amid natural plantings of juniper, primulas, gentians, and marsh marigolds. From a distance, the giant rocks look as if they have recently broken off the mountain, but once I reach the spot, it is obvious that they were dragged here by an extinct glacier that melted long ago after exerting its natural engineering on the landscape.

The boulders are of different colors: beige and gray, dull green and red, flecked with silver and yellow. Veins of gneiss running through the rock look like seams of crystalized treacle. One of the boulders has a crack down the middle through which I can see the waterfall beyond our camp framed within the fissure. Everywhere is evidence of erosion, water's corrosive touch—its freezing and melting, its constant flow. Even the gentle moisture on the breeze, over centuries, can mold the hardest surfaces as if they were malleable clay.

Only a few birds appear, a dark blue whistling thrush like those that frequent our garden at Oakville, a white-capped redstart, flaring his tail to show off the russet rump that gives him his name. A couple of monal pheasants sail out of the rhododendrons higher up, while a flock of snow pigeons keep their distance from me. Whenever they take to the air, their wings are like gray-and-white prayer flags.

I am looking for bharal and finally spot them on a snowfield higher up along the western rim of the valley. In early summer, before the goatherds and their flocks arrive, these wild sheep have the new grass to themselves. For an hour I watch them graze above me, more than thirty animals altogether, both ewes and rams. Eventually, they drift toward a south-facing pasture four hundred yards from our tents. The wind carries my scent in the direction of the herd, and they seem wary but allow me to stalk them.

These hardy ungulates are one of the species that field zoologist George Schaller wrote about in his book, *Stones of Silence*. He was accompanied by Peter Mathiesson, whose memoir *The Snow Leopard* chronicles their journey into Upper Dolpo in Nepal. Bharal are favorite prey of snow leopards, and I can imagine one of those elusive cats watching this herd from the shelter of the rocks nearby. Though I don't find any evidence of large predators beyond a twisted lump of old scat full of bleached hair that has lain under snow all winter, the bharal seem alert to danger.

Hoping to photograph the bharal, I creep closer, aware that they can smell me but trying to hide my profile in the rocks. During the annual rut in the fall, as Schaller describes, bharal perform impressive displays of head butting and rump nuzzling, behavior that places them in an evolutionary bracket somewhere between sheep and goats. But at this time of year, they are more intent on feeding than procreation. Eventually, after watching the herd for an hour, I notice a movement below me on a snowfield to my right. A single ram, separated from the herd, is coming up the valley. With the wind at his back, he cannot smell me, though he seems alert and agitated. Crouched behind a rock at the upper end of the snowfield, I watch him approach. He pauses, then trots up the ice, tail raised to signal his unease. I lift my camera slowly, waiting for him to come closer. The ram is now thirty feet away, moving at an angle up the snowfield. As I switch on my camera, it makes a faint click and whirr. Immediately, the bharal's head is cocked, his large flared horns and ears at attention. With three quick bounds, he reaches a rock directly opposite me and stands there, indignant and afraid. His alarm call is something between a sneeze and a whistle, shrill as the shriek of a bird.

The bharal's coat is almost identical to the mouse hare's fur. Though called blue sheep, they are mostly gray. Patches on his nose and flanks are ruddy brown, as if reflecting mineral pigments in the rocks. Though he has not seen me yet, the lone ram confronts my hidden presence, every sinew of his body ready to race away into the safety of the cliffs. With striped garters and streaks of black on his white hindquarters, he looks as if he has been formed out of rocks, completely adapted to this harsh terrain. Finally, when he joins the rest of the herd farther up the slope, he lets down his guard and begins to graze.

By our third day at base camp, the bharal had grown so used to us that they wandered in among our tents just like the peaceable herds that Shipton and Tilman described in the Nanda Devi sanctuary, back in the 1930s.

Reflections on a Lake

Preparing for our expedition to Bandarpunch, I took several shorter treks, including a four-day hike to Dodital Lake and Darwa Pass. While my primary purpose was to get in shape, this trip allowed me to retrace the traditional route to Bandarpunch that Martyn, Gibson, Tenzing, and Gurdial took during the late forties and fifties. It was also the same trek my father made in 1950 with a group of friends, climbing the ridge in front of Bandarpunch. The photograph I have of him, standing on a grassy slope, looking up at the peak, was taken on that journey, when he was twenty-four years old.

Instead of walking all the way from Mussoorie, as others did in earlier days, I was able to drive to Uttarkashi and on to Sangam Chatti, where two branches of the Assi Ganga flow together. The year before, catastrophic floods had ravaged the valley, and it was barely recognizable from earlier visits. Buildings and bridges were washed away, as well as most of a hydroelectric project being built below Sangam Chatti. Accompanying me on this trek were my nephew Aaron and his friend Maura, along with Suman, a young man whose home is the village of Agora, below Dodital. Over the past few seasons, Aaron and Suman have been taking anglers trout fishing on the Assi Ganga, until last year's flood washed most of the fish away. This year, they had been given permission by the Forest Department to begin restocking the Assi Ganga with trout from Dodital.

Though the lake has become a popular tourist destination, we went up ahead of the crowds in mid-April, before the route opened for mules and trekkers. It remains one of the most beautiful walks in Garhwal, a steady climb through forests of oak and rhododendron, with showy red flowers covering their branches and littering the path. I left Agora ahead of the others and had the trail to myself, meeting no other human being over the four hours it took to reach the lake. Though I could see flood damage in the valley, as well as charred sections higher up from recent forest fires, the trail remained virtually unchanged from when the early Bandarpunch expeditions traveled this way. At Manji, a seasonal shepherd camp was deserted, except for a troupe of thirty langurs that watched me approach with cautious disapproval. A flock of yellow grosbeaks took to the air, as if a patch of marsh marigolds had suddenly been transformed into birds. Turning a corner, I flushed a monal pheasant that perched in a rhododendron tree, its plumage so vivid and varied it seemed as if his creator had used every color in her paint box to tint the bird's feathers. In a few places, patches of snow blocked the path, and streams were overflowing after generous spring rains. This was one of the happiest walks I've taken in years, alone beneath a canopy of fir and spruce, the silence broken only by the Morse code of woodpeckers drilling holes in dead trees.

When I reached the lake, the lone person there was a sadhu I'd met twelve years ago. He pointed out the damage from the flood where debris had washed in from the stream above. Though his temple and hut were undamaged and even the wooden bridge at the lower end of the lake had been spared, he showed me where a wave of water had washed out of the lake and contributed to the flood below. Describing the cloudburst that happened just before dawn, the sadhu said it sounded as if a dozen helicopters had flown down the valley.

We camped on the grass embankment below the Forest Department bungalow. Once the sun went down, it grew cold, the lake in shadow, its clear water the color of moss agate. Dodital was as still as the sky except where trout dimpled its surface. During the night, the dew on my tent froze and I could hear a crackling sound, as ice crystals puckered its synthetic skin. Next morning, when I crawled out, the grass was white and my tent was crisp as a sugared biscuit.

In his published account of the 1950 Bandarpunch climb, Gurdial Singh writes about Dodital, where they camped and rested for several days before confronting the mountain. "Fabulously rich in brown trout, it gave Mr. Gibson an opportunity of which anglers dream, and to us—the dreamers of a different sort of dream—the chance of feasting on trout cakes and 'gourmandizing' on trout in baked, boiled or fried form."

Brown trout are not a native species of the Himalayas. *Salmo trutta* were brought to Garhwal from Scotland a century ago. Aaron has researched their genealogy, and DNA testing traces the fish back to Loch Leven, one of the primary sources of trout for stocking throughout the British Empire. Though Forest Department records confirm brown trout have been swimming in these waters for a century or more, the exact process by which they arrived is still unclear. Whether eggs or fingerlings were carried by ship to India, a journey of several months, including the slow riverboat passage up the Ganga, and then transported by mules or porters into these mountains, it is hard to imagine how the translocation of this species was accomplished. One theory is that brown trout were brought here by the Himalayan entrepreneur and adventurer, Frederick "Pahari" Wilson. After deserting the East India Company Army, he supported himself by hunting musk deer in Garhwal and later cut a deal with the Maharajah of Tehri to fell timber in these mountains and float it down the Ganga. He is also credited with building the first bridge across the Bhairon Ghatti gorge so that pilgrims could reach Gangotri (after paying him a toll). Wilson spent part of the year in Mussoorie, where he acquired several properties by extending mortgages to British officers and then foreclosing on their loans. Kipling modeled his title character in *The Man Who Would Be King* on Pahari Wilson. It seems likely that the trout in Dodital and rivers downstream may have been brought here from Scotland by this imperial renegade, considered beyond the pale of colonial society because he married not just one, but two Garhwali women.

In the 1920s, a fish hatchery was built below Sangam Chatti, and my father talked of camping there on his way up to Dodital. For trekkers it served as an important landmark along this route, and I remember passing the old tanks in which the fingerlings were kept. Last year's flood has washed it away completely, leaving no trace.

After a long winter, the fish in Dodital were hungry and, between three rods, we landed more than a hundred trout in four or five hours. Most of these were let go immediately, with the rest retained for restocking. Our permits allowed only catch and release. For a fisherman, seeing a fish rise to a dry fly no larger than a speck of lint on a mirror can be a semi-mystical experience. As I removed the tiny hook from its jaw, the trout's eye watched me accusingly. Though called brown trout, they come in different colors, almost as varied as the butterflies that sailed along the shore. Some were pink and rose, others gold, saffron, and yellow, as if bathed in turmeric. Beneath the water's surface they had a muted green hue, but holding them in my palm, I could see the speckled skin, as delicately patterned as tie-dyed silk.

While Aaron continued fishing the second day, I went on up to the Darwa Pass. Twice before, I've been to this ridge. Both times the clouds have disappointed me, hiding Bandarpunch from view. A young man from Agora, Annu, came with me and we set off just after 7:00 a.m. The first section of the trail was buried under gravel and rocks washed down from the flood, but once we climbed out of the valley, I recognized the route. Annu had crossed the Darwa Pass a couple years ago, accompanying a party of trekkers, but he had no clear memory of the trail. His primary interest was making videos of himself on his mobile phone whenever we stopped to rest, dancing to Garhwali tunes with a Bollywood beat, then showing me the results on the miniature screen. I couldn't blame him for being bored but wished I'd come alone.

As we neared the top, skeins of cirrus drifted overhead, and I raced up the final approach to the pass, hoping I wouldn't get there too late. Runnels of snow filled the gullies and I scrambled up as fast as I could, reaching the cleft in the ridge where shepherds cross over into the Hanuman Ganga valley. The north side of the Darwa Pass was covered in snow, and there above me stood the two summits of Bandarpunch. Though only a few miles away as the crow flies, they looked higher and more distant than I had imagined. Still breathing hard from the climb, I dropped my pack in the snow and stood near the spot where my father rested in 1950, the same year Tenzing put his footprints on the summit.

Already, the clouds were closing in, leaving the peak visible just long enough for me to take a couple of photographs. Within a quarter of an hour, the mountain was gone. Staring into the white vacuum, I wondered if I would ever reach the top.

Fear of Falling

Sitting on the other side of Bandarpunch five weeks later and thinking back on my trek to Darwa Pass, I try to imagine what I will see from the summit, looking down instead of up. If it happens to be clear, I should be able to survey the Hanuman Ganga valley and maybe even catch a glimpse of Mussoorie. If it is visible, I will recognize Landour ridge among the other ranges unfolding toward the plains. But I am getting ahead of myself. First, we have to climb the mountain and overcome whatever obstacles it presents. More than likely, at this time of year, the peak will be cloaked in mist just as it was two seasons ago when twenty members of our group reached the summit.

My optimism quickly wanes as we begin the second load ferry to advance base camp (ABC). I find myself struggling up grass slopes that the bharal climbed with such obvious ease. In the end, I reach ABC, though the last fifty yards are even worse than the near verti- cal ascent below. Titu has warned me that this final section requires a fixed rope and, when I see it, I understand what he means. A snow chute rises from an angle of 60 degrees to almost 80, where it passes through a chimney in the rocks. For experienced mountaineers, this minor hurdle wouldn't appear particularly difficult, but for someone like me, who has never clipped on a carabiner or crampons, it seems absurdly steep and treacherous, particularly since there is a drop of several hundred feet below.

The others have a higher opinion of my climbing skills than I do. Phurbu has fixed a rope, which trickles down the ice, looking more like a fragile spider's thread than something I would entrust with my weight. Nevertheless, up I go without a harness or jumar, grabbing the lifeline with my left hand and kicking into the frozen slope. Even in the polarized vision of my glacier glasses, the snow is blindingly white. At points it feels as if I am climbing a blank wall without any handholds, a vacant surface as empty as the air behind my back.

At the top, I flounder over a crumbling lip of icy shale, like an exhausted trout flopping onto land, every ounce of resistance spent in a desperate struggle to survive. Only after ten minutes of gasping for air and lying still can I appreciate where I am. Advance base camp lies almost 3,000 feet above base camp, at roughly 15,000 feet above sea level. It is a broad balcony of rock and snow pitching down to a precipice that falls away to the southeast. Through the middle runs a stream of melt-water edged with mud. The only splashes of color are purple primulas growing out of the frost-singed grass. I can see where tent platforms were excavated for earlier expeditions. Rusty tin cans and other refuse lie about, as well as the remains of fires where garbage has been burned. Unlike base camp, ABC is a precarious perch without any protection from the wind, though Phurbu assures me it is safe from rockfalls and avalanches. We stay for an hour and stow our gear under a blue tarpaulin, held in place with heavy stones.

The descent is worrying me, for I know that going down will be as much of an ordeal as coming up. Suddenly, mountaineering has lost its appeal—the physical risks involved and the cumbersome choreography of hauling equipment and supplies, the tedious process of moving from one camp to the next—taking two steps forward and one step back. While popular imagination, including my own, has always celebrated the heroics of solo alpinists and summit parties locked in an eternal battle of man vs. mountain, the truth is that most major ascents, even alpine style, involve a complex system of logistics and support. Far from being a primitive, ascetic pursuit, mountaineering is a thoroughly modern enterprise that owes more to the industrial age than any primal passion.

Human beings are not designed to climb mountains. They require all kinds of technology to accomplish these feats. Ironically, supplemental oxygen is probably the only substance not invented by man that is carried to the summit. Beyond that, Gore-Tex, neoprene, carbon steel, braided nylon, and bottled fuels provide the essential elements of a climb. Overcoming the obvious limitations of our bodies isn't easy, whether it be extreme temperatures that freeze our fingers or a shifting center of gravity that is constantly being adjusted according to the line of ascent. I have enormous admiration for rock climbers and mountaineers, but nobody can convince me that their acrobatics aren't contrary to the evolution of our species. Bharal and other mountain goats or sheep have adapted to this landscape, while man is more suited to less vertiginous heights.

All of these thoughts and anxieties pass through my mind as I dig my heels into the snow and lower myself down the chute. This time I face outward, staring at the consequences of a fall. While we pick our way to the bottom, I keep worrying about the others as well as myself. Titu comes down the snow chute without holding the rope. Kamal Singh seems unaware of the drop below his feet, as he leaps from one rock to the next. Phurbu and Tenzing shadow me at the steepest points, placing their bodies between me and the drop, though one misstep would send the three of us cartwheeling down the ridge. I am putting myself at risk but also the other members of our team. While I keep telling myself to focus on not being a liability rather than achieving heroic stunts, there is also a nagging fear that I am responsible for the lives and limbs of those who accompany me. Climbing Bandarpunch, no matter how grand a goal it might seem, is a selfish objective, a personal indulgence that puts everyone at risk.

Burnt Offerings

This morning, before breakfast, Phurbu begins building a cairn of ten large rocks placed one on top of the other. The uppermost stone is tapered like an arrow, pointing toward the mountains. In front of this, he constructs a small stone altar, where he stacks a pile of dry twigs collected from around our camp. The shape of the cairn is similar to a Tibetan chorten, a tiered spire that also serves as an emblem of the peak we hope to climb.

Once Phurbu is ready, he calls us together for a pooja. Soop Singh has brought a tray on which are placed a husked coconut, an apple, and a pomegranate, along with cashew nuts and raisins. Each of the men has decorated the cairn with wildflowers, yellow buttercups, saffron potentilla, and white anemones. The fire is lit with birch bark tinder, and white smoke begins to billow up in loose strands, braiding itself around the cairn.

Phurbu settles himself in front of the altar. He props up a pocket-sized tryptich of Buddhist deities, at the center of which is a photograph of the Dalai Lama. Opening a well-thumbed prayer book, he begins chanting softly in a low voice, as steady and muffled as the stream that flows nearby. I sit beside him, listening and watching without comprehension and yet in complete awareness of the purpose of this ritual. We celebrate a simple harmony of elements—earth and fire, water and air—the stones, the flames, the burbling stream, and the clean, white smoke that makes the wind visible. During the ceremony, each member of the team assumes an attitude of devotion, though there is no formality. Some sit, some stand, one or two fold their hands. From time to time, Phurbu gets up and adjusts the burning twigs without interrupting his throaty incantations. I can see that others are praying too, lips moving silently in several languages.

Eventually, Phurbu gestures to Soop Singh and directs him to take out coals with a ladle and put them on a flat stone directly in front of the cairn. Then a sprig of juniper is placed on top and it begins to smolder. Each of us is called forward and we place more juniper on the fire. The smoke has a sweet, resinous fragrance, the purest incense in the world. Closing my eyes, I feel its warmth caress my face. Phurbu sprinkles tsampa flour and kernels of rice on the flames. He gives us each a pinch of tsampa, which we throw together onto the burning altar. Some of the nuts and other offerings consigned to the fire are wrapped in birch bark. Finally, Phurbu takes a cup of water from the stream and uses a juniper sprig to sprinkle water on the altar. With the same sprig, he anoints us each, after which we are given water in our palms to drink. Soop Singh distributes prasad, blessed fruit and nuts, as well as halwa. The entire ritual takes twenty minutes, though the burnt offerings and juniper keep smoldering for most of the morning. At the end, in deference to Hanuman's presence on Bandarpunch, everyone shouts "Jai Bajrang Bali!"

Until now, Phurbu has been reserved, almost silent. His age and experience give him a dignity that everyone respects, and it is clear that he is the strongest climber in our group, a guide and guru on the mountain. During the rituals, he assumes a different role, becoming our priest and spiritual mentor. Though I feel an emotional resonance in the rituals, I do not offer any prayers of my own aside from mute reverie. By participating in the ceremony, all of us have offered veneration to the mountains and the deities who guard their slopes, asking for protection and success.

Afterwards, Nandan says to me, "They worship nature?" I'm not sure if he means it as a question or a statement. But, either way, he touches on the truth. Phurbu's Buddhist rituals, like all religious rites, have roots in animistic traditions. Earlier, Nandan had asked me, "Are you a Hindu . . . ?" then quickly added, "or Christian?" I answered with my stock response: "I'm everything and nothing," a glib reply that avoids the question even as it pretends to be an answer. Yet these Buddhist ceremonies combined with Hindu gestures bring me closer to the mountain. Phurbu's prayers have mingled with the constant incantations of the stream. The white smoke has evaporated into the clouds. The fire dissolves into ash. Seeing the cairn silhouetted against a field of snow on the slopes beyond, I think of my father. He would have appreciated this moment.

The rituals are comforting, intended to give us confidence to face the mountain. Today, again, is a rest day, our final acclimatization before we move on up toward the summit. Most of the team spends the day playing cards, sorting equipment, washing socks, and lounging in their tents. I have brought two books with me, one of which is Robert Macfarlane's *Mountains of the Mind*, a history of man's fatal fascination with mountains. The book arrived the day before I left Mussoorie, the only fortuitous outcome of our delayed departure.

Macfarlane's writing is provocative and disturbing. His chapters on early European perceptions of mountains describe the way in which evolving theories of continental drift explained the geology of high places. It also explores an appreciation for the sublime, which attracted both scientists and poets—the fusion of beauty and terror. Interspersed with this are the author's personal reflections as a climber and an underlying sense of dread that mountains evoke. The deaths of mountaineers on Mont Blanc and Everest, as well as lower but no less treacherous crags in Scotland and Wales, remind me again of the risks we are taking. The soothing fragrance of juniper smoke has dissipated, and my feelings of foreboding return.

Idleness begins to play tricks with my mind, sweeping away the reassurance of Phurbu's prayers and replacing it with doubts. Though the others invite me to play cards, I spend most of the day alone. My impatience is getting the better of me, and this game of "carrying high and sleeping low," is wearing thin. At one point, marking my place in the book and getting up to stretch my legs, I go to the edge of the meadow and see that the snow bridge we crossed five days ago has collapsed. The swollen river gnaws at the ice. We will have to take another route home, circling down to the Gujjar camp and crossing their bridge. It shows how changeable the landscape is, and I wonder if the glacier above us is opening up.

The altitude hasn't bothered me so far, but lying down and reading, I begin to feel breathless. As soon as I get up and walk around, the feeling passes, and I wonder if it's nothing more than anxiety. The snow chute still worries me, triggering a recurring fear of falling that I can't shake out of my head. The weather remains ominous, and, by afternoon, it begins to rain. The prickling sound on the taut fabric of my tent is like dozens of clocks ticking at once, seconds dripping away, a persistent itch of time.

Clouded Dreams

During the early hours of the morning, well before dawn, I wake up suddenly out of a terrifying dream in which I am falling. Still half-asleep, I sit up in my sleeping bag, feeling as if the earth has dropped away beneath me. In this nightmare, which seems so real it leaves me breathless, I lose my footing on the ice and skid toward the drop below, picking up speed while dragging others with me on a rope. Before we hit the rocks, my eyes open abruptly in the darkness, a hollow, hopeless feeling in my chest. The rain has stopped, and the night is black and silent. I know that I am in my tent, yet the immediacy of the dream sharpens my anxieties. Wrapping both arms about my knees, I tremble with fear.

After several minutes I am also shivering from the cold. As dawn approaches, temperatures plunge. Rolling back into my sleeping bag, I know I am alive and secure, though a lingering uneasiness keeps me awake. Lying there, I wonder why I am doing this. There is nothing to prove. Already, this expedition has cost me more than my last ten treks combined, but the money doesn't matter, even if I can't afford it. Bandarpunch has personal associations and a sentimental link with my father, but I never intended climbing this mountain as a tribute to his memory. Tucked in my journal is an old black-and-white photograph of Dad, but I have already decided not to leave it on the mountain. The gesture seems contrived. It is better to leave nothing behind. Maybe it is better not to go at all. I remember my father's voice during our last phone call, telling me to be careful. *Don't take any chances.* His warning, broken up by static, echoes inside my inner ear.

By the time the meniscus of my tent has brightened to the point where I can see my hands, I have made up my mind to listen to my fears and head back home. Already I am calculating the return journey. Emerging from my sleeping bag like a fungus growing out of a caterpillar, I begin to gather my things together. By the time Kamal Singh brings me a mug of tea, I am packed and ready to leave. Despite the fact that twenty-five people have walked up here with me, I'm quitting; despite the fact that the Indian Mountaineering Foundation has gone through innumerable bureaucratic contortions to make this possible; despite the fact that the chief wildlife warden of Uttarakhand has finally signed our papers. All of this means nothing at this moment. I am completely content in my cowardice, happy at the thought that never again will I have to climb that treacherous chute of snow, or the pathways of ice that lie beyond.

Last time I had no choice but to leave our expedition early because my father was dying. Now it is my decision alone, my failure, my inadequacy. A while later, when I explain my fears to Kunzang, he tries to persuade me to change my mind. I assure him that I will cover the cost of the climb and honor the agreement I have made with his employers. But he seems less worried about that than other consequences. "I think we shouldn't have taken a rest day yesterday," he says. Maybe he's right. Twenty-four hours of sitting around, worrying about the dangers ahead, has made me lose my nerve.

Phurbu joins us, solemn-faced, as if his prayers and rituals have been called into question. The cairn he built still points toward the mountain, though the fire has burned out. He tells me that he believes I can make it to the summit. "You are fit and healthy. We will help you get to the top. We have a strong team. It's not so difficult as it seems, and we will take no risks." His eyes are full of honesty and concern, but I shake my head. By this time, I'm conscious of the absurdity of my fears and the confusion I am causing. I try to reassure Kunzang and Phurbu that it has nothing to do with the team.

The morning brightens, though heavy layers of cumulus surround the upper ridges. My nightmare has faded. Yet, a part of me is already on my way home, tracing a path down the opposite side of the valley, to avoid the snow bridge that has washed away.

Finally, after the others have talked among themselves, Nandan comes to my tent. He speaks with formality, assuming his role as liaison officer. If I am turning around, he says, then everyone must go back. He reminds me that I am the leader of this expedition, and his duty is to stay with me. Nobody can climb the mountain once I retreat.

As he speaks, I realize that my fears and doubts will destroy any chance the others have of climbing Bandarpunch. Just as it was a selfish decision to undertake this expedition in the first place, so will it be an act of placing my own anxieties before the aspirations of the team, even if I am a client paying them to help me get to the top. My weakness threatens their success.

ABC

With tents set up, advance base camp is more hospitable than my first impressions allowed, though the slopes across from us keep shedding rocks, which sound like firing squads. Volleys of boulders cannonade down the cliffs. Since our last visit, the bharal have been up here to investigate, leaving cloven hoofprints in the frozen mud. Looking down from the ledge behind my tent, I can see base camp three thousand feet below, but soon the clouds come spilling into the valley and fill it up with a dense white tide. It is almost as if ancient glaciers have returned to cover the valleys, a broad expanse of white that looks perfectly solid, though I know beneath those clouds it must be raining steadily. Above the storm, we can see other mountains, like islands separated by estuaries of emptiness. Beyond the ragged summits of the Gangotri Group, I recognize the sharp profiles of the Bhagirathi peaks overlooking Gaumukh. Shivling isn't visible, but amid layers of clouds, contours are precisely outlined, creating a depth of field that delineates distances. To the human eye, light shapes the mountains in an instant, just as water does over time.

Compromising with my fears, I have told the team that I will come up to ABC with them, and we will send a group ahead to explore the route, after which I will make up my mind to proceed or not. My second ascent up the grassy cliffs and snow chute was no easier than before, but I am relieved to be here. After a lunch of *khichdi,* Phurbu and Titu set off with a load of equipment to investigate what lies ahead, while Tenzing stays back to give me a climbing lesson in using crampons, jumar, and descender. He fixes a couple of ropes on an ice field above our camp before showing me how to get into my harness. I wear Koflach climbing boots, a lime green color, stiff and awkward. Though I was taught all this two years ago, I have forgotten the knots and the sequence of clipping and unclipping.

The difference between trekking and mountaineering is like the difference between snorkeling and scuba diving. With my boots and crampons there is a secure attachment to the ice, though they feel as unnatural as walking with flippers on a beach. The harness grabs me around the thighs and is cinched at my waist. Tenzing knots a nylon strap that extends from my navel to my chin like an umbilical cord to which a jumar is attached. This simple mechanism allows me to move up a rope, but stops me from sliding down.

Trying to reassure me, Tenzing says that this is how clients go up Everest on fixed ropes. His father has been to the summit five times "by five different routes," he tells me. Tenzing is the youngest in our group, though Nandan and Titu are about his age, all of them younger than my own children. This lesson in mountaineering is as much an effort to persuade me to keep going as it is a training exercise. Though I haven't agreed to attempt the summit, the others have made it their mission to get me to the top. Tenzing's solicitous lessons give me confidence. Soon I am going up and down a hundred feet of ice, clipping on carabiners and using the jumar. This is certainly better, I tell myself, than grabbing at a loose rope with one hand, while kicking at a frozen slope. I feel brave enough to lean back against the descender and rappel down the incline. The only point at which I feel uneasy is when my crampons scrape the rocks beneath the ice, losing traction for a moment or two. I remember Gurdial's comment about climbing being nothing more than learning how to tie a few knots and putting on crampons.

All of the signs today have been auspicious. Soon after we reached ABC, shafts of light broke through the clouds and a circular rainbow appeared above us. This perfect ring of light seems ethereal, encircling the sun with a faint halo of colors like an omen from heaven. Each person in our party offers a different interpretation. Some say the rainbow signals fair weather for the next few days. Others believe it means that temperatures will drop tonight, but everyone agrees it signifies good luck.

When Phurbu and Titu return, they seem confident that tomorrow we can reach our summit camp. From what they've seen so far, the glacier has shifted, but the ice cliffs appear passable. Phurbu sketches out a map on his palm, showing me how we will negotiate our way up the ice. His index finger traces a path along his lifeline, as if circling a crevasse. Aware of my uncertainties, he explains that most of the route is easy, without any serious obstacles. I won't need crampons most of the way. Because of the clouds, they were unable to explore beyond the ice cliff, but I remember photographs of the summit camp taken on our previous expedition. These showed a broad expanse of level snow, as flat and wide as a dozen football fields. When I ask Titu, he confirms that the campsite is completely flat, and from there it is more a matter of walking than climbing. Compared to the exposed ledge on which we are camped and the ascent from base camp, it seems easy going from here on up, though I remind myself to be realistic. We are above 15,000 feet which means we still have more than 5,000 feet to ascend. From behind my tent, I can see the snout of the glacier to the right. It is broken up into huge slabs of blue and gray ice, like shattered glass, though I imagine farther on, where it winds its way around the summit cone of Bandarpunch, it is like a frozen river, easily navigable on foot.

The pendulum of emotions on this trip has been extreme, taking me from hours of fear and depression to moments like this when our objective seems simple and well within my reach. Our plan is to set off tomorrow morning and camp by midday, after which we'll rest for ten or twelve hours. The final push to the top of Bandarpunch will begin soon after midnight so that we can get there by dawn. Within the next thirty-six hours it will all be over. Settling into my tent after dinner, I am relieved that the others persuaded me to keep going and happily embarrassed by my earlier misgivings. Their optimism has infected me with a sense of exhilaration and I fall asleep to images of myself walking across a placid moonscape of snow and ice, my headlamp casting a silvery glow, roped securely between two others, confidently advancing toward the summit.

Tom Longstaff, one of the Himalayan pioneers, wrote in his memoir, *This My Voyage*: "To know a mountain, you must sleep upon it."

Gathering Storm

Several hours later, thunder rouses me from dreamless slumber. I am confused at first because the sound comes from below us in the valleys and then above, beyond the reef of ice that we must cross tomorrow. Flashes of lightning illuminate the struts of my tent, and heavy rain begins to fall before dawn.

We have no access to weather reports, and our group isn't carrying a satellite phone, which the government of India does not permit, fearing espionage or terrorist plots in the Himalayas. Our mobile phones stopped receiving signals after we crossed the pass above Sukhi. There is no way to tell if this rain is the beginning of the monsoon or just a passing squall. When I unzip the flap on my tent and peer outside, the clouds are as thick as matted wool and my headlamp barely penetrates the gloom. Whatever cheery predictions we made yesterday, based on a rainbow encompassing the sun, have been disproved. Just as I am about to zip shut the tent, something dashes through the mist, silent as a ghost, a sooty figure on four legs. The bharal are here to visit us, scavenging for salt and kitchen scraps. A young ram with stubby horns floats out of the mist, his wet fleece bedraggled, but shining eyes fixed on me, as if I am the interloper. Seconds later he flees the camp, followed by a dozen others. The bharal seem to leap away into nothingness, plummeting headlong down the cliffs.

Sheets of rain wash over my tent, which tugs at its ropes as the wind tries to uproot us. The lightning has ended, but there is distant thunder from all sides, as if the mountains were shuddering at their foundations. I can hear rockfalls too, dislodged by the rain. Even if I were to try counting wild sheep, it wouldn't send me back to sleep.

Two hours later, Phurbu confirms what I already know. We will have to wait another day because of the storm. For some reason, it doesn't worry me anymore, and I am content to lie here within my dry cocoon. I could be anywhere on earth. The Himalayas have vanished in the clouds, and this rocky patch of soil beneath my air mattress could just as easily be the prow of an ancient continent drifting toward another. Eons tick away instead of seconds. It doesn't matter how long we wait. The mountain will always be there.

Hours later, I sense that the wind has changed direction and the downpour eases. All of us emerge and gather for tea as clouds swirl about, taunting us with vaporous fingers. Gradually, it seems to be clearing, and Phurbu decides that he will take more equipment up to the glacier and try to fix a rope on the ice cliff below our summit camp. This will save us time tomorrow, he explains. What he doesn't say is that the monsoon has arrived, and we will soon be locked into a cycle of storms that offer only brief windows in which to climb.

Kunzang and Tenzing decide to go with him, along with Titu and Nandan. They ask, half-heartedly, if I would like to join them, but I can tell that I will be an impediment from here on up. I'll wait until the ropes are fixed. They set off slowly up the slope, a string of figures that grow smaller and are hidden for a while among the rocks, then reappear on a snowfield higher up. Folds of mist converge around them. They look as if they are walking on the clouds, before they vanish altogether.

Sitting with Soop Singh and Dhan Singh by a kerosene stove, we boil water to make tea and eventually prepare a simple lunch. Gokul is unusually silent and lets the others speak. Dhan Singh tells me that he comes from Loharkhet, the roadhead for the trek to Pindari Glacier, where I've been many years ago. He nods and smiles as I try to recall the stages of that trek—the forest rest houses at Dhakuri and Phurkiya, where we camped as a family in 1976. Dhan Singh corrects my memories of the trek and tells me there is a new route now, from a village called Khatti. "You can reach the glacier in just two days," he says. Soop Singh confirms this, telling me he's done the Pindari Glacier trek with several groups. His village is located in the same district, Bageshwar, but on the other side of the valley, toward Almora and Ranikhet. I ask if there are any tea estates nearby, but he shakes his head and says only apple orchards, though the crop is disappointing. Like their fathers and grandfathers before them, Dhan Singh and Soop Singh have no choice but to find work away from their families and villages in Kumaon. Even a hundred years ago, harsh conditions in this region forced men to leave their homes and join the army or seek employment in the plains. Being high-altitude porters and camp staff is an uncertain business, but whenever there is work, it pays relatively well. I ask if they enjoy their work, and both men smile and shrug, as if to say, *It's a job, nothing more or less.*

When the others don't return, I begin to worry, though Dhan Singh laughs when I suggest they might be in trouble. We wait until three o'clock to eat lunch, but still there is no sign of them. Whenever the clouds part, I study the snowfield where I saw them last, waiting for our team to reappear. Finally, around five, I spot a figure coming down alone. Minutes later, two more men appear, and within half an hour everyone is back in camp. Tenzing is the first to arrive. Before I can ask him how it went, he makes a gesture of frustration, throwing up both hands and waving in the direction of base camp.

"All of us will have to go back," he says. "There's no way up!"

Drinking hot lemon juice to revive themselves, they describe how they crossed the lower end of the glacier without any trouble, then fixed ropes on the ice cliff and started up. But instead of finding open fields of snow where Titu and the others set up camp two years ago, more ice cliffs and crevasses blocked their route, some of the crevasses fifteen to twenty feet wide. What used to be a featureless plateau of ice is now a fractured snowscape, impossible to cross without the right equipment. The glacier has broken up. "We would need ladders and much more rope," Kunzang tells me. "And ten more days, even if the weather clears." Titu and Tenzing have taken photographs, which they show me, revealing gnarled palisades of seracs and broad lesions in the ice, where bergschrunds have separated from the slope. "To climb down one side and up the other would take all day ... very technical and dangerous," says Phurbu, in case I have any illusions of arguing with him. For a brief moment, I wonder if they are exaggerating the risk to give me some sense of consolation before we turn back, but their exhausted faces do not suggest anything other than the truth. We have no choice but to abandon our attempt on Bandarpunch.

Consolation

Proverbial wisdom tries to convince us that important lessons accrue from failure. I suppose there is some truth in the idea that we learn more from disappointments than successes. For me, a subdued sense of resignation follows defeat. I do not think I will ever try to climb a mountain again, at least not one as high as Bandarpunch. The passion and drive that brought me here have abated. My encounters with the Himalayas will continue but at lower altitudes and under less severe conditions. I feel as if I am closing a chapter of my life before it has begun. But there is still the journey home, which remains half of the experience. Even in retreat, we must look ahead.

Rain returns during the night, and we have to wait until it stops before packing up camp and starting our descent. The morning is damp and depressing, but I feel a strange sense of calm as we bundle sleeping bags and pull up tent pegs. My earlier fears and premonitions may have been vindicated, but I am not concerned about being able to return home with a valid excuse for not climbing the peak. Instead, there is a recognition of having pushed as far as we could and knowing, despite the outcome, that our efforts were not wasted. Though it may seem as if everything we have invested in this expedition—physical and material resources, as well hopes and expectations—has been forfeited in a futile venture, this is not the case. Fulfillment comes from knowing that correct decisions have been made and whatever we have attempted has been undertaken to the best of our abilities. Even my personal weaknesses and fears seem consistent with a purpose greater than reaching the top: accepting defeat, but also accepting the limits that our minds and bodies will endure.

Most important of all is our encounter with the mountains and a renewed understanding of their magnitude, the beauty and danger of their sublime countenance. Each of us takes away something from the expedition—friendships, photographs, stories, new names for plants and animals. But there is also a deep respect and deepened reverence for high places.

We collect our garbage, as well as littered refuse left behind by earlier groups, and burn it in a shallow trough. Whatever we cannot set on fire will be carried back down the hill. The team is meticulous despite the rain, and everyone casts about for paper or plastic that might have been scattered by the wind. With the rain still falling, a generous amount of kerosene is used to keep the fire going. Burning up the excess fuel will also lighten our loads. Unlike the flames at Phurbu's altar that gave off fragrant white smoke, these burnt offerings send up black banners of defeat. Amid the drizzle and clouds, I watch the flames consume a cardboard carton that Gokul carried up.

Before our departure, he makes an enormous breakfast including a seventeen-egg omelet, all in the interest of reducing weight for our descent. The equivalent of three load ferries has to be taken down the hill. As Phurbu says, "Nobody wants to climb back up here again." The final gesture before we start down is leaving mounds of salt and flour on the rocks, so that the bharal will find something to eat when they return.

We go down slowly and Phurbu is the last in line, collecting the anchors and fixed rope. I am spared a heavy pack, but everyone else carries more than eighty pounds, double a normal load. Disappointment at turning our backs on the mountain shows on the faces of my companions "Hanuman has hidden his tail," Kunzang says with a rueful shrug. Halfway down, as some of us are resting on a scarp of moraine, Gokul regains his sense of humor. He sings out in English from above us as he lumbers down, under a lopsided pack: "I am a donkey, you are a monkey!" Everyone begins to laugh hysterically, as if it were the only joke we've heard for days.

A short while later, there is more slapstick humor when Kamal Singh and Dhan Singh decide to take a shortcut down a snowfield, still hoping to find keeda ghaas. They plan to slide their heavy packs in front of them. But before they can accomplish this, both men slip and the rest of us watch them tumbling and sliding down the ice, along with duffle bags and empty jerry cans—a comical reenactment of my nightmare. They slide three hundred feet or more, but both men land safely in a heap at the edge of a stream.

Departure

On our last evening at base camp, we have a feast. Phurbu and Tenzing make *momos* and *thukpa*, while Gokul bakes a cake, frosting it with the message, "See you again, Steve." Next morning, three of us leave—Titu, Soop Singh, and myself. We will go ahead and contact the porters, who are expecting us to return next week. As we say farewell after breakfast, Phurbu presents me with a white scarf, placing it around my neck. Email addresses and mobile phone numbers are exchanged, though none of these have any relevance here. After two weeks together, we embrace and part, promising to meet again in Mussoorie or Delhi.

Our trail takes us around the south side of the valley, angling across steep meadows to the Gujjar camp. We stop for a brief conversation with two of the herdsmen, tall imposing men with regal profiles and thick beards. Their huts are flimsy shelters. Women are churning butter while barefoot children eye us curiously from behind strips of torn plastic spread over bamboo frames. All of them are members of a single extended family. Their winter home is in the Shivalik foothills south of Dehradun. Each spring they travel with their herds, following an old mule track near Mussoorie and crossing over at Suokholi, the same route that climbers used to take before the motor roads were built. How much longer these nomads can continue this annual migration it is hard to know, but here in the Son Gad watershed they have reached the high meadows that will sustain them and their sixty buffalos for another season. The older man, about my age, with a white beard and a loose turban, asks me, "Why do you people try to climb these mountains . . . Is it to take photographs?" The answer I give him is that we are possessed by a kind of craziness or *pagalpan*, as well as *shauk*, a word that means both sport and passion. He looks skeptical, and we laugh together.

After crossing a bridge of birch boughs below their huts, we keep moving quickly down the valley. A few hours later, climbing out of the Son Gad gorge, we pass another abandoned Gujjar camp beneath a grove of wild hazelnut trees that lap at the moist air with their serrated leaves. Though the sky is overcast, it doesn't rain until we cross the pass. At first the drops aren't heavy—a fine mist that beads the hair on my forearms, though the rain gathers force as we descend. At moments, I feel a slow sadness gathering like the clouds in the valley, my emotions as changeable as the climate. Have I forgotten something, left something behind? Far below me, I can see the rooftops of Sukhi and the motor road where a pilgrim coach maneuvers around a hairpin bend.

Our journey is almost over, yet none of us could have predicted what happens next.

Flooded Mountains

Within twenty-four hours, the rain becomes a torrential monsoon storm that lasts for three days and three nights without cessation, dumping four times the normal rainfall, almost sixteen inches (400 millimeters) of precipitation every twenty-four hours, setting a record for the month of June. Rivers rise more than fifty feet, gouging out long sections of the road. A huge reservoir in the sky has burst its banks, inundating the Central Himalayas in a sudden onslaught of moisture. Homes collapse and fields are washed away. Villagers flee to higher ground, only to find the ridges above them sinking into the valleys. Hotels built along the banks of the Ganga are torn from their moorings and swallowed by the flood. Statues of Hindu gods made out of reinforced concrete are swept away in the relentless current. Billboards fall like playing cards, and whole sections of riverside towns disappear into the Ganga. For some it must seem like the end of the world. Others never know what hit them and are killed instantly beneath mudslides or drowned in their sleep. The devastation is made worse because of poor planning, shoddy construction, badly engineered roads, and jerry-rigged guesthouses, most of them illegal, where pilgrims crowd together for shelter, as many as twenty or thirty in a room. Roofs collapse, walls implode, and foundations drop away into whirlpools. Ninety-three bridges, some of which have stood for more than a century, are consumed by the rivers they span. Water rises so high that pylons on either side are ripped free from the rocks. Buses and cars are carried away in the flood, tossed about as lightly as flotsam. Power lines and telephone cables snap, and communication towers fall. Trees are torn from the earth, and whole sections of the mountains slough off, avalanches of earth and forest.

Unaware of what is coming, Titu and I hire a jeep from Sukhi and drive downriver through heavy rain for most of the night, escaping only a few hours ahead of the flood. By the time we reach Mussoorie, much of the Bhagirathi valley is cut off. If we had continued with our attempt on Bandarpunch, we would have been stuck on the mountain in the storm. Suddenly, our expedition and adventure becomes meaningless, set against the cataclysm of the flood. All of the four main sources of the Ganga and their temples, visited by hundreds of thousands of pilgrims each year, have become totally inaccessible. The worst damage is at Kedarnath, where a glacial lake bursts a couple of miles above the temple, sending a deadly slurry of mud and rocks streaming into the heart of the pilgrim complex, burying rest houses where yatris lay asleep, filling rooms to the ceiling with dirt and debris. The main temple, made of stone, remains undamaged, though all around it every other structure is flattened.

Four days go by before I am able to contact our team. When I finally get through to Nandan's mobile phone, he reports that they have been able to reach Sukhi but are now stranded, along with thousands of pilgrims who had been visiting the Gangotri shrines. Every day the newspapers and television carry more and more disturbing stories of settlements vanishing and walls of water carrying away everything in their path. Rescue operations begin. The army and air force are called in to carry food and water to the region, while bringing out the elderly and injured. Helicopters fly back and forth, but the huge number of people makes it an impossible task, especially with the rain still falling. Corpses are buried under mudslides or washed down into the rivers. Nobody knows for sure what the death toll might be, but estimates rise quickly into the tens of thousands.

Finally, twelve days after abandoning our attempt on Bandarpunch, we get word that Kunzang and the rest of the team have reached Delhi. While stranded, they assisted with the rescue operations, using their ropes and mountaineering equipment to help yatris negotiate the hazardous route out. Eventually, after walking to Uttarkashi, they were able to get transport home. Gokul calls me the day after they escape. It is a relief to hear his voice and familiar laugh. When I ask if they are all okay, he says, "Of course! Why, were you worried about us?"

Invoking Tragedy

The devastation in Uttarakhand was headlined as a "Himalayan Tsunami" by journalists and politicians hard-pressed to describe the scale of destruction. The comparison is not far-fetched, for huge waves of water poured down the valleys. Narrow gorges added to the velocity and force of the current, which had nowhere else to go. Though the violent storms took everyone by surprise, there was nothing new about these floods. Only a year before, the Assi Ganga overflowed and washed out sections of Uttarkashi. Similar catastrophes have occurred in the past. In 1978, a landslide near Gangnani blocked the river for a couple of days before it burst and swept away parts of the towns and settlements downstream. Hundreds died, and survivors were said to be picking fish out of trees as if they were fruit. In 1880, Pahari Wilson, who built his palatial home in Harsil and floated deodar logs down the Ganga, was rumored to have drowned in a similar flash flood on the Bhagirathi. He was presumed dead and his obituaries appeared in the papers. A week later, however, Wilson came sauntering down the Mall Road in Mussoorie, just as his two wives had gone into mourning.

The people of Garhwal are familiar with these natural disasters, which often happen at the outset of the monsoon along smaller streams as well as major rivers. What made this flood so catastrophic was the uncontrolled expansion of towns and settlements near the river banks. Over the past two decades low-lying areas in the Ganga's watershed were converted into yoga ashrams, eco-retreats, vedic resorts, and labor colonies. All of these lay in the path of the swollen torrent. Added to this, the ever-increasing volume of pilgrim traffic has multiplied in recent years—an annual deluge of devotees from the plains seeking Ganga's blessings. In hindsight, a great deal might have been done to limit the damage and suffering, but the flood itself was as inevitable as earthquakes, a violent process of erosion that has, over countless epochs, created these valleys and sculpted the mountains.

Of course, none of this mitigates the loss of life and property that occurred during the 2013 Uttarakhand floods, but as I read or listened to news reports and heard helicopters flying over our house in Mussoorie, I couldn't help but think of the bones at Roopkund. Five hundred years ago, an anonymous party of pilgrims died in the Himalayas seeking a path to god. Since then, many others have lost their lives, including victims of altitude sickness at Mount Kailash, their spiritual quest ending in physical anguish and mortal finality. There will always be those who ascribe these deaths to the vindictive fury of deities like the goddess Nanda. But invoking divine retribution for the collective sins of modern society is a simplistic, ignorant explanation that defies reason and belittles faith.

In the wake of the floods, the Raj Jaat Yatra, the royal pilgrim-age of Nanda Devi was canceled, partly in deference to those who were killed but also because damaged roads made much of the route inaccessible. Three months after the natural disaster, spontaneous myths began to circulate about shrines that were spared and miracles of survival sustained by devotion and prayer. Despite these fatalistic interpretations of events, we must understand that the mountains lie beyond our control no matter how many terraces, temples, roads, or dams are built. Instead of trying to tame and subdue the Himalayas, we must approach them with compassion and logic as well as consid-eration for the intangible mysteries of faith. Rather than conquering and colonizing high places, or laying claim to precarious territories while destroying the natural bounty of these ranges, we must become like the mountains instead, part of something much greater and infi-nitely more eternal than ourselves.

Reaching for Closure

On the wall of my study is a watercolor painting by my art teacher, Frank Wesley. He gave it to me in 1974, when I graduated from high school. It is a miniature, roughly three inches by five inches. From a distance, the painting looks like a dark rectangle of the deepest blue, almost black. Only when you observe the painting closely does the scene reveal itself, a mountain landscape at night. As your eyes adjust to the subtle shades and contours on paper, it is possible to make out a series of forested hills unfolding toward a distant ridgeline that blends into the sky. The night is moonless but several stars appear, even a dot of firelight from a village on one of the slopes enveloped by darkness.

This painting has stayed with me from the day I got it, and I have always hung it in my study wherever we have lived—Delhi, Hawaii, Cairo, Boston. Now it is back on my wall in Mussoorie. Frank was born in Azamgarh, in western Uttar Pradesh. He trained in Bengal, Japan, and America, then finally settled with his family in Australia. Most of his work is rooted in India, and he is best known for having painted images of Jesus and other Biblical figures within a rural Indian context. During the time he taught at Woodstock, both Ameeta and I were his students, and it was the only class we took together. Many of Frank's paintings are large works in oil and acrylic, but his miniatures are the pictures I appreciate most. He was an outdoorsman as well as an artist, and his work expresses a close understanding of natural history. Even in the dark pigments of the painting on my wall, the Himalayan trees are easily recognizable, banj oaks and chir pines.

Though Frank may have painted these mountains from his imagination, I have always located this scene as the view from Flag Hill on a clear night, looking out over the ridges above Patreni in an easterly direction. Exposing barely any light, the painting remains enigmatic, a dark riddle of indigo and midnight blue. Yet details become visible through careful observation, faint lines of terraced fields near a village in the forest, where the artist's brush has picked out the color. Frank taught us this technique, which he called a Lucknow wash—soaking the paper and then covering it with successive coats of paint. As the paper dried, he removed some of the color using a brush dipped in water, creating areas of brightness that emerge from beneath the painting's surface.

Whenever I look at this miniature, I can feel the darkness surrounding me, the enclosing solitude of night in the mountains. Though much remains hidden, we can see things after sunset that are invisible during the day—the stars, of course, but also the layered shadows of foliage and rock, muted colors that emerge after dusk. And the black profile of a tree that is lost among others during the day. This nocturnal scene suggests much more than it reveals; illuminating my presence in the picture like a shadow hiding behind a veil of light.

⁓

Climbing Flag Hill in the dark, my feet kick up pieces of flint that spark underfoot. Early in the morning, an hour before dawn, a lopsided moon hangs above Landour. Its light is barely enough to silhouette the ridge. As I weave my way through a steep maze of limestone boulders, brambles tug at my jeans. Whenever I turn off my headlamp after checking the path, I have to wait for my eyes to adjust, pupils dilating while the ridge regains definition. On this walk, I am guided by memory as much as sight. To the east, I can see only blackness except where the sky contrasts faintly with the farthest mountains beyond Nali and Surkanda Devi. Scattered constellations of electricity mark distant villages while the Dehradun valley to the south is a shimmering galaxy of lights. There is no sign of daybreak, but the birds have already sensed the morning. A collared owlet is calling . . . its flute-like ellipsis punctuating the night. A whistling thrush screeches and then sings uncontrollably like a needle sliding across vinyl. Sibias stammer and chirp, and a koklass pheasant crows loudly down the slope. None of the birds is visible in the dark, but their cries give shape to the forest around me. It is late September once again. Bar-headed geese will soon begin crossing the Himalayas southward, retracing the flyways above Flag Hill, their soft honking like plaintive voices, almost human.

I have come here by myself but do not feel alone. By the time I reach the wind-bent deodar tree on the shoulder of the ridge, I can just make out the prayer flags waving from its branches, a spiritual semaphore signaling rescue. The stars have been extinguished by loose layers of clouds. As I walk toward the top of the hill, I can smell the dawn before I see it, a sour-sweet infusion of dew and dead leaves, the resinous sap from the pines, musty spores of ferns curling up and turning brown. All five senses converge, as my feet find a path in the dark and I hear my way through the trees. My sixth sense is also alert but suggests no danger.

This year, conservationists set up a series of camera traps on Flag Hill to capture images of the wildlife in this forest. A barking deer grazed in the leafy shadows. A young goral sniffed at the rocks where I often sit and watch others of his kind grazing on the slopes to the north. A man from Kolti village tripped the camera as he walked by, carrying a gunny sack full of pine cones. Ten minutes later, according to the digital imprint on the pictures, a long, curved tail and spotted haunches appeared in one frame, following the villager's footsteps. At a second camera, two hundred yards farther on, the leopard stopped and took his own portrait, sitting in the middle of the path with a look of supreme indifference. His rosettes and golden fur caught the evening light. Climbing Flag Hill this morning I could have set off a dozen camera traps, flashing my own image in the dark, but nobody is watching, except perhaps the leopard following in my tracks.

Frank Wesley's painting surrounds me with layered shades of indigo. Wet ferns brush my legs, and the mountains wash away into darkness. Solitude is accompanied by the whisper of prayer flags on the breeze, bodhisattvas dissolving into clouds, wind horses chasing a storm, conch shells echoing silent tides of the Tethys Sea. . . . I find the rock I always sit on, cushioned by moist grass. The sky to the northeast is a fraction brighter than it was a moment ago, and the clouds are tinged with silver and bronze. Mountains stand like unread myths upon a bookshelf. My pupils contract with the dawn. An itch runs up my arm from the scar on my wrist. I breathe in light and air . . . as our teacher's paintbrush rinses out the night.

Acknowledgments

Many people assisted me in completing the journeys I have described. In addition to those who are mentioned in the book, I would like to thank Rabi Thapa of Sacred Summits, Sunil Kainthola of Mountain Shepherds, Chewang Motup and Yangdu Goba of Rimo Expeditions, and Krishnan Kutty, director of the Hanifl Center for Outdoor Education and Environmental Study at Woodstock School. Winterline Foundation has generously supported the Mussoorie Writers' Mountain Festival, which has allowed me to explore the Himalayas through the words and images of many remarkable writers, mountaineers, and artists. Subhadra Sengupta sent me Indra's advice to Rohita, for which I am grateful. Special thanks to Shibani Alter, our daughter, who is my technical advisor on all things digital, and to Jayant Alter, our son, who helped outfit my expeditions with the latest and lightest gear. I am grateful to Jill Grinberg, my literary agent, who encouraged me on this project from the beginning. Many thanks to Cal Barksdale, executive editor at Arcade, and David Davidar, publisher of Aleph.

A condensed version of the chapter "Recovering Memory" appeared in *Outlook* magazine in 2009.

Permission to quote from the following sources is gratefully acknowledged:

Blackberry Books for the poem by Nanao Sakaki from *How to Live on Planet Earth: Collected Poems of Nanao Sakaki* (2013).

"View from a Train" by Stephen Spender from *New Collected Poems*, published by Faber & Faber, 2004. Reprinted by kind permission of the Estate of Stephen Spender.

Mamang Dai for her poem "Voice of the Mountain" from her collection *The Balm of Time*.

Glossary

ananda: happiness, contentment

Avalokiteshvara: Buddhist deity of infinite compassion

"Bam Bam Bholey!": Hindu slogan in praise of Shiva

Bauji: colloquial form of "babuji," an honorific denoting age and learning

bergschrund: crevasse where glacial ice separates from a mountain slope

bhajan: hymn

bharal: Himalayan blue sheep, *Pseudois nayaur*

bindi: cosmetic dot worn on the forehead by women

Bon, Bonpo: ancient shamanistic tradition in Tibet predating Buddhism

bugyal: high meadows

chaan: seasonal shelter built by herdsmen

chakkar: circuit: the chakkar road in Landour circles the top of the hill

chorten: Tibetan shrine containing relics, with tiered roof and a dome

chuba: full length, wraparound dress worn by Tibetan women

dakini: celestial nymph in Tibetan mythology

darshan: being in the presence of, or observing the divine

descender: mechanism used in mountaineering for descending on a rope

Ganga: Ganges river

gompa: Tibetan monastery and religious complex

goral: goat antelope, *Naemorhedus goral*

Gujarat: Western state of India bordering Maharashtra

Gujjar: Muslim herdsmen who migrate to the Himalayas in summer

"Jai Bajrang Bali!": Hindu slogan in praise of Hanuman

jumar: mechanism used in mountaineering as a secure brake while climbing a rope

kakad: barking deer, *Muntiacus muntjak*

keeda ghaas: "insect grass," a fungus that grows out of dead caterpillars, used in Chinese medicine

khichdi: rice and lentils cooked together

khukuri: Nepali knife used by ghurka soldiers as a weapon and for ritual sacrifices

kora: Buddhist term for sacred circumambulation

lung-gom: trance walking

lungi: unstitched lower garment wrapped around the waist

Maharashtra: Western state of India bordering Gujarat

mandala: sacred diagram of the cosmos

mani stones: stones with carved prayers, often *"Om mani padme hum,"* in praise of the sacred jewel in the lotus.

Manjushree: Buddhist deity of enlightenment

momo: steamed or fried dumpling filled with vegetables or meat

NRI: Non-Resident Indian

Om: sacred syllable chanted by Hindus and Buddhists in prayers and meditation

"Om Namah Shivaya!": Hindu slogan, "In the name of Shiva!"

padyatra: pilgrimage or symbolic journey on foot

parikrama: Hindu term for sacred circumambulation

pathal: cleaver

pika: small rodent commonly found in the mountains, also known as mouse hare

pooja: rituals of worship, both Hindu and Buddhist

prasad: sanctified food given to devotees during rituals

Raj Jaat Yatra: royal or major pilgrimage of Nanda Devi, held every twelve years

shakti: feminine power; the force or energy of female deities

shikar: hunting

Tantric: mystical and occult practices in Hindu and Buddhist tradition

tapasya: acts of devotion, penance and self-abnegation

"Tashi Delek!": Tibetan greetings, meaning "Blessings and good luck!"

terma: hidden scriptures or ritual objects representing ancient teachings

tertons: Buddhist saints and teachers who are blessed with the ability to discover scriptures and sacred objects hidden by earlier teachers

thukpa: flat noodles, often served with meat and sauce

trishul: trident

tsampa: roasted barley flour, often mixed with butter tea, a staple diet in Tibet

Yama: god of death and lord of the underworld

yatra: journey or pilgrimage

Sources

Aitken, Bill. *The Nanda Devi Affair*. Delhi: Penguin, 1994.

Atkinson, E.T. *The Himalayan Gazeteer*. Delhi: Cosmo, 1973 (First ed.,1886).

Avedon, John. *In Exile from the Land of the Snows*. New York: Vintage, 1986.

Chatwin, Bruce. *The Songlines*. London: Vintage, 1998.

Conze, Edward, et al., *Buddhist Texts Through the Ages*. Translated by Arthur Whaley. New York: Harper & Row, 1954.

Eck, Diana L. *Darsan: Seeing the Divine Image in India*. New York: Columbia University Press, 1996.

Ehrlich, Gretel. *Questions of Heaven*. Boston: Beacon Press, 1997.

Emerson, Ralph Waldo. "Brahma" in *The Chief American Poets*. Edited by Curtis Hidden Page. Boston: Houghton Mifflin, 1905.

———. *The Solace of Open Spaces*. New York: Penguin, 1986.

Fleming, Robert L. Jr., Dorje Tsering, and Liu Wulin. *Across the Tibetan Plateau: Ecosystems, Wildlife, and Conservation*. New York: W. W. Norton and Future Generations, 2007.

Govinda, Lama Angarika. *The Way of the White Clouds*. New York: Overlook, 1966.

Hoagland, Edward. *Walking the Dead Diamond River*. New York: Lyons & Burford, 1993.

Kala, D. C. Kala. *Frederick Wilson ('Hulson Sahib') of Garhwal*. Delhi: Ravi Dayal, 2006.

Kalidasa. *Kumarasambhava: The Birth of the War God*. Trans. Ralph T. H. Griffith. London: W. H. Allen, 1853.

Keay, John. *The Great Arc*. London: Harper Collins, 2000.

Leopold, Aldo. *Sand County Almanac*. New York: Ballantine, 1987. First edition, 1949.

Lhalungpa, Lobsang P. *The Life of Milarepa*. Delhi: Book Faith India, 1997.

Lightman, Alan. "Does God Exist?" *Salon*, 02/10/2011.

———. *Mr. g*. New York: Pantheon, 2012.

Longstaff, Tom. *This My Voyage*. New York: Scribners, 1950.

Lopez, Barry. *Arctic Dreams*. New York: Bantam, 1996.

MacDonald, Bernadette. *Brotherhood of the Rope*. Seattle: Mountaineers Books, 2007.

Matthiessen, Peter. *The Snow Leopard*. New York: Viking. 1978.

McCrindle, J. W. and R. C. Mazumdar. *Ancient India as Described by Megasthenes and Arrian*. Calcutta: Chuckervertty, Chatterjee & Co., 1960.

Macfarlane, Robert. *Mountains of the Mind*. London: Granta, 2003.

Norgay, Tenzing. *Tiger of the Snows*. With James Ramsey Ullman. New York: Putnam, 1955.

Oakley, E. S. and Tara Dutt Gairola. *Himalayan Folklore: Kumaon and West Nepal*. Kathmandu: Ratna Pustak Bhandar, 1977.

Oakley, E. S. *Holy Himalaya*. Nainital: Gyanodaya Prakashan, 1990.

Pathak, Shekhar. *Asia Ki Peeth Par*. Nainital: Pahar, 2006.

Perrin, Jim. *Shipton & Tilman: The Great Decade of Himalayan Exploration*. London: Hutchinson, 2013.

Pundeer, Surendra. *Gods of Jaunpur*. Trans. N. C. Tripathi. Dehradun: Samay Sakshaya, 2003.

Roerich, Nicholas. *Heart of Asia*. New York: New Era Library, 1929.

Roskelley, John. *Nanda Devi: The Tragic Expedition*. Seattle: Mountaineers Books, 2000.

Sax, William. *Mountain Goddess*. New York: Oxford University Press, 1991.

Schaller, George. *Stones of Silence*. Chicago: Chicago University Press, 1988.

Shipton, Eric. *Upon That Mountain*. London: Hodder & Stoughton, 1943.

Shor, Thomas K. *A Step Away from Paradise*. Delhi: Penguin, 2011.

Smetacek, Peter. *Butterflies on the Roof of the World*. Delhi: Aleph, 2012.

Snelling, John. *The Sacred Mountain: A Complete Guide to Tibet's Mt. Kailash*. Delhi: Motilal Banarasidass, 2006.

Thoreau, Henry David. "Walking" in *Henry David Thoreau: Collected Essays and Poems*. Edited by Elizabeth H. Witherell. New York: Library of America, 2001.

Unsoeld, Willi. "Nanda Devi from the North" *American Alpine Journal*, 1977: 300–313.

———. "Nilkanta, Garhwal Himalayas, 1949." *American Alpine Journal*, 1956: 75–80.

Von Essen, Carl. *The Hunter's Trance*. Great Barrington, MA: Lindisfarne Books, 2007.

Western Tibet and Mt. Kailash Trekking Map. Map Point Nepal, 2005.